/

THE USE OF DRAMA
IN THE REHABILITATION
OF VIOLENT MALE OFFENDERS

THE USE OF DRAMA
IN THE REHABILITATION
OF VIOLENT MALE OFFENDERS

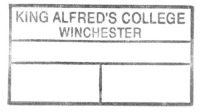
Michael Balfour

Studies in Theatre Arts
Volume 19

The Edwin Mellen Press
Lewiston•Queenston•Lampeter

Library of Congress Cataloging-in-Publication Data

Balfour, Michael.
  The use of drama in the rehabilitation of violent male offenders / Michael Balfour.
    p. cm. -- (Studies in theatre arts ; v. 19)
  Includes bibliographical references and index.
  ISBN 0-7734-6849-8 (hc)
    1. Prison theater. 2. Violent offenders--Rehabilitation. 3. Behavior modification. 4.
  Acting--Psychological aspects. 5. Criminology--Great Britain. I. Title. II. Series.

  HV8861.B35 2003
  365'.66--dc21

                                                                            2003052729

This is volume 19 in the continuing series
Studies in Theatre Arts
Volume 19 ISBN 0-7734-6849-8
STA Series ISBN 0-7734-9721-8

A CIP catalog record for this book is available from the British Library

Front cover: Mask image reproduced with kind permission from the Metropolitan Police Authority

The Edwin Mellen Press   The Edwin Mellen Press
        Box 450   Box 67
  Lewiston, New York   Queenston, Ontario
   USA 14092-0450   CANADA L0S 1L0

           The Edwin Mellen Press, Ltd.
           Lampeter, Ceredigion, Wales
           UNITED KINGDOM SA48 8LT

         Printed in the United States of America

For Ginny

Contents

List of figures

Geese Theatre Fragment Masks

(Copyright: Geese Theatre UK's versions of 'The Fist', 'Mr Cool' and 'The Brickwall' (or Stonewall) are based on original concepts and designs by John Bergman and Geese Theatre USA. All other masks are original concepts by Geese Theatre UK. All pictured masks were designed and constructed by Sally Brookes. All mask and design concepts are copyright with all rights reserved and not to be reproduced in any manner.)

TIPP Centre Challenging Violence Programme. Design ideas by Jocelyn Meall.

Acknowledgements

When I originally started on this study, I was interested in the contemporary use of theatrical masks. As a result of talking to and observing the mask work of Geese Theatre Company I was drawn to the contradictions and paradoxes of theatre practice in prisons and probation. I am therefore indebted to Clark Baim, Alun Mountford and the other Geese members for their patience and generosity in enabling me to interview and observe the company in rehearsal and performance.

The other major influence on this monograph has been the opportunity of working for and with the TIPP Centre over the last 3-4 years. More than keeping me from penury during my time as a post graduate student, it has offered me a wide range of rich and varied experience which has directly informed my writing. This monograph could not have been achieved without the friendship and support of the TIPP Centre - James Thompson, Paul Heritage, Kate Lodge, Bridget Eadie, and Jacqui Burford - who have all helped me in different ways. Thanks also to Professor Baz Kershaw, who showed great patience and editorial good-sense in the many stages it has taken me to complete this work.

But most of all I thank the group members who have participated in drama workshops over the last four years. It is with humility that I acknowledge that I have probably learnt more from listening to them, than they have to me.

Preface

I have been an inmate in prison only once. In 1960, Manchester Crown Court sentenced me to an indefinite term of confinement at Her Majesty's Pleasure in Strangeways Prison. The magistrates had no option: as a CND Committee of 100 member arrested during a demonstration I refused to give my name in Court. Even in England, as in too many swathes of the globe now, having no name led to reduced rights. Forget rehabilitation and reform, my lack of identity apparently gave the jail a more or less clean slate to brutalise me, so long as it left no visible marks. The details of that are not important - much, much worse has been suffered by incarcerated others - but the principle at stake is paramount in the creation of a humane system of criminal justice. Even at the ugliest heart of the punitive prison there has to be some glimmer of daily justice for the recidivist impulse to be rescued from itself.

Many years later I returned to prison to run a drama workshop. The prison was situated in an ancient castle, so it was a warren of dark passageways and heavy doors. One of the workshop group - a man serving a long sentence - wrote a short play which dramatised how the warren was used to punish prisoners: if a individual's journey from A to B took too long then he would lose some of the remission time attached to his sentence. This system of punishment was probably a fabrication, but the fact that the prisoner felt compelled to invent it spoke volumes about the resentment and resistance that prison too frequently produces. The drama group recorded the play and, although I do not know if it changed their future behaviour in any way, the pleasure it gave them to 'state their case' in xiv

dramatic form was surely a positive experience. The production of the play introduced a little more humanity into the prison.

Humanity and justice, in a system angled towards retribution and punishment, are especially difficult principles to pursue. They raise complex issues about rights and responsibilities, rehabilitation and restitution. It is a distinctive mark of the quality of this book that Michael Balfour is very alert to those complexities, while being exceptionally clear-headed about how drama and theatre in the criminal justice system might make a positive difference in prisoners' lives. As one of the pioneer practitioners of TIPP - theatre in prisons and probation - in the UK, his acute sense of the difficulties of such work is not surprising. But the clarity of analysis he brings to bear on it could only be achieved through an assiduous and thoroughgoing balance of successful practice and subtle theory. The book deals with some especially tough terrain, but the agility with which he traverses it is paradoxically pleasurable. More crucially, it deserves to be read for its steadfast commitment to creativity as a source for increasing justice and humanity in prisons.

Baz Kershaw
University of Bristol
September, 2002

Introduction

Theatre in prisons and probation (TIPP) represents a new field in theatre practice in Britain. It has developed in response to a growing recognition within the criminal justice system that the arts can play a directly functional role in the 'primary task of reducing offending, through education and challenging behaviour, offering new ways of thinking, and redirecting energies'.[1] In particular, criminal justice agencies have acknowledged that imaginative and engaging styles of education are crucial to rehabilitative work with offenders. [2] .

This monograph investigates the potential efficacy of a drama-based educational programme for violent offenders, and evaluates whether drama can contribute to a very specific rehabilitative and educative goal. Central to the monograph is the possibility that drama-based techniques are an effective learning tool for groups of violent men; that the conveyance of specific social skills may contribute to individual change - in terms of a reduction in violent behaviour. The commission by the Home Office and a Probation Service of a drama-based programme targeted specifically at criminal violence, reflects a concern within the criminal justice system in dealing with the increasing problem of violence against the person. In the 1980's in Britain the male rate of such offences rose by 40%, while the rate against females rose by 90%. [3] The figures for female assaults are

---

[1] Community Sentences Committee (1994) *Probation and the Arts, A Briefing Paper*, Association of Chief Officers of Probation, Wakefield, p.1
[2] ibid, p.1
[3] Davidoff, L. and Greenhorn, M. (1991) 'Violent Crime in England and Wales', paper presented at the British Criminology Conference, York, p.4

partially explained by a much greater awareness and willingness by the Police Service to make convictions in cases of domestic violence. The 2001 British Crime Survey suggests that violent offences now account for 14% of all recorded crime.[4]

The study will trace the development of TIPP practice in a number of ways; by assessing drama-based approaches to rehabilitative work with offenders; by examining the contribution made by Geese Theatre Company, the largest and most established company working in the field; and by looking at potentially efficacious practices and areas of difficulty for the field. With this as a background, the monograph will go on to analyse, as its main case study, the devising and implementation of a new TIPP programme, the Pump Challenging Violence programme developed by the Theatre in Prisons and Probation (TIPP) Centre, University of Manchester in collaboration with the Practice Development Unit (P.D.U.), of Greater Manchester Probation Service.[5]

In this introduction I will provide an outline of the main areas of investigation that will be explored in this monograph under the following headings:

- A background to rehabilitative approaches in the criminal justice system.
- The development of theatre in prisons and probation (TIPP).
- An outline of the main issues.
- Drama with offenders: phenomenological, egalitarian and dialogical principles.
- Working with criminal justice agencies - common goals.
- The 'What Works?' debate. Working within the system - potential conflicts.
- Structure of the study.
- Methods and methodology.
- What outcomes are hoped for in the study.

---

[4] http://www.crimereduction.gov.uk/sta index.htm, p.1
[5] The programme was funded by the Home Office, and after extensive piloting and evaluation is a Probation approved 'anger management' course for violent offenders used throughout Greater Manchester. The course has also been run in partnership with Cheshire Probation Service and the Prison Service (HMP Manchester). Background information about TIPP Centre and the PDU in appendix 1.

A background to rehabilitative approaches in the criminal justice system.

The criminal justice system is an extremely complex field with multiple goals and perspectives. I will be exploring the theoretical territory of criminology in Chapter One, but in order to fully appreciate why and how prison theatre has developed, it is important, briefly, to outline the criminal justice's historical efforts to implement more radical approaches to working with offenders.

The liberal consensus of the mid-1960's and 1970's was crucial in promoting radical initiatives and programmes in prisons and probation. Advocates of the rehabilitation perspective proposed an alternative to the traditional punitive function of the justice system. The radical view of the criminal justice system was manage themselves. One of the predominant explanations of crime causation was defined as 'an expression of the offenders' frustration with their place in society and their inability to do anything about it through conventional means'. [6]

The rehabilitation philosophy held that people were 'at the mercy of social, economic and interpersonal conditions and interactions'; and that 'it is the duty of society to help them compensate for their social problems'. [7] The rehabilitative perspective argued for the need to empower people through helping them find legitimate ways of living in society. In practical terms, this period saw a huge increase in a range of 'intervention' programmes, including job training, psychological counselling, education and some arts activities (although documentation of the latter is scarce). The Probation Service in particular launched anti-crime and delinquency prevention programmes which emphasised community development, job training, and educational enrichment. In addition 'a

---

[6] Senna, J.J. and Siegal L.J. (1990) *Introduction to Criminal Justice*, St.Paul, MN, West Publishing, p.156
[7] Clear, T. and O'Leary, V. (1983) *Controlling the Offender in the Community*, Lexington, Mass., Lexington Books, p.35

multitude of programmes were created at every level of government to offer social services to known offenders who desired to 'go straight''. [8]

At its height, between 1965-1975, the rehabilitation view rejected the concept of punishment because of what it saw as its inherent brutality and futility. Its use implied that 'society had given up on the offenders and precluded the hope that they would ever be turned into law-abiding members of society'. [9] Advocates of the rehabilitation viewpoint wanted not only to present alternative methodologies, but to question the traditional ideological principles underpinning the criminal justice system.

By the mid-to-late 1970's the development of rehabilitation and oppositional views was checked by a shift towards more conservative, punitive policies. The return to power of the Conservatives in Britain and Republicans in the US in the 1980's marked a considerable shift towards more punitive efforts and policies in the criminal justice system in both countries. The liberalisation of the system undertaken by prison education departments and the Probation Service was also hindered by a series of research studies which indicated that programmes designed to rehabilitate known offenders did not work as well as expected. [10] The failure of rehabilitation programmes to generate unqualified support eroded confidence in the ability of some criminal justice agencies' to improve the lives of convicted criminals and offer alternatives to potential offenders. The cost of funding effective rehabilitative efforts, coupled with a growing public fear of violent crime, helped further erode the dominance of the rehabilitation philosophy in the criminal justice system. [11]

It is important to stress at this juncture that criminology and penal policy are characterised by a 'pendulum of fashion' between competing theories,

---

[8] Senna, J.J. and Siegal L.J., (1990) op. cit., p.156
[9] ibid., p.156
[10] In particular: Lipton, D., Martinson, R. and Wilks, D. (1975) *The Effectiveness of Correctional Treatment*, New York, Praeger.
[11] Senna, J.J. and Siegal L.J. , op. cit., p.156

explanations and treatments of crime and the offender. [12] Thus the path of theoretical perspectives is, as discussed in Chapter One, not so much 'progressively linear', but 'a continuous circuit of *deja vu*'. [13] In practical terms this means that although questions about rehabilitation remain, there are still sections of the justice system that continue to argue for and implement progressive policies. For example, most prisons still maintain an education department, a small probation team, and counselling services. And the Probation Service continues to operate a wide range of community-based programmes for offenders. So despite the negative attitude towards rehabilitation programmes, it has been possible for criminal justice agencies to let theatre organisations 'in through the back door', in the hope that 'before they have been noticed' it may be possible to demonstrate their usefulness to the general aim of reducing offending behaviour. [14] Before discussing the broader issues of interaction between probation and theatre practitioners, it is relevant to understand some of the background as to why theatre practitioners were interested in prison/probation work, and the development of different approaches to the field over the last two decades.

The development of theatre in prisons and probation.

In the U.K. there are currently half a dozen theatre organisations working exclusively with offenders on probation or in prison, and over a hundred and fifty artists and/or companies who work regularly in a criminal justice setting. [15] In the last fifteen years there has also been a growing number of international criminal justice projects set up by a variety of theatre and arts practitioners. There is a British Network of Prison Theatre which exists to influence and inform Home

---

[12] Young, J. (1994) 'Incessant chatter: recent paradigms in criminology', in McGuire, M., Morgan, R.and Reimer, R. (1994) *Oxford Handbook of Criminology*, New York, Clarendon Press, p.70
[13] ibid., p.70
[14] Tomalin, D. (1996) Interview with the author.
[15] Arts organisations in U.K.: Geese Theatre Company; Clean Break Theatre Company; The TIPP Centre; Leap; Insight Arts Trust; Escape Artists; arts activities in prisons are collated by the Unit for Arts and Offenders.

Office policies and a European Network which was formed after the 2nd European Conference on Theatre and Prison, held in Manchester in 1996. Academically, the theory and practice of prison theatre is being taught in 5-6 U.K. universities at both undergraduate and postgraduate level.

The emergence of theatre in prisons and probation is not an isolated event. It's roots lie in the development of community arts and the theatre's 'search for a useful and effective *role* within society and an exploration especially of its potential both as an educational medium and as a force for social change'. [16] TIPP practice has many influences, though it is difficult to trace a uniform line of inheritance. Generally, it connects with the history of the community arts movement, but more specifically the development of a 'cultural expansionism' in alternative theatre in the mid to late seventies. [17] I believe it is relevant to provide a brief overview of these movements, and how/why they have informed the development of theatre in prisons.

In the late sixties in Britain community arts and alternative theatre emerged as part of a much wider, radical, cultural and social activism. These new movements were an aspect of a sustained economic boom which 'people had come to believe was permanent'. [18] The influence of the 'counter culture' and the general optimism of the times, led to a belief in new ideas and radical approaches to art and learning. The attempt was not just to create aesthetic alternatives, but to invent methodologies that were in opposition to the status quo, in an effort to 're-fashion society'. [19] The community arts movement was in reality a 'fluctuating group of (mainly) young artists' who were working in ways which were, at the time, unorthodox. [20] One of the far-reaching influences of this period was the

---

[16] Jackson, T. (ed.) (1980) *Learning Through Theatre*, Manchester, Manchester University Press, p.ix
[17] Kershaw, B. (1992) *The Politics of Performance*, London, Routledge, p.252
[18] ibid, p.9
[19] ibid, p.16
[20] Kelly, O. (1984) *Community, Art and the State: Storming the Citadels*, London, Comedia Publishing Group, p.9

concern to take art 'into the streets' and 'give it back to the people'. Community and theatre artists began to work in areas which included 'financial, cultural, environmental or educational deprivation'.[21]

The ultimate purpose of these approaches was to make theatre 'for the people'; to empower the spectator; to make art participatory. One of the guiding notions was that 'everybody can do everything'. The aim was to 'de-mystify the art form, especially to strip it of the mystique of professionalisation, and to promote greater equality between the stage and the auditorium'. [22] The belief was that theatre was a means of bringing change in individuals and groups through direct experience of theatre art. The drive to establish theatre outside of traditional theatre buildings, was perhaps first begun with Brecht in the thirties. Viewed from this 'expansionist' perspective, alternative theatre aimed to promote subversive 'counter culture' values in a popular context, and:

> ....to promulgate them to a widening span of social groupings. Hence, the movement continually searched out new contexts for performance in a dilating spectrum of communities. [23]

The move away from traditional theatre spaces led to the mushrooming of new trends and strands: theatre in education (although strictly speaking this began in 1965 at the Belgrade Theatre); remedial drama which led to drama therapy; [24] feminist theatre; street 'agit prop' theatre; reminiscence theatre; 'pub' theatre; gay theatre; and prison theatre amongst many others. Some of these strands carried forward the subversive values of the wider alternative movement whilst

[21] ibid., p.10
[22] Kershaw, B. (1992) op. cit., p.103
[23] ibid., p.18
[24] Jennings, S. (1990) *Dramatherapy with Families, Groups and Individuals. Waiting in the Wings.* London. Jessica Kingsley, p.4

attempting to create popular appeal; others reinvented and developed ideologies in order to reflect and adapt to the context in which they were working:

> ..alternative groups aimed to promote radical socio-political ideologies in relatively conservative contexts. Thus, complex theatrical methods had to be devised in order to circumvent outright rejection.[25]

Theatre in prisons represents a particularly useful example of how fraught this ideological negotiation can be. Because the context of prison is so profoundly disciplinarian and establishment-orientated, *any* advance in evolving an oppositional culture of creativity, egalitarianism, libertarianism, and empowerment needs to be seen as a significant achievement. I will discuss this issue later, as it is a problematic that informs and shapes the whole study.

The TIPP field is both complex and diverse in its approaches to working with offenders. A precise definition of TIPP practice is difficult, partly due to the complex interaction between drama and educational method, but also because the work is constantly changing and evolving in response to practical experience. Underlying the different approaches, whether implicitly or explicitly stated, is a crucial orientation to a rehabilitative goal. [26]

However, some arts organisations have chosen to work in partnership with criminal justice agencies (Geese Theatre, the TIPP Centre), while organisations like Clean Break Theatre Company, view working with agencies as inappropriate. Clean Break's argument is for an independent and autonomous link between the

---

[25] Kershaw, B. (1992) op. cit., p.18

[26] The arts organisations currently practising exclusively in prisons and probation were all founded under very different circumstances. Geese Theatre Company, for example, were a franchise of an American company, and imported their methods and ideas from the US, while Clean Break Theatre Company were established by two women ex-offenders, and set out a belief that the arts should be used as a method for empowering and developing skills with offenders. The TIPP Centre was created after a conference for theatre and probation practitioners interested in working together on projects.

arts and prisons, and an emphasis on the prisoners' goals rather than the goals of the agency or system. [27] While this approach to the TIPP field is valid, it tends to deny the responsibility of offenders in addressing their offending behaviour. The approach described in this monograph will focus on drama-based work that is explicitly concerned with engaging in social issues connected to offending behaviour, while working in partnership with criminal justice agencies. The decision to focus on this area does not deny the efficacy of a different approach, it merely highlights a concern with a project that has specific educational aims and objectives.

As part of the research, I spent time observing the devising of a show by Geese Theatre Company, one of the first British theatre organisations to work exclusively in prisons and probation. Soon after I worked for the Theatre in Prisons and Probation (TIPP) Centre primarily on the devising of the Pump programme, but also to develop and run other projects. Although there are differences in the way these two organisations function, their approach is broadly similar in that they work alongside existing criminal justice agencies. The educational programmes and projects that they devise are generally focused towards issue-based work which promotes thinking and debate around offending behaviour, such as: looking at the consequences of crime; victim empathy; understanding internal and external pressures which lead to criminal behaviour; exploring the effect of drugs (both dealing and using) and alcohol; promoting and developing social skills to deal with interpersonal problems. In other words practitioners like the TIPP Centre and Geese Theatre seek to enable participants to find creative resolutions to problems linked to criminal behaviour. These issues

---

[27] Clean Break's constitution prioritises the needs of female ex-offenders released from prison: 'Following release from prison offenders often lack confidence in their abilities. The stigma attached to their criminal past acts as an obstacle to their gaining access to employment and to mainstream education. The company seeks to expand the employment opportunities and personal choices of women ex-offenders. The company believe that theatre is a vital means by which individuals can develop their skills, creativity and self-esteem. Info: Clean Break Theatre Company Annual Report.

are closely and very often directly linked (through commissions) to the agenda of the Probation Service. Indeed for both Geese and TIPP the partnerships with probation form one of the main funding planks on which much of the work is based. So it is important to bear in mind that this close symbiotic relationship influences many of the projects, in financial terms as well as setting a particular methodological and theoretical agenda.

TIPP practice orientated to directly addressing offending behaviour is characterised not by a formulaic approach, but by a range of practical techniques and styles that can be pragmatically selected for a workshop. These include image theatre, forum, role-play, role-reversal, re-enactment, character development, improvisation exercises and social skills training. Additionally TIPP companies use elements of traditional TIE and theatre practice (actors in role); educational drama (participants actively involved in improvisations); and simulation (structured role-play and decision-making exercises within simulated 'real-life' situations). I will explore the use of drama-based techniques in more detail in Chapter Two.

An outline of the main issues.

The theatre in prisons and probation field needs to be approached with an understanding of the present theories of criminology, and the paradox of creative work within a system orientated as much to punishment as to rehabilitation. In particular this monograph will explore the conflict between creative intervention programmes and the disciplinary methodologies of justice and punishment. The monograph will address a number of issues. Firstly, how can a drama-based educational programme contribute to a progressive change in thinking and behaviour of convicted violent offenders? Secondly, can theatre practitioners and criminal justice agencies combine their different methods to create efficacious work? Thirdly, in what ways can theatre challenge, transcend, resist the traditionally conservative environment of the criminal justice system?

These issues reflect an interest in three areas of 'interactional' analysis, namely, the individual (facilitator-participant), the micro-social (theatre organisations-criminal justice agencies) and the macro-social (theoretical processes and structures). The 'individual and the social' and the 'macro and the micro' are themes which will recur throughout this monograph. There is a complex interrelationship between an offender and a theatre practitioner, an arts organisation and a criminal justice agency, and an arts-based rehabilitative approach within a diverse theoretical environment - such as the criminal justice system. Each area of analysis has its own properties. Individuals, I will argue, have the property of agency: of being able, sometimes, to choose to do otherwise and to create relationships and new social forms. The macro-social context has its own properties: structures, organisations, agencies, institutions and social processes. The efficacy of theatre in prisons and probation needs to be assessed with this complex interaction between the micro and macro born in mind.

One of the related reasons for being interested in the micro and macro is that it raises important issues about the nature of relationships between individuals and social forms. For example, the question of primacy in the relationships between the individual and the social. Which is the crucial determinant of social interaction - the individual or social structures and practices? Nowhere is this question more intriguing, perhaps, than in the relationship between offender and criminal justice agency and/or institution. How do interactions at a micro and macro level contribute to influencing an anti-social individual to reform and conform? How do we measure the efficacy of one approach over another? And in what ways do individuals influence the micro-and-macro elements of the criminal justice system?

These general questions are both complex and difficult to address. However, in the next three sections of this chapter I will introduce some key issues which relate to these questions. Firstly, I will look at the interaction between facilitator and participant and the way in which phenomenological, egalitarian and dialogical principles are proposed and tested in this monograph. Secondly, I will explore the relationship between arts organisations and criminal justice agencies - by outlining some common goals and criteria set out by probation researchers for devising educational programmes. In particular I will refer to the 'What Works?' debate. Thirdly, I will deal with the issue of TIPP practice navigating the fraught ideological territory of the criminal justice system, and the ways in which TIPP can learn from the previous experiences of the community and alternative theatre movement.

Drama with offenders - phenomenological, egalitarian and dialogical principals.

In this monograph I focus on the strengths and weaknesses of theatre in prisons and probation: strengths, in which practical solutions are sought to interpersonal social problems; weaknesses, in that little theoretical or practical emphasis is placed on the macro-social context in which problems arise. For example, in relation to the problem of domestic violence, Novaco and cognitive-behavioural psychology suggest ways in which facilitators might work with groups of violent men to change angry and aggressive attitudes, in an attempt to reduce the risk of violent abuse in relationships and find alternative patterns of social interaction. [28] Although such progress would be a major achievement, the pro-feminists argue that cognitive-behavioural programmes for violent men can do little about the power relations between men and women in the context of a patriarchal society. [29] Some pro-feminists argue that applications such as social skills training can ameliorate abusive situations but cannot address the root causes of those

---

[28] Novaco R W. (1975) *Anger Control*, Massachusetts, Lexington Books; Novaco, R W. (1976) Treatment of Chronic Anger Through Cognitive and Relaxation Controls, *Journal of Consulting and Clinical Psychology*, **44**, p 681.
[29] Dobash, R.E. and Dobash, R.P. (1979) *Violence Against Wives*, New York, The Free Press; Dobash, R.E. and Dobash, R.P. (1981) 'Community response to violence against wives: charivari, abstract justice and patriarchy', *Social Problems*, **28**, 5, pp 563-581; Dobash, R.E. and Dobash, R.P. (1990/91) *The CHANGE Project Annual report 1990 and 1991*, University of Stirling.

situations.[30] In defence, cognitive-behaviourists might argue that it is better to do something in the short-term, and that pro-feminists underestimate the extent to which 'local' social interactions in men's groups determine 'global' macro-relations between men and women.

The development of the TIPP Centre's Pump programme for violent men was informed by both Novaco/cognitive behavioural psychology and pro-feminist perspectives. The interaction between these theories will be explored in detail in Chapter Three.

The Pump programme was also informed by phenomenological, egalitarian and dialogical principles. The Phenomenology model is, in its most fundamental form, a philosophical study which concentrates on the detailed description of conscious experience.[31] Its use in this monograph provides a necessary through-line in the understanding of how people perceive, reflect and bestow meaning in their social interactions. [32] The phenomenological view suggests that the consciousness of the world involves and somehow depends upon self-consciousness. Thus if there is an attempt to try and help violent offenders alter their behaviour, then it is relevant to help him become more aware of his own consciousness of the world. Therefore one of the objectives of using drama with offenders is to develop perceptions in relation to their own and others' perceptions, and to further their understanding of social processes. In dramatic terms, the awareness of plurality in social interaction may be presented by looking at events from other people's point of view, through techniques such as image tableau, re-enactment, role reversal, and social skills training. The phenomenological principle underlining this process is to suggest that meaning in reality is always 'deferred, elsewhere, multiple and shifting, and

---

[30] Gondolf, E (1984) 'How Some Men Stop Battering: An Evaluation of a Group Counselling Program.' Paper presented at the second *National Conference for Family Violence Researchers*, Durham, NH.; Gondolf, E and Russell, D. (1986) 'The Case Against Anger Control Treatment Programs for Batterers', *Response*, **9**, No 3

[31] A more detailed definition of phenomenology is available in Chapter One.

[32] Curtis, B. (1978) *Phenomenology and Education*, ed. Bernard Curtis and Wolfe Mays, London, Methuen, p.xiii

therefore a process and not a product'. [33] In other words the phenomenological moral imperative is not about instructing offenders about right and wrong, but about working with participants to find creative solutions to a moral environment that is forever in process. For example, The Pump programme has a stated anti-violence stance, but attempts to challenge violent behaviour not by moral instruction, but through critical problematisation of behaviour. It is therefore necessary that a violent incident is made the subject of investigation and dialogue, and theatre techniques can be used to look at what happened and how it happened. The purpose of this is not to re-enact the situation in the hope of catharsis, but to problematise and question the social interactions which led to the violence. As Freire notes, the process is to 'reflect on the 'wherefore' of the fact and on its connection with other facts in an overall context'. [34]

From this viewpoint it is possible to argue that 'the arts offer a language with which to engage an offender in dialogue'. [35] The principle of dialogic and egalitarian approaches to education through theatre is an important one, as it offers a rationale for both respecting and challenging the participant. The dialogic methodology explores problems with critical analysis, and in criticising 'gives human beings their place within their own reality as the true transforming Subjects of reality'. [36] This line of argument assumes that we are autonomous, that we can choose and be held accountable for our actions. As I will discuss in Chapter One, in criminological terms, this is a far from simple assumption.

This monograph will consider whether theatre practitioners can resist, transcend or influence criminal justice agencies, whilst seeking to become accepted by them. What are the constraints imposed by the agencies? e.g. differing attitudes to

---

[33] Reinelt, J.G. and Roach, J.R. (1992) *Critical Theory and Performance*, Michigan, University of Michigan Press, p.111

[34] Freire, P. (1974) *Education for Critical Consciousness*, London, Sheed and Ward, p.124

[35] Community Sentences Committee (1994) *Probation and the Arts, A Briefing Paper*, Association of Chief Officers of Probation, Wakefield, p.1

[36] Freire, P. (1974) op. cit., p.123

what efficacy means; different 'philosophy' and attitude toward offenders; the 'acceptability' (or not) of drama techniques; how one measures efficacy? One of the crucial topics I discuss is the process of negotiating this kind of terrain between probation and theatre. This is developed by assessing the common goals and conflicting points between theatre and probation practitioners, with reference to the research, development and evaluation of The Pump programme; and through the exploration of the contradiction between forms of creative expression and the constraints of compulsory 'moral education' within a punitive-orientated context.

Working with criminal justice agencies - common goals.

It is important that we consider not only the context of the target group, but also the criminal justice agencies (Probation, Prison Education Department), the wider socio-political culture of the justice system, and the society it is designed to serve. As Foucault argues, the technologies of the punishment system are inextricably bound up with political concerns. [37] And as this monograph focuses on a process that explicitly aims at encouraging individual change it therefore follows that the development of the programme should also be subject to scrutiny from a political perspective. These specific issues I deal with in Chapter One. However, a related point is the question of why criminal justice agencies believe that they may share common goals with an art form that, historically, has been as much anti-establishment and radical as conservative?

One response to this question is that criminal justice agencies engaged in rehabilitative work, the Probation Service and Prison Education Departments, share common ground with TIPP practitioners in wanting to help disadvantaged and marginalised people in society. The Probation Service, in particular, has a pragmatic need to find ways of delivering moral issue-based work that will

---

[37] Dreyfus, H. and Rabinow, P. (1982) *Michel Foucault, Beyond Structuralism and Hermeneutics*, Chicago, Harvester Wheatschaf.

engage a challenging variety of people. Drama is one of several identifiable methods that can be used as an engaging educational 'participatory' tool, as an alternative to discussion groups or paper and pen exercises. The Probation Service may set the learning agenda, while the theatre practitioner devises suitable projects which fit the agenda. But within this type of commission there may be space for a theatre practitioner to bring his/her own agenda; for example the application of egalitarian and dialogical principles, arts-based aims and objectives as opposed to 'educational' goals; knowledge through the body (through doing and being), through experiential and creative work.

Nonetheless, theatre practitioners have had to work hard to convince agencies of their compatibility with criminal justice aims and objectives. Prison-orientated theatre organisations have had to create a space for themselves in the resources and budgets of prison regimes and Probation Services. In common with other community-orientated theatre there was never going to be a ready made theatre space. Theatre has had to take place on the wing (open to the jeers of non-participants), in cluttered classrooms on the education block, in tiny, converted cells used for interviews, or at best in the prison chapel (an open space dominated by religious artefacts in which swearing is discouraged or banned). The design of a prison may incorporate space for education (limited and never a priority for the regime) but rarely a space for creative arts. [38] Similarly in probation the most commonly assigned room for drama will be the waiting room filled with ragged, stained furniture, yellowing leaflets about drug help-lines, and a broken pool table. The amazing fact is that theatre has slowly been able to adapt into these spaces, and that after several years of tough, challenging work it has become an accepted practice in these environments both by participants and criminal justice workers.

---

[38] 'Rarely' because since 1996 HMP YOI Hindley in Lancashire has designated one of the rooms on the education block as a theatre studio (a room with no furniture) and have employed two staff to run regular drama workshops.

However, in order for agencies like the Probation Service to include TIPP practice in their timetable, they need to be able to prove the efficacy of drama-based educational programmes. The 'What Works?' debate suggests significant goals which educational programmes need to achieve if they are to be considered efficacious by the Probation Service and Home Office. [39] The 'What Works?' debate was crucial in the way the TIPP Centre's Pump programme was researched, developed and evaluated, and will provide an essential contextual introduction to probation-orientated concerns.

The 'What Works?' debate.

One of the main starting points that this, or any study of its kind, needs to acknowledge is the fact that proving the efficacy of arts educational work is an arduous and complex task. The nature of creative efficacy in a prison context is also deeply political. Theatre companies with an overtly 'serious' educational or moral task engage in work which makes significant judgements about the nature of crime and criminals. Performances or drama workshops in prisons are aimed at altering an audiences/participant's ideas and attitudes in the hope/belief that this will affect future actions.

An understanding of the theoretical landscape in criminology is an essential part of being able to traverse the socio-political nature of the criminal justice system, and of gaining a more informed and developed insight into the varying nature of crime and criminals. Without this type of knowledge it is difficult to fully appreciate how we can *accurately* assess the relationship between programme effect and subsequent behaviour of programme participants. For example, the most commonly used Probation method has been to administer pre-and-post psychometric questionnaires, and whilst the initial results from the first pilot programmes of The Pump have proved generally positive - which politically is

---

[39] McGuire, J., and Priestly, P. (ed.)(1995) *What Works: Reducing Re-offending*, Chichester, Wiley.

very useful - I will argue that the type of results produced by positivistic means are inconclusive and should generally be viewed with scepticism.

A more recent evaluation technique has been to analyse a number of projects with similar aims and objectives together.[40] This method was used in an influential academic paper by Lipton, Martinson and Wilks, published in 1975, of 231 treatment outcome studies of offenders.[41] The study included evaluating programmes involving psychotherapy, education, group therapy, behaviour modification, and counselling among other approaches. It was from this research that one of the authors, Robert Martinson, published 'What Works? - Questions and Answers about Prison Reform'. The key message of this paper was that the effectiveness of rehabilitation programmes was called into question, with the doctrine 'nothing works'.

Since Martinson's paper was published researchers and organisations have fought hard against its findings; developing programmes, using better evaluation techniques and hosting events that widen the debate on what constitutes effective work with offenders.

The use of meta-analysis, which is the aggregation and side-by-side comparison of the results of a large number of separate programmes, has played an important part in recent criminology studies. The studies reported by Andrews et al. (1990) and Lipsey (1991) have made a significant contribution to identifying factors in programmes that show a high effect in terms of a reduction in criminal behaviour. Whilst the evidence to date does not offer definite answers to the What Works? debate, it provides useful guide-lines for planning work with offenders, demonstrating that there are a number of readily identifiable programme features

---

[40] Andrews, D.A., Zinger, I., Hoge, R.D., Bonta, J., Gendreau, P. and Cullin, F.T. (1990) 'Does correctional treatment work? A clinically relevant and psychologically informed meta-analysis', *Criminology*, **28**; Lipsey, M.W. (1991) 'Juvenile delinquency treatment: A meta-analystical inquiry into the variability of effects', in K.W. Watcher and M.L. Straf (eds.) *meta-analysis for Explanation: A Casebook*, New York, Russell Sage Foundation.
[41] Lipton, D., Martinson, R. and Wilks, D. (1975) op.cit.

which are more likely to be effective than others. Some have been drawn from the original Lipsey research, others are from more recent research: [42]

1. Target high risk offenders; offenders who are most likely to re-offend again. The indiscriminate targeting of treatment programmes is counterproductive in reducing recidivism.
2. Concentrate on offence behaviour or behaviour closely linked to it.
3. Use programmes with a clear and directive approach based on specific well-researched models and linked with the learning style of the group.
4. 'More structured and focused treatments (e.g. behavioural, skill-orientated) seem to be more effective than the less structured and focused approaches, e.g. counselling'.[43] The most successful programmes, while behavioural in nature, include a cognitive component in order to focus on the 'attitudes, values and beliefs that support anti-social behaviour'. [44]
5. Implement programmes in the community; interventions have a stronger effect in community rather than in prison/residential setting.
6. Maintain high programme integrity; what is planned is carried out in practice. The treatment is carried out by fully-trained staff and there is effective management of a sound rehabilitative programme.
7. Select type and style of programme carefully; Andrews et al. (1990) suggest that some therapeutic approaches are not appropriate for general use with offenders. Specifically, they argue that 'traditional psychodynamic and nondirective client-centred therapies are to be avoided within a general sample of offenders'. [45]

The meta-analysis surveys conducted by Andrews et al., and Lipsey suggests that when the above conditions are met, programmes may be able to reduce the likelihood of recidivism in the order of 20 to 40 per cent. On this basis it is fair to conclude that it is not the case that 'nothing works' but that if programmes are

---

[42] Hollin, C. R. (1992) *Criminal Behaviour: A Psychological Approach to Explanation and Prevention*, London and Washington D.C., Falmer Press, p.131
[43] Lipsey, M.W. (1991) op.cit.
[44] Gendreau, P and Andrews, D.A. (1990) 'Tertiary prevention: what the meta-analysis of the offender treatment tells us about "What Works"?, *Canadian Journal of Criminology*, 32, pp.173-84.
[45] Andrews, D.A., Zinger, I., Hoge, R.D., Bonta, J., Gendreau, P. and Cullin, F.T. (1990) 'Does correctional treatment work? A clinically relevant and psychologically informed meta-analysis', *Criminology*, 28, p. 376

based on key principles, as outlined above, that there may be a significant reduction of recidivism.

The results from meta-analysis must be regarded with the same caution as the outcomes of other evaluation techniques. The analysis will only be as good as the quality of the data the researchers choose to look at and the way in which the data is coded and recoded. Therefore the meaning and interpretation of the data is only a starting point for discussion. Nevertheless, the meta-analysis makes it possible to suggest positive recommendations for the design of successful rehabilitation programmes aimed at reducing offending.

Even if theatre practitioners can navigate themselves effectively through the territory of working with offenders and in partnership with relatively sympathetic criminal justice agencies, there remains the much rougher terrain of the criminal justice system. The orientation to rehabilitative forms of drama-based education needs to be understood within the context of the theories of the criminal justice field. The rehabilitative perspective is one of many within the complex field of criminology, and has implications about the way crime and the criminals are regarded. It also needs to be emphasised that the rehabilitative perspective is a complex and sometimes contradictory area of criminological research and practice. For example, it may refer to drug therapy, psychological therapy, skills-based programmes (to enhance employment opportunities), basic education (literacy, numeracy) as well as programmes addressing issues related to offences. The main issue therefore is not only *what* one's position is, but *how* and *why* this position has been selected, and the ways in which theatre can resist, inform and/or transcend the traditionally punitive elements of the system.

Working within the system - potential conflicts.

A significant part of the history of prison and probation theatre is the history of its direct and indirect relationships with the state. For companies like Geese Theatre and the TIPP Centre the criminal justice agencies have been an important and regular source of funds. The relationship between these agencies and theatre practitioners have been governed, or constrained, by the function of the justice system, and ultimately by the nature of the state's view of crime and criminals. This difficult type of relationship is not unique to prison theatre, and as Owen Kelly observes, may be extended to the community arts movement (and alternative/oppositional theatre) in general:

> The history of community arts is the history of a movement of naive, but energetic, activism which, bereft of analysis, drifted into the arms of those groups it set out to oppose. Fuelled by a liberal pragmatism, which claimed it was better to do *anything* than to risk doing nothing, it seized whatever money was offered, with little thought for the possible consequences. Addicted to [grant] aid, which was provided at all times in amounts and in ways which suited the funding agencies, it could only scream for a regular increase in the dosage. [46]

There are similarities too, in Kelly's objection to '...the imposition....of the values of one particularly powerful group' and that these values are a 'compulsory imposition of centrally controlled systems of value...' [47] Although Kelly was debating the distinction between the democratisation of culture and cultural democracy, these arguments about the relationship between the state and the arts may be equally relevant for theatre in prisons and probation. For example, in the argument for arts in the criminal justice system lays the inherent contradiction between the system's orientation towards punishment and the deprivation of rights, and the desire of arts practitioners to empower and encourage responsibility. Perhaps this contradiction is weakened when arts practitioners' are funded by the state agencies and end up in the ideological arms of those they 'set out to oppose'. [48]

---

[46] Kelly, O. (1984) op cit., p.43
[47] ibid., p.101
[48] ibid., p.43

Theatre which constantly has to negotiate and alter its aesthetic methodology, in order to integrate effectively into its context, may risk neutralising its ideological agenda. The attendant risk is that the development of an alternative methodology and/or ideology may be crippled by a 'liberal pragmatism' which relies on:

> ....'common sense' definitions which can be manipulated and twisted, with the result that [community] artists are increasingly told what to do, how to do it, by people whose motivations often directly contradict the alleged aims of the community arts movement. [49]

Kelly's warning, directed at the community arts movement, may be equally valid for theatre in prisons and probation. The point that Kelly makes is that vigilance and analysis is crucial, but it is a mistake, in my opinion, to view the system and/or state as a monolithic, monological operation. The agencies within the criminal justice system operate from a range of theoretical and ideological perspectives, many of which are not in accord with each other. The complexity of the system and the multifarious purposes of its agencies highlight the 'incessant chatter' of multiple paradigms of criminology. [50] This problematises any view that there are 'centrally controlled systems of value' which are imposed by the justice system on a prison or probation population. [51] This does not negate the need for analysis and vigilance in negotiating relationships, it simply suggests that all organisations are subject to a reflexive process, in which the agendas of each are in a constant dialogical process. Fortunately or not, the economic dependency which Kelly is so openly sceptical of in the funding of the community arts movement, is something which prison theatre has not experienced. Like most arts organisations in the nineties, the funding base for prison specific work is small but drawn from a wide variety of sources i.e. as well as income from criminal justice

---

[49] ibid., p.3
[50] Young, J. (1994) op.cit., pp.69-124
[51] Kelly, O. (1984) op.cit., p.43

agencies, a proportion of funding comes from Foundations, Trusts, the National Lottery, fund-raising, and sponsorship.

The achievements of TIPP practice in making 'radical, cultural interventions' in the last fifteen years are arguably relatively small in comparison to other strands of alternative theatre, both in terms of developing new aesthetics and methodologies, and a clear oppositional socio-political perspective. [52] But these achievements need to be measured against an understanding of the complex nature of the context, and the theatre practitioner's need to walk 'a knife's edge between resistance to, and incorporation into, the status quo' of the criminal justice system. [53]

Structure of the Study.

The monograph begins with a contextual overview in Chapter One of issues related to criminology and the criminal justice system in the U.K. There is a consideration of criminological explanations for the causation and treatment of crimes in society. I look at the two distinct images of the criminal offender which have dominated criminology: one whose behaviour is determined; the other whose behaviour is the result of rational choice. After outlining the historical and theoretical background to the study of criminal behaviour, the chapter will concentrate on some of the main issues relating to rehabilitative and educative work in prisons/probation.

Chapter One also introduces why phenomenology, in its broadest definition, is useful in creating a link to theories of perception, specifically in relation to theories of male violence. The relationships between consciousness, behaviour and the environment are also discussed with reference to rehabilitative approaches to offender education, and more specifically theories of socialisation (Mead, 1934; Foucault, 1984; Piaget, 1965) and moral development (Kohlberg et al. 1978;

---

[52] Kershaw, B.(1992) op.cit., p.8
[53] ibid., p.8

Colby et al. 1978; Durkheim, 1961). These sociological, political, and philosophical points of reference re-emerge later on in the monograph, when theories of violent offenders are considered, and in particular in the discussion of how the TIPP Centre devised a practical approach informed by these various theoretical perspectives.

Chapter Two is divided into three sections. The first section looks at ways in which traditional drama techniques, such as role-play, re-enactment, role reversal and social skills training have been used in an attempt to challenge offenders' anti-social attitudes and to encourage victim empathy. In the second section I will give an account of Geese Theatre Company, and assess the implication of the company's theoretical and practical perspective of the offender as having therapeutic needs. In the final section, I propose a phenomenological, egalitarian, dialogical model that, in my view, provides a more reflexive and appropriate methodological approach.[54]

The third chapter links phenomenological notions with theories about how violent men form fixed psychological constructs and perceptions about the world, and how these inform their behaviour. I will contrast Novaco's anger treatment model with the pro-feminist's 'belief's' model, discussing the ways in which these sometimes contradictory approaches were incorporated into the TIPP Centre's Pump programme. [55] In particular the TIPP Centre programme will be used to problematise the process of resisting and/or negotiating a narrowly determined agenda set by the Probation Service and Home Office.

The fourth chapter will acknowledge the need for arts projects to be evaluated. I will assess the outcomes and findings from the Pump programme evaluation, derived from research work carried out by the TIPP Centre, Greater Manchester

---

[54] Freire, P. (1974) op.cit.
[55] See Novaco R W. (1975)op.cit.; pro-feminist theory: Dobash, R.E. and Dobash, R.P. (1979) op.cit; Dobash, R.E. and Dobash, R.P. (1981) op.cit.; Dobash, R.E. and Dobash, R.P. (1990/91) op.cit.

Probation Service, and a consultant psychologist from the University of Liverpool. The chapter will also highlight concerns and criticisms of a relatively positivistic approach to evaluation, discuss alternatives and finally, look at the ways in which the Pump programme has been developed and re-assessed in response to the evaluation.

Methods and methodology.

Given the complexity of both the criminological and theatrical fields it is not surprising that it has not been possible to use a single method to address all the issues. Exploring the complex nature of criminal violence, and the ways in which drama-based education may help to positively influence aggressive perceptions and behaviour, has required a range of different analytical methods.

The monograph offers a general review of criminological theoretical literature, and gives an overview of my orientation to theoretical perspectives on crime and criminals. It also gives an account of the way in which a number of drama-based methods have been used in an attempt to change anti-social attitudes of offenders, and in particular assesses the strengths and weaknesses of TIPP rehabilitative work with reference to Geese Theatre. I also examine a case study of a programme for violent offenders, developed by the TIPP Centre. The project (the Pump) seeks to develop and learn from past experiences of TIPP practice, and I shall be analysing the extent to which the project achieves these aims. There is also a presentation of findings from the evaluation of the case study (questionnaires, drama-based evaluation, written feed-back) and an assessment of the constraints and alternatives to positivistic methods of research.

The choice of method used for each of these chapters has depended on a number of factors. In part, the choice was reflexive to the kind of subject matter being investigated and the kind of issues being explored. The choice of method was also based on assumptions about the nature of crime and society. If I had been adopting a positivist line I would have been looking for 'hard data' and trying to establish laws of cause and effect, and would have chosen methods designed to yield these. Although positivistic methods are present, this monograph inclines more towards a hermeneutic approach, concerned with interpretation and unpacking meanings underlying the social world, and therefore adopts qualitative methods and conceptual analyses as the basis for investigation and research.

The term research needs to be further clarified. In this monograph the research applies to two broad areas. Firstly, social research; the application of systematic and interpretative principles of behaviour to the problems of people within their social contexts. Secondly, educational research, which applies the same principles to the problems of facilitating and participating in drama-based workshops within the formal criminal justice framework and to the clarification of issues having direct or indirect bearing on these concepts.

The aim of the overall methodology, in Kaplan's words is:

> ..to describe and analyse these methods, throwing light on their limitations and resources, clarifying their presuppositions and consequences, relating their potentialities to the twilight zone at the frontiers of knowledge. It is to venture generalisations from the success of particular techniques, suggesting new applications, and to unfold the specific bearings of logical and metaphysical principles on concrete problems, suggesting new formulations. [56]

I have therefore selected a methodological approach that suggests a theoretical hypothesis, which is tested and problematised in practice, and revised according to its 'limitations' and 'potentialities'. My aim in adopting this methodology is to arrive at 'dependable solutions to problems through the planned and systematic collection, analysis and interpretation of data', in order to ensure that drama-based education of the type described in this monograph develops a sense of progression and understanding. [57] However, my aim is not to present a replicable model of

[56] Kaplan, A. (1973) *The Conduct of Inquiry*, Aylesbury, Intertext Books, p. 53
[57] Mouly, G.J. (1978) *Educational Research: the Art and Science of Investigation*, Boston, Allyn and Bacon, p.55

practice that is suitable for the whole range of theatre practice in prisons/probation. Rather it is to illuminate and make transparent the contradictions and benefits of creating and implementing drama-based work in the criminal justice system.

What outcomes are hoped for in the study?

TIPP practitioners have demonstrated, I believe, an extraordinary determination, belief, imagination, and skill in creating 'relevant theatre' and drama 'for' and 'with' offenders. [58] However, after fifteen years TIPP is still subject to the changing political and social tides, a feature which is not helped by a lack of a credible rationale. The achievement and potential of TIPP practice, for me, is undeniable. However, critical assessment is needed, in order to make qualified assertions as to the nature of these achievements and the crucial qualities of its working practice. It is also necessary to distinguish between 'good' practice that seeks to establish rapport and a dialogical relationship with its participants and the system, and 'bad' practice that empowers the practitioner, but not, relatively speaking, the participants. [59]

This monograph is intended to make a positive contribution to such an assessment, by focusing on a specific project (The Pump programme) that serves as an example of some of the achievements and contradictions that working in prisons and probation may present to an arts practitioner. The aim then is to help clarify the nature of TIPP practice; and whilst I will be arguing for a specific approach to the work, the argument is based on a crucial element of reflexivity to a context that by its very nature is complex and challenging.

I therefore hope that the contradictions of creative work in a system which, by design, is meant to be repressive will be illuminated in this monograph. I will

---

[58] Bergman, J. and Hewish, S. (1996) 'The Violent Illusion, Dramatherapy and the Dangerous Voyage to the Heart of Change', in *Arts Approaches to Conflict*, ed. Marian Liebmann, London, Jessica Kingsley Publishers, p.93

[59] This latter issue is discussed in detail in Chapter Two.

argue that it is crucial that arts educationalists have a secure understanding of the specific environment of their work; a clear theoretical and practical rationale; and are able to form reflexive and dialogical relationships with criminal justice agencies and participants. I take this approach because in the final analysis there seem to me to be two crucial orientations to theatre in prisons and probation: either one simply does not do the work because of the contradictions present, or the paradox of the context is born in mind and the attendant tensions are made transparent and worked through in practice. It is the latter territory which I aim to explore in this study.

Chapter One

The theoretical territory

- theories relevant to working in the criminal justice system.

Introduction.

If theatre is to traverse the theoretical territory of the criminal justice system, it is important for it to take into account the complexity of its landscape. This chapter will provide a theoretical framework for my monograph, and seek to explain my view of crime and offenders. The position I will argue for is of a multi-causal explanation of crime and criminal behaviour. Central to the monograph is a belief that, with some offenders, education and drama techniques may contribute to a change in criminal behaviour. This assumes a degree of agency and autonomy in an individual's capacity to change his/her behaviour, an assumption which is questioned by some criminology paradigms (positivism - criminal behaviour determined by genetic inheritance and/or biological factors; social realism - crime is a result of poverty, poor education, lack of opportunity). Therefore it is relevant to explain to what extent these other factors may contribute to human behaviour, and how the numerous theories may influence practical drama work with violent offenders. To what extent theatre may be informed by and inform criminological theories will also be discussed, with particular reference to how and in what ways drama may contribute to the theoretical territory.

The chapter will supply information about the following areas of study:

- Set out a definition of criminal law
- Provide an overview of criminology
- Discuss the theoretical and historical background to the explanation and prevention of crime
- Give an account of the rehabilitative perspective on criminal justice
- Consider the link between theories of socialisation and behavioural programmes for offenders
- Definitions and applications of phenomenology
- The contribution of theatre to the theoretical territory of the criminal justice system

The use of the term 'offender' in this monograph needs to be qualified. Implicit in much of the work in prisons is a dangerous process that labels one person an offender and another a 'normal' citizen. Without denying the fact of crime I feel it is wrong to label someone purely by a singular deed they have done. A human being is more than the sum of his/her actions. The label of offender, no matter what offence has been committed, is ultimately a tag which needs to be redeemable. There is a dangerous assumption in much writing on criminal justice that encourages a reader to see an offender as only an offender, rather than a human being. It is far too easy to give people labels which take something away from their humanity. The only other term used by criminal justice workers (not including slang) is the 'client', which I think is respectful but inaccurate. After all someone who breaks the rules of society is not a consumer, just as someone who is an inmate is not a 'guest' at her majesty's pleasure. Unfortunately there is no suitable term that is both descriptive and free from stigma. But in a chapter looking at roles it is important to be aware of how language works to restrict and label individuals.

Definitions in law.

From a British empiricist legal perspective criminal behaviour is an <u>act</u> that violates criminal law. In law the first element of the *corpus delicti* ('body of the crime') is referred to as *actus reus* (guilty act). The emphasis on an act is important. The *actus reus* must be a measurable act; thought alone is not a crime. However planning, conspiring, and soliciting for criminal purposes are considered an actus reus even if the actual crime is never carried out or completed. Clive Hollin illustrates three different areas in which an *actus reus* might be unlawful: an act against another person (e.g. assault); against property (e.g. burglary) or not acting when legally required to do so (e.g. driving within the speed limit; parents' legal duty to protect a child). [1]

The second element basic to the commission of any crime is the establishment of the *mens rea,* translated as 'guilty mind'. *Mens rea* is the element of the crime that deals with the defendant's intent to commit a criminal act and also includes such states of mind as concealing criminal knowledge (*scienter*), recklessness, negligence, and criminal purpose. [2] A person ordinarily cannot be convicted of a crime unless it is proven that s/he intentionally, knowingly, or willingly committed the criminal act.

There are many instances where this definition is difficult; take, for example, the fact that children under a certain age cannot be prosecuted for criminal acts (although the age varies from country to country). To complicate the matter further it is possible to prosecute someone who has committed a criminal act even though they were not in a conscious state of mind to show they intended the act, for example someone who is deemed mentally ill or insane. There are also other exceptions, for example, in cases where self-defence was used: the intention of the defendant may have been to hurt the person who had attempted to assault him/her,

---

[1] Hollin, C. R. (1992) *Criminal Behaviour: A Psychological Approach to Explanation and Prevention,* London, The Falmer Press.
[2] American Law Institute (1985) *Model Penal Code,* Philadelphia, American Law Institute.

but the injury was caused in order to protect himself/herself and/or his/her property.

In simplified terms, then, the definition of criminal behaviour is an intended action that breaks the laws of a particular society. The law then identifies behaviours which a society does not tolerate. Using this perspective the law is the consensus of a society, which technically, represents a mutually agreed code of conduct. There are other perspectives and arguments in regard to this definition which will be dealt with later in the chapter, however for now it is enough to regard this perspective, called classicism, as the basis for mainstream British/Empiricist thinking on law.

An overview of criminology.

Criminology is a composite, eclectic and multidisciplinary field, and an area of study that has 'a long past, but a short history'. [3] Discourse about crime and punishment has existed, in one form or the other, since ancient times, but it is only during the last 120 years that there has been a distinctive 'science' of criminology. And it is only in the last fifty to sixty years that a discipline of criminology has been academically established in Britain.

Criminology draws upon a number of academic disciplines to develop insights into the potential causes and prevention of criminal behaviour. Siegal and Senna have noted how these different disciplines have applied themselves to criminology, for example sociologists study the social and environmental factors associated with criminal delinquency; psychologists have researched if the 'typical' offender's criminal behaviour is a result of some emotional or mental health problem; law academics have focused on the effects of changes to the legal system, and the relationship between social control and civil liberties; historians

---

[3] McGuire, M., Morgan, R., and Reimer, R. (1994) *Oxford Handbook of Criminology*, New York, Clarendon Press, p. 27

have examined the development of criminal justice agencies. [4] Thus a wide range of information and data has been taken from various disciplines and consolidated to serve as a knowledge-base for this area of study. [5]

Given the multidisciplinary and diverse nature of the subject it is hardly surprising that modern criminology has highly differentiated theoretical, methodological and empirical concerns. Attempts to explain the causation, prevention, and punishment of crime draw on the whole gamut of theoretical perspectives (psychoanalysis, functionalism, interactionism, ethnomethodology, Marxism, econometrics, systems theory, postmodernism, etc.) and ideological concerns (feminism, social-welfarism, left and right realism, etc.,). Each of the competing theories has its own intellectual history and is backed up with substantial research. This not only creates confusion amongst criminologists but also filters through to the media and politicians. Young has noted that in popular discussions on crime there is often a switch in theoretical ideas mid-argument. [6] One of the examples he gives is of someone defining vandalism as a wilful act of damage (implying conscious intent), but going on to *explain* vandalism as a product of the vandal's poor home life (implying that the behaviour is determined). The 'switch' between theories can also be exemplified in the speaker's perspective on justice and crime control. If the cause of the criminal act is because the vandal is from a poor family, then is it logical to severely punish that person rather than 'treat' the socio-economic circumstances?

The complexity of theories is compounded by the existence of different types of crime and offender e.g. sex offences, violent offences, fraud, burglary, non-payment of fines, car crime, illegal drug selling/using. Nevertheless early criminologists were invariably trying to identify singular factors whose presence

---

[4] Siegal, L.J. and Senna, J.J. (1990) *Introduction to Criminal Justice* (5th ed.) St Paul, MN, West Publishing, p.4
[5] ibid., p.4
[6] Young, J. (1981) 'Thinking seriously about crime' in *Crime and Society: Readings in History and Theory*, London, Routledge.

or absence would predispose individuals toward criminality. There are too many different, complex individuals committing too many crimes for far too many reasons to allow for a single causal element.

The promiscuity of theoretical discourse, combined with the raiding of other disciplines for ideas (sociology, psychology, genetic science etc.), makes contextualising one's work in this field an important but delicate, walking-on-egg-shells process. As Young notes, criminology has a chronic tendency towards 'myopic' partiality:

> This one-sidedness can involve taking the criminal at one single point of time and denying the past circumstances which brought about the crime or the future possibilities. It can involve a fixation on the distant past, so that present circumstances are annulled. It can involve a focus on micro-structure of society and its legislation and ignore the rule-breaker altogether - and, of course, it can focus on the criminal as if he or she were independent of humanly created rules. It can produce criminal actors whose actions are proscribed by their bodies; it can produce those who exist outside of the physical world of space and opportunity. It can be bone-headedly deterministic or can imbue human nature with pure reason. It can attempt to explain the criminological universe in terms of race, or class, or gender, or age, but scarcely ever a genuine, meaningful cultural synthesis of them all. [7]

Criminology's history is not one of steady progress and refinement because, as in other academic fields, it does not exist in a social or political vacuum: the dominant ideas of a period (whether establishment or radical), the social problems of a particular society, the government in power and shifting political pressures - all shape its discourse. This is not to suggest a relativism of theory, rather it points to a reflexivity. Young's clarification is useful here: 'theory emerges out of

---

[7] Young, J. (1994) 'Incessant chatter: recent paradigms in criminology', in McGuire, M., Morgan, R. and Reimer, R. (1994) *Oxford Handbook of Criminology*, New York, Clarendon Press, p. 70

a certain social and political conjuncture: this generates points of sensitivity and areas of blindness which inhibit the development of a general theory...' [8]

But it is important to note that whatever coherence criminology can muster, it does so because it is orientated towards a scientific goal and also an institutional field. The convergence and formation of diverse approaches are directed both at a theoretical field and an administrative task. The interdisciplinary criminology field is one that, at least in part, aims to reduce criminal behaviour in society by explanations of crime, predictions of criminal behaviour and endeavouring to influence criminal activities and the policies of justice agencies.

Where then might a theatre practitioner fit into this multi-agency field? This is a question I will be attempting to answer in different, but hopefully generally coherent ways throughout this monograph. A theatre practitioner working in prisons or probation needs to understand and be aware of the context s/he is working in. As soon as s/he enters the confines of a criminal justice institution, s/he will be judged as operating from a particular theoretical viewpoint. For example the work in this monograph describes a project that was designed to contribute to the reduction in likelihood of further violent offences by offenders already convicted of such crimes. The combination of cognitive-behavioural methodologies with theatrical techniques in a short educational programme implies a belief in the agency and free will of individual group members. This is an assumption that cannot be taken for granted. And indeed it would be foolish to deny the existence of other influential factors that can act on individuals and lead to them becoming violent. The practical work described in this monograph needs to be seen as one of several approaches that might contribute to changing the behaviour of violent people (more specifically men). For some participants education, through short programmes, might be helpful, for others, perhaps with

---

[8] ibid., p.71

mental health problems, or those in need of drug therapy, this type of approach may have limited value or be inappropriate.

It is important for a theatre practitioner to be clear about his/her rationale within this field. When asked to justify himself/herself, s/he needs to be aware of, if not have an informed opinion on, the full gamut of theoretical perspectives. The criminal justice system is alive with a hotchpotch of half-baked theories and practical dogma about crime and the criminal offender. Without a basic compass and map a theatre practitioner new to this area could easily become disorientated and lost. It is for this reason that I now turn to some fundamental criminological paradigms.

A brief treatment of some theoretical paradigms.

Two different images of the criminal actor have persisted during the last 100 years of criminology. The first is of a wilful hedonist who takes deliberate decisions to break the rules of a consensus. The second is of one who has been predisposed to crime by forces within or external to him/her (possessed by demons, psychologically 'sick', hereditary criminal personality). It is notable that the most diverse theories converge with these two images in the most unlikely of pairings; for example the conservative and the anarchist hold that an offender operates with free will (for one it is a lapse in moral reasoning, for the other the criminal is a hero); whilst the Lombrosian and the social reformer believe that the actor's behaviour is determined (one argues for biological factors, the other for the influence of poor socio-economic environments). These two equally abstract images of the wilful and the 'propelled' actor reverberate throughout the history of criminology, despite their tenuous link to social reality.

Voluntarism.

At one end of the theoretical continuum there are paradigms which are characterised by a belief in the wilful offender (or individual voluntarism) such as classicism, conservatism and humanist reformism. Whilst it is misleading to indiscriminately use these generic terms to denote absolute paradigms of thinking, they provide a useful framework of different forms of inquiry. For example, classicism, although referring to such different thinkers as Beccaria and Bentham and eighteenth-century thought more generally, maintain similar views of a rational, free-will offender. [9] Classicism holds that the social order is maintained by a contractual legal consensus and that the definition of crime is a violation of the consensus; the extent of crime is marginal and is the result of individual irrationality which can be corrected through punishment and deterrence.

Conservatism differs from classicism in a number of small, but important points. [10] Conservatism maintains that the social order is essentially a _moral_ and _traditional_ consensus (class system, family values) and that threats to the social order may be considered a crime. Conservatism sees the cause of crime as the result of selfishness, greed and the pursuit of personal gratification, and correspondingly believes punishment must be rigorously enforced, to teach a lesson to individuals, and to act as a general deterrence to the rest of society.

The classical and conservative picture of the wilful law violator lies behind endeavours to punish the criminal and protect society. The fundamental argument is that the proper amount of legal punishment is enough to deter crime. Those who are not deterred by the threat of punishment should, upon proof of guilt and conviction, be punished severely so that they will never violate the law again. The weapon used to enforce this view is harsh and long sentences or, in some countries, capital punishment. An example of this retributive view was President

---

[9] There are a number of influential textbooks which discuss the history of criminology, and identify 'the classical school'; Radzinowicz, L. (1986) _A History of the English Criminal Law and its Administration_, from 1750, 5 vols., London, Stevens; Radzinowicz, L. (1966) _Ideology and Crime_, London, Stevens; Taylor, I., Walton, P., and Young, J. (1973) _The New Criminology_, London, Routledge and Kegan Paul; most of these writers identify Beccaria as one of the earliest pioneers of 'classicism': Beccaria, C. (1963 [1764]) _Of Crimes and Punishments_, Indiana, Bobbs-Merill. First published in Italian as Dei Delitti e Delle Pene.
[10] Haag, E. van den (1975) _Punishing Criminals_, New York, Basic Books.

38

Clinton's '3 strikes and you are out' campaign which held that if convicted three times an offender would be given a life sentence - no matter what the crime (the first casualty of this policy was a man who was given a life sentence for stealing a pizza). Classicism and conservatism tend to a retributive view of policy, advocating that the focus of justice should be on the victim of crime rather than the criminal. The role of the justice agency should be to protect the innocent from criminal acts. The main aim of the justice system is to take criminals out of the community, until they are fit to return.

Like classicism, humanist reformism maintains that an act of crime breaks a social contract, and that as a result society has the right to redress the wrong-doing. However, emerging out of the 'excess of violence' in the eighteenth-century, reformism proposed that the limit of punishment was 'the humanity of each subject'; punishment should be transparent to the crime and as non-arbitrary as possible; punishment should be a deterrent, a recompense, and a lesson. [11] The influence of reformism on the current system has meant that although a greater proportion of people are going to prison, the sentences they receive for similar crimes are less likely to vary widely than in previous years.[12] The emphasis is on the examination of penal codes in an effort to simplify the classification of offences and create a more rational approach to sentencing.

Positivism.

At the other end of the theoretical continuum is the image of an individual whose behaviour is more or less determined by internal or external factors. Positivism is traditionally the anti-monograph of classicism. Essentially positivism holds that behaviour is governed by biological, physiological and psychological factors. The

[11] Dreyfus, H., and Rainbow, P. (1982) *Michel Foucault, Beyond Structuralism and Hermeneutics*, Chicago, Harvester Wheatsheaf, p.147-148
[12] Siegal, L.J. and Senna, J.J. (1990) op.cit., p.469

criminal actor is one who violates the behavioural consensus, due to genetic /physiological incapacity or ineffective inculcation.

Positivism is a diverse theoretical approach that describes a range of criminological work which has been carried out within an empiricist framework. However it emerged from quite specific claims of Lombroso and his *scuola positiva* in the late nineteenth century (the born criminal, the constitutional and hereditary roots of criminal conduct, criminal types, etc.). [13] Lombroso put forward the view that the criminal is born and not made, and that each criminal could be distinguished from non-criminal people by the 'stigmate' [14]: in other words, certain physical abnormalities which would be found only in criminals. Lombroso although not the first to 'discover' the 'criminal type' is now often used as a reference point to identify theories which seek to locate criminality as a naturally occurring entity. For example, Thompson wrote in 1867 about 'the criminal class' describing these individuals as 'morally insane' and 'defective in physical organisation ...from hereditary causes' in a way that appeared altogether 'Lombrosian' before Lombroso. Thompson:

> All who have seen much of criminals agree that they have a singular family likeness or caste....Their physique is coarse and repulsive; their complexion dingy, almost atrabilious; their face, figure, and mien, disagreeable. The women are painfully ugly; and the men look stolid, and many of them brutal, indicating physical and moral deterioration. In fact there is a stamp on them in form and expression which seems to me the heritage of the class. [15]

Although Lombroso's theories have been largely discredited, the general proposition that heredity plays a part in the causation of crime has continued to develop. The contemporary view is that what each of us inherits is a biological

---

[13] Smith, P. (1968) *Cesare Lombroso, Crime Its Causes and Remedies*, Montclair, N.J. p.31
[14] Young, J. (1994) op.cit., p. 71

system that may provide an orientation or tendency to respond in a certain way to our environment. [16] However, positivism also tends to acknowledge the influence of other factors. For example Erikson's position is expressed in his idea of 'triple book-keeping' ; that in order to understand identity we need to look at its biological basis, at a person's development and at the social context in which he or she lives, each in relation to the others - and on the understanding that none of these are fixed. [17] From a rational point of view, positivists do not regard criminals as being separate from the rest of the population. Instead, criminals are seen as representing the extreme end of a continuous distribution, 'very much as a mental defective represents the extreme end of...intelligence'. [18]

One of the main methods used to explain the role of inheritance in criminal behaviour has been the twin study. The basis of twin studies lies in the difference between Monozygotic (MZ) twins (who share 100 percent of their genes), and Dizygotic (DZ) twins (who are no more alike than ordinary siblings). The overall finding of Lange's studies was that just about twice as many monozygotic as dizygotic twins are concordant. [19] In other words, when one twin is criminal, then among identical twins the other one has twice the chance of being criminal that he would have if the twins were fraternal. More modern and sophisticated studies also tend to indicate that genetic factors can influence delinquency, and specifically more than other factors such as shared environments, and individual environmental factors. [20] The conclusion that researchers make from these

---

[15] Thompson, J.B. (1867) 'The effects of the Present System of Prison Discipline on the Body and Mind', *Journal of Mental Science*, 12, p.341

[16] Rowe, D.C. (1990) 'Inherited dispositions toward learning delinquent and criminal behaviour: New evidence', in L. Ellis and H. Hoffman (Eds) *Crime in Biological, Social and Moral Contexts*, NY, Praeger.

[17] Stevens, R. (1991) 'Personal Identity', Block 5, D103, *Identities and Interaction*, Milton Keynes, The Open University Press, p. 29

[18] Eysenck, H.J. (1970) *Crime and Personality*, St. Albans, Paladin, p. 74

[19] Lange, J. (1921) *Verbrechen Als Soshicksal*, Leipzig, Verlag.

[20] Rowe, D.C. and Osgood, D.W. (1984) 'Heridity and sociological theories of delinquency: A reconsideration', *American Sociological Review*, 49.

'scientific' results is that heredity must play an important, and possibly vital part, in predisposing a given individual to crime. [21]

A number of criticisms have been made about these findings. Firstly, genes are chemical structures which interact with 'all of what we are and can thus indirectly affect endpoints as complex as behaviour, but there is no gene for a particular behaviour'. [22] Secondly, criminal behaviour is a social and legal construct rather than a behavioural act that can be properly defined and measured; thirdly, 'few human behaviours have the quality of fixed action patterns that inheritance determines in other animals..'. [23]

Perhaps one of the reasons why the inheritance explanation is often opposed, is that it suggests a certain 'therapeutic nihilism' [24]. In other words, it is believed that because heredity produces certain effects it is therefore impossible for anything to be done about them; heredity sets definite limitations on powers of manipulation. However, Eysenck argues that by understanding precisely how heredity works, what it does to the organism, it is possible to arrange a rational method of drug therapy which 'makes use of the forces of nature, rather than trying to counteract them'. [25] Perhaps this is the main reluctance towards heredity explanations, an unpalatable solution, a political 'hot potato', that completely undermines the existing system and calls for the ruling out of punishment, and proposes that each criminal act should be dealt with as an individual medical prognosis.

Social democratic positivism also holds a determinist view of behaviour, but prefers to see crime as the result of external and environmental factors. [26] Social democratic positivism was part of a widespread post-war consensus that one of

---

[21] ibid.; Eysenck, H.J. (1970) *Crime and Personality*, St. Albans, Paladin.
[22] Plomin, R. (1990) *Nature and Nurture*, Pacific Grove, CA, Brooks/Cole, p.30
[23] Hollin, C. R. (1992) op.cit., p. 30
[24] Eysenck, H.J. (1970) *Crime and Personality*, St. Albans, Paladin, p. 71
[25] ibid., p. 72
[26] Young, J. (1994) op.cit., p. 73

the causes of crime was impoverished social conditions. It was part of a more general conviction that through political interventions anti-social conditions could be improved resulting in a consequent reduction in anti-social behaviour. During the post-war period in Britain much work was done to demolish slums, increase educational standards, create full employment, and introduce comprehensive welfare reforms. The root cause of crime, the social democratic positivism argument holds, is poverty, deprivation, lack of education. The general theory holds that criminals themselves are victims of poverty, lack of hope, alienation, family disorganisation, racism and other social problems. Crime can be controlled by enabling people to cope with their life situations, and helping them to lead law-abiding lifestyles. The social democratic view believes that it is far cheaper, more efficient and humane to help offenders establish themselves in the community rather than punish them with a prison sentence and lock them into a life of crime. In its most basic form social democratic positivism merely argues that when affluence rises, crime will decrease. [27]

A double crisis.

The swing between the traditional arguments of classicism and positivism has been a constant feature of criminology and policy implementation in post-war Britain. However in the last ten years, policies drawn from any one theoretical paradigm have proven questionable in their effectiveness to explain and prevent crime. For example, what Young refers to as the 'etiological crisis' came about as a result of most 'advanced' industrial countries in the post-war period experiencing rising affluence and increased welfare spending, combined with huge increases in crime and delinquency. [28] Although all sorts of justifications were made about this, including denying the crime wave existed, the situation very much undermined the social democratic argument. For example, between

---

[27] ibid., p.72
[28] ibid., p. 72

1951-71 in Britain there was a 64 per cent increase in disposable income, whilst crime in that period rose by 172 per cent. [29]

Although social democratic theories are still a major component of contemporary social thought, the changed prospects for policy based on social intervention gave way to a corresponding growth in neo-classical methods of intervention. An increased police force, the building of more prisons, and a 'more effective' justice system began to inform British policy. For example Rab Butler's 1959 White Paper introduced the biggest prison building programme for young adult offenders, with 16 new institutions 'designed to administer a "short, sharp, shock" to the evidently more recalcitrant young offenders of the new age'. [30]

This is the neo-classical response to the criminal who wilfully breaks the law; to impose increasingly stiff prison sentences, and in harsher settings. The 'short, sharp, shock' regimented prison programmes aim to reduce subsequent criminal activity by 'hard punishment' and deterrence. Criminals are processed through a militaristic-style 'boot camp' approach to punishment intended to be both physically and psychologically gruelling. The argument being that when criminals are forced to conform to rules or are compelled to work regularly, they learn 'good habits' which are transferable to their lives on release. Foucault writes with great insight on this method, describing how the human body of the criminal is objectified in order to be manipulated and controlled. [31] The type of procedure used in 'boot camps' is what Foucault refers to as 'technologies'; the joining of knowledge and power, with the aim of 'forging a docile body that may be subjected, used, transformed and improved'. [32] This is done in several related ways: through drills and training of the body, through standardisation of actions over time, and through the control of space. The link to military tactics of discipline is clear and overt; the focus is on the formal organisation and

---

[29] ibid., p. 72
[30] Fyvel, T.R. (1963) *The Insecure Offenders*, London, Penguin, p. 17
[31] Foucault, M. (1979) *Discipline and Punish*, London, Penguin.

disciplined response of the constituent parts of the body, the automatic reflex of hands, legs and eyes.

The 'boot camp' programmes also emphasise, more than other prison regimes, the allocation of time. The theory is that prisoners are made to 'sweat' for their crimes, to be 'exhausted, and worked hard' as a punishment for their delinquency. Control of a prisoner's time is not applied sporadically or even at regular intervals. There is a constant, regular physical and mental application. Ironically, just as this 'boot camp' approach is beginning to re-surface in Britain (it was first tried in the 1950's), the American 'camps' have been closed after exhaustive and damaging evidence of their lack of effectiveness. [33] The 'camps' were redundant either because there was a dramatic rise in violence and resentment towards staff, or because prisoners were actually enjoying their experience. The other outcome, or fear, was that the 'camps' trained criminals to be faster, fitter, and more disciplined in their offending behaviour, totally inverting the *raison d'etre* of the regime. The effect of these neo-classical practices on the arts and education in prisons is a concern to appear 'useful' or 'effective'. The language used to justify artistic activities in prison becomes functional, for example drama may become 'social skills'; performance may become 'life-skill rehearsals'; the arts are justified as tools of the prison to increase self-esteem and team building - everything must be justified in pragmatic, physical terms. We will find these considerations relevant to the way in which the Pump programme was developed and promoted to the Probation Service and the Home Office.

However, the crisis in theory has also occurred with neo-classical perspectives. Apart from anything else, the cost of prison in the U.K.(and most other countries) is escalating. In 1946 there were approximately 15,000 prisoners and 2,000 staff,

---

[32] Rabinow, P. (1984) *Foucault Reader*, London, Penguin, p. 17
[33] The Guardian (1996) 'U.S. Boot Camps Closed Down', 6th April, p. 21

in 1991/2 there were approximately 50,000 inmates and 34,000 staff. [34] A little over £1.4 billion (nearly 16 per cent of total public spending) was spent on law and order services, with the average prisoner costing the public purse £438 per week. [35]

The concept of prisons as an effective medium of deterrence or punishment has been questioned by some researchers [36] particularly because prisons statistically have such a poor record in terms of the subsequent behaviour of inmates (approximately two-thirds of all young offenders and almost half of all adults are reconvicted at least once within two years of release). [37] These facts about prison have led some researchers to sum up that: 'The notion that punishment can reduce the rate of crime in society is little more than an irrational and unfounded hope.' [38] And yet the difficulty with these arguments is a lack of sufficient alternatives. Prison may be a 'detestable solution', but what else would society replace it with? [39]

The discrediting of both positivism and classicism in the last fifty years is not always evident in political rhetoric or contemporary policy. But most current theories have by now reacted to the double-barrelled crisis in etiomology and penalty with the tendency to identify multiple causes of crime; each individual criminal act is seen as a function of a varied number of social, psychological, or environmental factors, with no two sets of factors necessarily being exactly alike. Thus most recent theories don the Emperor's new clothes in their attempts to solve old problems, wearing cloth woven together by old criminological discourses from the 1960's and 1970's. Young points out that, surprisingly, they

---

[34] Home Office (1947) *Report of the Commissioners of Prisons and Directors of Convict Prisons for the Year 1946*, Cmd. 7271, London, HMSO; Home Office (1992) *Prison Statistics England and Wales 1990*, Cmnd. 1800, London, HMSO.

[35] Home Office (1992) op.cit.

[36] McGuire, J. and Priestly, P. (1985) *Offending Behaviour*, London, B.T. Batsford.

[37] Home Office (1992) op.cit.

[38] McGuire, J. and Priestly, P. (1995) *What Works: Reducing Reoffending*, Chichester, Wiley, p. 14

share some common ground: 'they all play down the role of the police in the control of crime; they are all critical of the existing prison system; and they all reject traditional positivism and classicism'. [40]

The Rehabilitation Perspective.

Alongside the development of explanatory theories about criminal behaviour there has been a corresponding concern with forms of treating and/or preventing criminals from committing further offences. The image of the voluntaristic or determined actor has influenced the way in which criminals are treated once incarcerated.

As this study is related to an investigation of an educational programme, I would like to concentrate on exploring the rehabilitative perspective in the criminal justice system. However, the reader should be aware that the rehabilitation perspective is only one of many approaches that attempt to prevent, deter and/or change an offender's criminal activities.

The notion of rehabilitation for offenders is linked to the image of the determined actor, who whilst having some degree of agency, is propelled by social misfortune or biological deficiency. Rehabilitation programmes consist of some explicit activity designed to alter or remove conditions operating on offenders which are deemed responsible for their illegal behaviour. One positivistic approach to rehabilitation work is to view the criminal on a parallel with the neurotic or psychotic individual, except his personality pathology is expressed in an illegal fashion. This view holds that offenders need to be 'rewired' by a psychiatrist or some other psychotherapeutic technician who can delve inside their psyches. In general this approach focuses more on the individual and less on his social circumstances.

---

[39] Rabinow, P. (1984) op.cit., p. 215
[40] Young, J. (1994) op.cit., p. 80

The criminal is a person whose:

> ...behaviour is a function of cognitive elements buried deep within the "layers of personality". These deep-seated tensions are dimly perceived by the individual, or may be unperceived by him, but can be made apparent by a skilled psychiatrist. [41]

Once the 'patient' becomes sufficiently aware of his dysfunctions then, with the psychiatrist's help, he is back on the road to mental health. Undoubtedly there are some people who will fit the psychiatric picture of the abnormal offender, so these forms of psychotherapeutic activities may be useful. For example the Parkhurst Special Prison Unit (now closed) succeeded in reducing violent assaults by 90 per cent. [42] This was not achieved by swapping DNA or lowering testosterone levels, but by helping these extremely violent men to 'escape from their childhood prison':

> ...the stark fact is, inside every man, there is a violent infant....Violence is a disease. Disease, however, can be cured. [43]

The style of rehabilitation programme which I will be exploring in this monograph, focuses on the individual and his or her ability to change their life situation. It does not deny socio-economic factors, nor does it suggest that an offender has no responsibility over his or her actions. Probation rehabilitative programmes deal with an offender's belief systems and the interpretative frameworks by which they 'make sense' out of sensory perception and direct their behaviour. If offenders are to be directed away from unlawful acts they must learn to recognise and change certain self images, attitudes and beliefs.

---

[41] Johnson, B. (1996) 'Violent, man and boy', in *The Guardian*, 13th February, p.6
[42] ibid., p.6

The emphasis in probation rehabilitation programmes focuses on the idea that offenders are characterised by various definitions, rather than a uniform set of attitudes and beliefs, which separate them from non-offenders. [44] The key principle in this area of work is to look at the offender's definition of a criminal situation, and particularly at the set of justifications and rationalisations that are made.

I have indicated that the work in this monograph fits into a rehabilitative perspective of crime and the offender. This perspective allows for Erikson's notion of 'triple book keeping'; that in order to understand criminal behaviour different theories of causation are needed. [45] For example, individual voluntarism, social context, and the effects of biology all need to be understood in relation to the other. These theories may be difficult to integrate, but each contributes different but complementary insights into the reasons for crime.

The theories I have discussed also present very different concepts about how to deal with crime. Rehabilitation, individual psychoanalysis and even drug therapy have been mentioned as possible 'cures' or ways of changing offenders into law-abiding citizens. And it is this notion of change which I would now like to focus on. The rehabilitation perspective in probation work links an offender's deficit of social skills to offending behaviour, and explores alternative ways of social functioning that are legitimate. One of the underlying assumptions in this approach is that an offender has a deficit or lack of social skills. For example participants on an anger management programme have a lack in self-control, in offence focused work there is a deficit in empathy for victims and an insufficient notion of consequences (for self and other people). This notion of social skills deficit suggests that a process of social education has not transpired 'properly' in an individual, and that rehabilitation seeks to redress the balance and enable an

---

[43] ibid., p.6
[44] McGuire, J. and Priestly, P. (1985) *Offending Behaviour*, London, B.T. Batsford.
[45] Stevens, R. (1991) op.cit., p.42

offender to adapt or re-adapt more successfully to society. This is a central theoretical and practical premise of probation work, and one that informs the way in which drama is developed in this context. As we will explore later, the emphasis in drama work in probation is to acknowledge the socio-economic and political pressures, but to focus on an individual's efficacy in that context. Crucially, a great deal of drama work is informed by the probation notion of choice and agency. The function of the aesthetic experience is therefore to re-engage with the decisions of a criminal act and highlight consequences of actions in order to encourage greater degrees of social responsibility and moral maturation. This brings us to a rather threatening concept: that society engages the science of criminology as a 'disciplinary technology', with the aim of socialising deviant citizens into behaving according to moral (or legal) 'norms'. [46] Whether or not this process is indeed a threatening one, depends on one's perception of how socialisation connects with the 'culture' and ideologies of a society.

Socialisation and moral development.

The central debate in this section concerns the socialising interaction between a 'culture' and a developing child. If a child is to acquire the values and behaviour of a functioning member of human society some interaction is needed between a culture's socialising agents and a child's capacity for growth. In the literature of moral-development this interaction often seems to puzzle writers. How does culture transmit its standards and values to a young child? [47] How does a child

---

[46] Dreyfus, H., and Rainbow, P. (1982) op.cit., p.152

[47] Mead, G.H. (1934) *Mind, Self and Society*, Chicago, University of Chicago Press; Foucault, M. (1984) op.cit.; Piaget, Jean (1965) *The Moral Judgement of the Child*, New York, The Free Press; Kohlberg, L., Scharf, P. and Hickey, J. (1975) The Just Community Approach to Corrections: the Niantic Experiment, in L. Kohlberg (Ed) *Moral Development and Behaviour*, New York, Holt, Rinehart and Winston; Durkheim, E. (1961) *Moral Education: A study in the Theory and Application of the Sociology of Education*, New York, Free Press; Durkheim, E. (1974) *Sociology and Philosophy*, New York, Free Press; Colby, A., Gibbs J, and Kohlberg, L. (1978) *The Assessment of Moral Judgement: Standard Form Moral Judgement Scoring*, Cambridge, Mass., Moral Education Research Foundation.

make sense of behavioural regularities that s/he observes in the social world; regularities which will be demanded of the child itself? There is a diversity of opinions on this in the moral-development literature and only occasional agreement. For example the socialising culture, for some, is thought of as a negotiable, loosely organised collection of rules or standards for regulating conduct; [48] for others it is aligned with absolute and oppressive state power. [49] In this section I will be exploring a number of these contrasting theories of moral development and socialisation, but will be focusing on how they specifically relate to rehabilitation work in prisons and probation.

Mead argues that the process of becoming a social being depends on a capacity for self representation, and emerges from an ability in role-taking and reflexivity, abilities acquired as a child learns language and develops in a social environment.[50] Mead believes that a new born baby is only a potential social being, and that without culture he/she would not be shaped into human history. He believes that for a baby the world is an initially meaningless and confusing place, but as s/he becomes more competent at symbolising the world in general, s/he also learns about himself/herself as separate selves with a particular identity. 'Only when the individual can symbolically designate objects in the environment can the self be designated as one of those objects'. [51] Mead places special emphasis on the role of parents in the socialisation process. He argues that the parents or guardians are the most *significant others* for a child, surrounding the maturing self with attitudes, evidence and information about the nature of itself.

---

[48] D'Andrade, R.G. and Romney, A.K. (1964) Summary of Participants' Discussion, *American Anthropologist*, **66**; Levi-Strauss, C (1969) *The Elementary Structures of Kinship*, Boston, Beacon Press; Much, N.C., and Scheder, R.A. (1978) Speaking of Rules: The Analysis of Culture in Breach, in Damon, W. (Ed) *New Directions for Child Development: Moral Development*, **2**, 19-39, San Francisco, Jossey-Bass Publishers.

[49] Foucault, M. (1979) *Discipline and Punish*, London, Penguin.

[50] Mead, G.H. (1934) op.cit.

[51] Hewitt, H. (1984) *Self and Society: A Symbolic Interactionist Social Psychology* (3rd ed.), London, Allyn and Bacon, p.67

> Individuals do not learn about themselves or experience themselves directly...we see ourselves as others see us. In the simplest sense, we learn to use the name given to us by others; more subtly, all the terms of value, respect, hatred, liking, hope, social location and definition that people apply to themselves, they learn from members of their family and the other groups to which they belong...The child does not learn to hate or respect himself by responding directly to his own conduct. Rather he learns both the terms of reference he should use and their specific application to him from others who are significant to him as he grows up. [52]

According to Mead, the social self is developed by internalising the attitudes of the family and other groups to which it belongs. In doing so the child becomes socialised into a culture of attitudes, language, values and beliefs. The self is constructed then through a process of self-representation, taking on new roles and the environment of representations and attitudes experienced by the developing self.

In a slightly more complex model Gerson and Damon argue that a number of behavioural and conceptual complexities have obscured the actual connection between the moral judgement and social conduct. [53] Although they assume a connection between the two, it is neither one of simple concordance nor one in which moral judgement unilaterally determines conduct. In their model Gerson and Damon argue that many different types of moral and non-moral knowledge interact in a manner that shapes both the individual's moral judgement and his or her social conduct. The various types of knowledge derive from the individual's actions and goals within social contexts. Accordingly, such knowledge is determined not only by the specific nature of the social context but also by the individual's capacity to act. This capacity, in turn, directly reflects the individual's development status: a combination of his/her past history, present abilities and

---

[52] ibid., p.55
[53] Gerson, R.P., and Damon, W. (1978) Moral Understanding and Children's Conduct, in Damon, W. (Ed) *New Directions for Child Development: Moral Development*, 2, 19-39, San Francisco, Jossey-Bass Publishers.

potential for continual growth. In short, their definition of moral development is the achievement of increasingly more complex but adaptively more adequate modes of thought to a varying set of social demands. [54]

A contrasting view of the same process is expressed by new deviancy theory, which holds that human beings are born free but gradually lose their freedom through socialisation, as structures of society transmit representations designed to control behaviour and maintain the social order. [55] For the criminal, the looking-glass self is someone who acts, and whose behaviour is reflected back as being criminal. The criminal actor is thus labelled, and s/he begins to reorganise his/her view of themselves in relation to the world, adopting the identity suggested by society's view of their conduct. Centrally, new deviancy theory makes the assumption that an individual is fundamentally changed during the socialisation process because natural, pre-socialised tendencies are incompatible with the demands of adult society as transmitted in the socialisation process. In this view deviancy is normal and conformity must be explained. However, Damon argues that given the central role culture has played in human evolution, it is more realistic to assume a compatibility between a child's natural tendencies and the demands of an adult society; thus conformity is normal and deviancy must be explained. [56] Damon goes on to stress that not only is conformity to culture normal, but the internalisation of culture is essential to the normal development of personality. 'Man has a deep, organic need for his culture, and the feeling of belonging to and participating in a viable, on-going group gives substance to personality and meaning to life'. [57]

[54] Damon, W. (Ed) (1978) *New Directions for Child Development: Moral Development*, 2, San Francisco, Jossey-Bass Publishers.
[55] Akers, R (1968) 'Problems in Sociology of Deviance: Social Definitions and Behaviour', *Social Forces*, 46, Spring; Pelfrey, W. (1980) *The Evolution of Criminology*, Cincinnati, Ohio, Anderson Publishing Co.
[56] Damon, W. (1978) op.cit.
[57] Hogan, R., Johnson, J., and Emler, N.P. (1978) 'A Socioanalytical Theory of Moral Development',

These speculations about human socialisation can be described as a form of individualism, which is a socioanalytical theory that argues that there is an evolutionary basis of morality.[58] Hypothetical human motives or drives such as a need for social attention and approval, the need for structure and organisation, and a need for aggressive self-expression (competitive tendencies, status seeking) are seen as being unconscious and inherent to all human beings. [59] In view of this emphasis on how moral development is over-determined and how an individual evolves in response to a need for culture, it is necessary to find an explanation as to why some people become deviant and others do not.

One response might be to argue that failures in moral development begin with poor attachment bonds between a child and its significant others. This produces insecurity, hostility and 'low rule attunement'. [60] Disturbances in the attachment bond spill over into the next phase of development, disrupting peer relations and further isolating the child. By adolescence such children are socially isolated and insensitive to social expectations and to the rights of others and may potentially become criminal offenders.[61] This explanation of criminal behaviour, from a socioanalytical perspective, echoes many of the criminological notions of crime causality, i.e. that deviancy is subject to determined factors such as unconscious drives and environmental learning.

in William Damon (ed.) *New Directions for Child Development: Moral Development*, **2**, San Francisco, Jossey-Bass Inc., p. 4

[58] Campbell, D.T. (1975) 'On the Conflicts Between Biological and Social Evolution and Between Psychology and Moral Tradition', *American Psychologist*, **30**; Erikson, E.H. (1950) *Childhood and Society*, New York, Norton; Hogan, R. (1975) 'Moral Development and Personality', in D.J. DePalma and J.M. Foley (eds.) *Moral Development: Current Theory and Research*, Hillside, N.J., Erlbaum Associates.

[59] Lovejoy, A.O. (1961) *Reflections on Human Nature*, Baltimore, John Hopkins University Press.

[60] ibid., p.15

[61] Goldstein, A. (1988) *The Prepare Curriculum*, Champaign, Research Press.

Socialisation, moral development and rehabilitative interventions.

I have been describing some of the theories of socialisation and moral development, and how they propose different perceptions as to the cause of deviancy. To extend this analysis, and develop it towards the central concerns of this monograph, I would like to focus on some educational initiatives that have sought both theoretically and practically to address problems of moral maturity and social skills deficit. In particular, theorists such as Piaget and Kohlberg have explored people's patterns of reasoning about moral decisions, and identified different levels of maturity and development.[62] These theories are particularly relevant to this monograph because they form the foundation of learning theories which inform the work of cognitive psychologists working in prisons and probation. These theories may also be seen to have influenced the methodology of theatre practitioners operating with an overtly educational or rehabilitative agenda.

The moral development literature is often ambiguous in its definition of what constitutes deviancy and what exactly moral maturity is. In spite of a tendency to tolerance and pluralism, when it comes down to moral actions, it is likely that, in general, people will commend some behaviours and disapprove of others. Therefore when it comes to dealing with a criminal deviant, is it just a question of teaching 'correct' values? If what needs to be accomplished is right thinking and straight acting, educating for moral maturity is simply plugging in right answers to questions of 'would I' or 'should I' and then devising will power exercises for the fortitude to follow the right path.

Piaget, Kohlberg, and Colby emphasis the *process* of moral thinking in their practical work. Piaget and Kohlberg in particular maintain a belief that moral judgement develops through a series of cognitive reorganisations called stages. Each stage has an identifiable shape, pattern and organisation. As Kohlberg points

---

[62] Piaget, J. (1965) op.cit.; Kohlberg, V.J. (1975) op.cit.

out, an indication of moral maturity is not how forcibly one says that stealing is wrong, but what reasons one gives for holding that view. Moral development is not a process of imprinting rules and virtues but a process involving transformation of cognitive structures.

In a prison and probation context moral development exercises look at rationalisations, justifications and developing a participant's empathetic understanding of the consequences of criminal behaviour - for the victim of crime, the offender himself/herself, and for the offender's family. The goal of such exercises, whether they be discussion or drama based, is to stimulate the movement toward a more developed sense of moral maturity. This rather modest hypothesis, that consistent exposure to moral dilemmas results in moral development, has been tested out quite widely.[63] The findings from these studies show that whilst the capacity for moral reasoning can be increased, there is not necessarily a correlation between reasoning maturity and behaviour. The significant factor in encouraging more responsible behaviour was shown to be the environment in which the individual currently lived. This was particularly clear when Kohlberg set up a moral education programme in a Connecticut prison.[64] What became immediately apparent was that once the group began discussing real-life dilemmas, the contrast became apparent between how the group thought the conflicts should be resolved and how they actually were resolved. Life in prison reflected the lowest stage of moral reasoning: everyone acted either to avoid arbitrary punishment or to further his or her own instrumental interests. Inmates who in discussions suggested higher stage resolutions to real-life conflicts admitted they could not act on these resolutions and hope to survive in prison society. The need to create a prison environment in which inmates could learn to

---

[63] Blatt, M. and Kohlberg, L. (1971) 'The Effects of Classroom Moral Discussion Upon Children's Level of Moral Judgement', research report in *Collected Papers on Moral Development and Moral Education;* Rest, J. (1976) 'The Research Base of the Cognitive Developmental Approach to Moral Education', in T.C. Hennessy (ed.) *Values and Moral Development*, New York, Paulist Press.

act on their higher stages of reasoning led to Kohlberg setting up a 'just community', in which the inmates and guards agreed to work together to democratically arrive at decisions about how to govern their community and how to enforce the rules they made (see also Barlinnie Special Unit and HMP Grendon). [65] What Kohlberg and his colleagues identified was that moral acts are undertaken within a certain ideological context and community atmosphere. Yet the classical model is of a lonely person of morality, acting alone and relying only on their inner moral principles to determine which moral action to take.

This brings us back to the importance of significant others in the process of socialisation and moral development. But it also shows that when the moral atmosphere of our immediate environment changes our behaviour may alter too. This is particularly significant for the theatre practitioner who has little or no control over the environment in which s/he is working. It suggests that the effect of arts educational work, or indeed any work, will be restricted by the 'moral atmosphere' of the prison. But what Kohlberg's work offers is that environmental atmospheres can be changed, and that arts educational work can play a part in these 'atmospheric' changes.

Definitions and applications of phenomenology.

It would be a major philosophical task to undertake a detailed definition and explanation of phenomenology. But in its most fundamental form, phenomenology is a philosophical study which concentrates on the detailed description of conscious experience. We will find the consideration of phenomenology relevant to the development of the TIPP Centre project.

---

[64] Kohlberg, V.J. (1978) op.cit.
[65] Kohlberg, L., Scharf, P. and Hickey, J. (1975) The Just Community Approach to Corrections: the Niantic Experiment, in L. Kohlberg (Ed) *Moral Development and Behaviour*, New York, Holt, Rinehart and Winston.

Bernard Curtis observes the following as distinguishing features of phenomenology: [66]

1. A belief in the importance, and in a sense the primacy, of *subjective consciousness*.

2. An understanding of consciousness as active, as *meaning-bestowing*.

3. A claim that there are certain essential structures to consciousness of which we can gain direct knowledge by a certain kind of *reflection*. Exactly what these structures are is a point about which phenomenologists have differed.

In this section I will discuss how these general features link to: the principles of applying phenomenological critiques to an aesthetic experience; and understandings of human beliefs and actions (with reference to violent men).

Phenomenology and consciousness.

The central focus of phenomenology is to seek understanding of consciousness; of the internal mechanisms which perceive the world, and which, in turn, influence external behaviour. A person's behaviour, or some of it, remains outside the competence of 'natural' science unless we first understand the motivational aspects of the person: the ways in which the person perceives the world; the ways in which the person arranges those perceptions; the ways in which these perceptions link to reflexivity and emotion - in short it is the study of a person's consciously-held beliefs which may extend and develop understanding of what an individual is and how they are formed.

---

[66] Curtis, Barnard (1978) *Phenomenology and Education*, ed. Bernard Curtis and Wolfe Mays, London, Methuen, p.xiii

The notion of the subjective-consciousness can be illustrated by considering perception. Conscious perception involves consciousness of the presence 'outside consciousness' of the thing we see, hear, etc., and also our consciousness of seeing or hearing it. We can distinguish as aspects of conscious perception both an awareness of an external world of coloured, audible, tangible, etc., things and an awareness of one's consciousness illuminating this world for oneself. Moreover we are conscious of the unity and regularity of the world of things, and conscious of the unity and 'transparency' of our own consciousness. This ability to reflect on oneself may be described as the capacity for *reflexivity*, or *self-objectification*. This is something which develops as we grow, as one can see from a child who gradually becomes self-aware. Hewitt refers to this as the moment when a person begins to 'mind their own conduct', [67] while Mead talks about 'being another to oneself'.[68]

Curtis argues that by reflecting upon what it is to see something it is possible to discover these aspects or component parts of seeing. [69] One feature of this account is that by reflecting upon consciousness we are reflecting also upon the external world it is conscious of, and vice versa. This kind of reflection upon consciousness, upon the way in which, for example, the experience of seeing presents itself in consciousness, is central to phenomenology.

The second important feature of phenomenology is the identification that consciousness is active and meaning-bestowing. In chapter three, I cite Dodge's identification of steps in the effective processing of social information. [70] These are, firstly, the encoding of social cues, secondly, the cognitive representation of these social cues, thirdly, the searching for appropriate ways of responding, and

---

[67] Hewitt, H. (1984) op.cit., p. 61

[68] ibid., p. 69

[69] Curtis, B. (1978) *Phenomenology and Education*, ed. Bernard Curtis and Wolfe Mays, London, Methuen.

[70] Dodge, K.A. (1986) 'A Social-information processing model of social competence in children', in M. Permutter (Ed.) *Minnesota Symposium on Child Psychology*, Hillsdale, N.J., Erlbaum, p.18

fourthly, the decision on the best way to respond. What Dodge is highlighting, is that subjective consciousness is constantly active in interpreting and processing information from the external world, and that the way in which an individual arranges external signs or cues effects reactive behaviour. Even a simple act of perception involves interpretation, as does every act of knowing, and all interpretations involve *decision*. This point is one of the main features of phenomenologically linked notions in cognitive behavioural theories and forms an important element in interventionist strategies with violent men.[71]

The third phenomenological claim that Curtis identifies is that there are *essential structures* to consciousness of which we can gain direct knowledge by a certain kind of *reflection*. If it is assumed that a young child is conscious before learning 'public' words, and if it is meant by this that the child bestows meaning and uses signs to express to himself/herself the meaning s/he bestows, then clearly signs are not always the same as or related to public words. However, children who are denied access to all public language (gesture, behaviour, specific language skills), will probably have a limited development for using signs to express and bestow meaning. It seems, therefore, that only within very narrow limits can the human consciousness discover its own signs from within its own resources to express and bestow such meaning as it can. The developments of individual consciousness and of the meaning which it intends seem closely dependent on public language, born from previous learning and experience. This reflexivity, informed by past experiences, filters perception; an important point when considering why some people choose to use violence, when others in similar situations do not.

---

[71] Beck, A.T. (1976). *Cognitive Therapy and the Emotional Disorders*, New York: International Universities Press; Kelly, G.A. (1986) *A Brief Introduction to Personal Construct Theory*, London, Centre for Personal Construct Psychology; Novaco R W. (1975) *Anger Control*, Massachusetts, Lexington Books.

Phenomenology and aesthetics.

The phenomenological principles may be relevant to extending psychological understanding of consciousness, but in what way do they provide a critique for understanding the aesthetic experience? In chapter two I present an explanation and analysis of why and how drama may be used as an effective tool in 'bracketing' and exploring contrasting modes of perception.

It was not until 1953 in Dufrenne's *The Phenomenology of Aesthetic Experience* that phenomenological ideas, as outlined by Husserl, were used as an analogue to investigate the features of aesthetic experience. [72] The analogy involves the conscious or in some cases spontaneous operation of suspending the efficacy of aspects of existence as significant of the course and content of conscious experience. [73] Both Merleau-Ponty and Sartre argue that the 'reduction' is continually being performed, at least in part, by consciousness in living contact with its surrounding world. [74] Therefore, the process of 'reduction' is perceived by some phenomenologists as a 'natural' method of processing social information, which includes: the encoding of social cues and the cognitive representation of these social cues. This also links back to the definition outlined by Curtis, of subjective-consciousness and the active meaning-bestowing consciousness.

Herbert Read usefully provides a definition of the process in aesthetic perception, he identifies three stages: [75]

1. The mere perception of material qualities - colours, sounds, gestures and many more complex and undefined physical reactions.

2. The arrangement of such perceptions into pleasing shapes and patterns.

---

[72] Husserl, E (1931) *Ideas: General Introduction to Pure Phenomenology*, translated by W.R. Boyce Gibson, New York, Humanities Press, p.27-32.
[73] ibid.
[74] Merleau-Ponty, M. (1962) *Phenomenology of Perception,* trans. C. Smith, New York, Humanities Press; Sartre, J.P. (1966) *The Psychology of Imagination*, trans. B. Frechtman, New York, Washington Square Press.
[75] Read, Herbert (1982) *Meaning of Art*, London, Faber and Faber, p 24-25

3. The aesthetic sense may be said to end with these two processes, but there may be a third stage which comes when such an arrangement of perceptions is made to correspond with a previously existing state of emotion or feeling. Then we say that the emotion or feeling is given *expression*. The work of art comes into existence with the act of incarnation - that is to say, at the moment the artist finds the words (or other media) to express his emotion or 'state of mind'. Emotion and expression are then an organic unity that cannot be separated.

If we contrast Read's definition with Curtis', we can see that both the philosophical and aesthetic notions of phenomenology are closely linked. For example, Read's first stage of 'mere perception' links to Curtis' of the unstructured subjective consciousness; Read's second stage links to the idea of meaning-bestowing - of constructing and arranging perceptions; and Read's third stage of expressing previously felt emotions resonates with Curtis' 'certain kind of reflection' which is structured by previous experiences.

Linking phenomenology to theories of violent behaviour.

Some of the implications which the phenomenological viewpoint has for educational programmes for violent offenders can be stated in broad terms as follows. The view about the primacy of consciousness seems to claim that consciousness of the world involves and somehow depends upon self-consciousness. Knowing about one's own subjective consciousness accompanies and in some respects even precedes knowing about the world outside consciousness, including knowing about other people. Thus if there is an attempt to try and help violent offenders alter their behaviour, then it is relevant to help him become more aware of his own consciousness of the world. Furthermore, to recognise that consciousness is meaning-bestowing is to recognise, for example, that being conscious of seeing something is a matter of making sense of seeing it,

62

and that to extend the possibility and scope of meaning-bestowing is to extend and increase awareness. Finally to claim that consciousness has an essential structure is to claim that consciousness' making sense of things is structured in crucial ways. The precise nature of the structure is a complex argument, for example, whether and how consciousness can be shown to be efficiently caused by things outside consciousness; whether and how consciously-held beliefs can be shown to be determined by society; these are fundamental questions on which phenomenologists have differed. In seems clear, though, that any essential structure of consciousness would play a crucial part in a theory of education for violent offenders. For example, in chapter three the pro-feminist perspective will be discussed in relation to the effect of patriarchal structures on consciousness. Pro-feminist writers argue that male domestic abusers perceive their violence as part of a socially 'approved' need to control women, and therefore rationalise, minimise, and deny that the rules that govern their behaviour are implicitly wrong, or against the codes of society. [76] Some violent men may argue that there is a socially imposed need to control women, that to punish and control their partners is simply a prerogative of the husband/male partner.

The feature of a phenomenological approach to theories on violent behaviour, as evidenced by cognitive behaviourists is that in all cases the gains for the offender outweigh the losses or else he would not behave in that way, in other words their violent behaviour makes sense to them. [77] Pojman identifies these in more general terms as 'knowledge [that] is known in a way appropriate to the knower', and

---

[76] Scheter, S. (1982) *Women and Male Violence,* London, Pluto Press; Holmes, Mark and Lundy, Colleen. (1990) 'Group Work For Abusive Men: A Profeminist Response',*Canada's Mental Health*, Vol. **38**, December 1990; Dobash, R.E. and Dobash, R.P. (1979) *Violence Against Wives*, New York, The Free Press; Dobash, R.E. and Dobash, R.P. (1981) 'Community response to violence against wives: charivari, abstract justice and patriarchy', *Social Problems*, **28**, 5, pp 563-581; Dobash, R.E. and Dobash, R.P. (1990/91) *The CHANGE Project Annual report 1990 and 1991*, University of Stirling.
[77] Kelly, G.A. (1986) op.cit.; Novaco, R.W. (1975) op.cit.; Beck, A.T.(1987). *Recidivism of Young Parolees*, Washington D.C., Bureau of Justice Statistics Special Report; Bush, J. (1995) Teaching Self Risk Management to Violent Offenders, in McGuire, J. (Ed.) *What Works: Reducing Reoffending*, Chichester, John Wiley and Sons.

goes on to argue that only what is learned through experience, personally appropriated, is truly known. [78]

This is an important point, which is echoed by research about violent men:

> Attitudes, beliefs and thinking patterns in the minds of violent individuals support and promote their violent behaviour. Violent people may truly believe, for instance, that if they abandon violence the world will overwhelm them. They may form the habit of thinking of themselves as victims. They may nurture underlying feelings of righteous anger and resentment toward the world. They may believe they are entitled to hurt others because of the hurt they have suffered. These kinds of attitudes, beliefs and thinking patterns can make violence seem to be a normal, justified, and necessary behaviour. [79]

I have talked briefly about the view among phenomenologists that experience is structured by thought and *vice versa*. And all experience is reflective in the sense of being structured by thought, and some of it is reflective in further degrees as we become self-conscious of our structuring of the world. But our awareness of the structure of our beliefs might not extend to being articulate about the relationships between our beliefs, and such awareness is perhaps even more likely not to extend to being able to explain why we hold the beliefs we do by offering supporting reasons for holding them. Also, our awareness of the fallibility of our beliefs might not extend to regarding the structure of our beliefs about what we are perceiving as being other than unambiguously 'given' in the things in the world that we are perceiving. To understand the development of an individual consciousness we must understand how it is based on (at least to some degree) self-consciousness of its own unity and continuity of belief and action. Curtis

---

[78] Pojman, L.P. (1978) 'Kierkegaard's theory of subjectivity and education', in *Phenomenology and Education*, (ed.) Bernard Curtis and Wolfe Mays, London, Methuen, p. 4

[79] Bush, J. (1995) 'Teaching Self Risk Management to Violent Offenders', in McGuire, J. and Priestly, P. (Eds.) *What Works: Reducing Reoffending*, Chichester, John Wiley and Sons.

argues that the individual consciousness grows by extending in range and complexity of belief and in awareness of its own history of action. [80]

Contributions of theatre to the theoretical territory.

The practical experimental work described in this thesis is an attempt to explore a basic hypothesis that, through using theatre and drama techniques, ways of perceiving and behaving can be developed so that people who use violent behaviour can discover alternative and more positive forms of expression. It is my assertion , that, to some degree, violence is something which is learnt. It is part of the socialisation of the individual that takes place through contact with *significant others* (parents, peer groups) and to some degree communicated by the cultural representations available in society i.e. masculinity, aggression and competition. Whilst I would refute the idea that there is a gene for say, domestic violence, it is harder to deny that certain aggressive tendencies might be inherited. It is the complex interactions of inheritance, personality, and social environment that influence identity and behaviour. Criminal violent behaviour is without doubt determined by a large and heterogeneous array of social, psychological and biological factors. Learnt behaviour through socialisation is not the only factor, nor does it suffice by itself to produce such behaviour. But it is not therefore unimportant; an explanation of part of a phenomenon is not to be discarded because it does not deal with the total phenomenon.

The attempt to develop a 'technology' involving behavioural modification is, as Foucault rightly points out, a highly suspect occupation. The notion of 'human engineering' of any kind is a thorny ethical issue, and one which I have had to think through with great care over the last four years. At times I have felt deep discomfort at the thought that I was part of a process attacking one set of values and arguing for them to be replaced with another - deemed more morally superior.

---

[80] Curtis, B. (1978) op.cit.

My way through this difficult argument has been to believe that the criterion for the goodness/badness of values lies not in their antecedents, but in their consequences. That the values or beliefs in themselves are not as important as the behaviour they endorse. Therefore, for the theatre practitioner operating with a specific educational agenda, the goal of his/her work with offenders is to explore rationalisations, justifications and motivations for criminal behaviour, in the hope that this encourages a more developed sense of responsibility, maturity and empathetic understanding of the consequential effects deviant actions have on other people.

The arts are part of the co-ordinating creative intelligence of human society. The condition of the enjoyment of arts is leisure to look, to become receptive, to become reflexive, to absorb; leisure to form a connection. Aesthetic leisure is an area in which things are absorbed and re-personalised. However in a system in which all activities must be purposeful and useful, there is a danger that the dramatic/artistic imagination is an anachronism, an irritant which:

> ....disturbs the chemical sleep of habits of such a system by making it conscious of the degradation of its mechanisation, by the appearance of extraordinary desires; by overshadowing it with the super-reality of theatre, by unsettling it with a thirst and a hunger for external beauty. [81]

Theatre projects which result from partnerships between agencies within the criminal justice field may share common goals, i.e. to reduce offending behaviour and victimisation. So it may be that theatre can help to hit certain educational targets, but it may also go beyond the pragmatic goals of the criminal justice system. Within the commission there may be space for a theatre practitioner to bring his/her own agenda, specific arts-based aims and objectives; not just thinking skills but knowledge through the body (through doing and being) through

---

[81] Collins, Cecil (1944) *The Vision of the Fool*, London, Penguin, p.9

experiential work which links feelings and thoughts. The system may endorse and commission theatre if it can prove itself to be a respectable, earnest and education based activity. The system needs to be able to justify everything by its usefulness. However if theatre can prove its effectiveness and usefulness, it may also be able to transcend these criteria, by contributing to the system not merely a philosophy of the useful, but a quality of consciousness of life and an endless regard for human identity; both these elements should live in the basic premise of theatre in prisons and probation.

Chapter Two
Drama with offenders
- the function of drama and the role of
the theatre practitioner in the criminal justice system.

Introduction.

ygUDu

ydoan

yunnuhstan.....

lidl.....bas
tuds weer goin

duhSIVILEYEzum

e.e. cummings
Reprinted in Tony Parker's Violence of our Lives.

The poem is an imitation of a drunk American soldier, sitting in a bar. It should be read out loud, very slowly, and slurred. The irony of the poem is that the drunk is such a pathetic, thoroughly uncivilised figure, that his moral superiority appears foolish and self-righteous. The poem was an attack on the lack of rationale for the American involvement in Korea. The drunk, however, could also symbolise the criminal justice system, hunched over a metaphoric glass, telling the world what to do about those liddle bastuds - we are going to civilise them! To civilise and make them lead law abiding lives. Either through retribution, punishment, deterrence or rehabilitation - whatever it takes. As part of the criminal justice system, theatre practitioners need to be wary of joining the drunk at the bar, and ought to be clear about their rationale and function within the system.

The aim of this chapter is to explore the ways in which drama-based methods have been developed to serve a rehabilitative function in work with offenders. For arts organisations like Geese Theatre and the TIPP Centre this is a key task: 'translating a non-arts objective into an arts-based method', and creating an approach to practical work with offenders which is effective in both an artistic and probation sense.[1] As Thompson notes, 'doing drama in a prison does not automatically become a drama approach to offending behaviour'.[2]

The chapter is divided into three related sections. In the first section I will look at the ways in which traditional drama techniques, such as role-play, re-enactment, role-reversal, and forum theatre, have been adapted for use in the probation/prison context to enhance social skills training, challenge anti-social attitudes, and develop 'perspective taking' or empathy for victims. [3] To this end, I will be concentrating on drama techniques that are particularly relevant to challenging offending behaviour.

The second section of the chapter will focus on the work of Geese Theatre Company, the longest established national touring theatre company to work exclusively in prisons and probation. Geese Theatre and the TIPP Centre are the two main UK arts organisations to have adapted drama-based methods to rehabilitative work with offenders. Over the last seventeen years in the U.S. and U.K., Geese Theatre has pioneered 'relevant theatre' for inmates and probationers

---

[1] Thompson, J. (1996) 'Stage Fights' in *Arts Approaches to Conflict*, ed. Marian Liebmann, London, Jessica Kingsley Publishers, p. 74
[2] ibid., p.74
[3] McGuire, J. and Priestly, P. (1985) *Offending Behaviour*, London, B.T. Bateman, p. 91

focusing on offending behaviour issues. [4] The company has developed from political consciousness-raising performances to offence-focused shows and cognitive-behavioural drama-based programmes. [5]

Geese Theatre usefully highlights the ways in which theatre with a rehabilitative agenda has changed and adapted its orientation to inmates and criminal justice agencies over the past two decades. I will provide an overview of the company, and assess the ways in which the goals of arts and criminal justice agencies have been combined, e.g. in the use of masks, and the Violent Illusion Trilogy. [6] I will also highlight areas of difficulty within the drama with offenders field. In particular I will focus on an injunction hearing brought against two dramatherapists in the US by the American Civil Liberties Union. I will use the issues raised by the case to explore the role and function of a drama practitioner within the criminal justice system.

In the final section I propose an egalitarian and dialogical model that, in my view, provides an appropriate reflexivity to, and rationale for, working with offenders. The idea of a dialogical, egalitarian role in education is not new. Theatre practitioners (e.g. Dorothy Heathcote, Augusto Boal and practitioners from the T.I.E., D.I.E. and Community Theatre movement), group work leaders in social work environments, educational reformists in the sixties, can all be seen to be influenced by a long standing Marxist and Libertarian educational tradition. [7] One of the key areas in which these traditions have influenced educational theory and

---

[4] Bergman, J. and Hewish, S. (1996) 'The Violent Illusion, Dramatherapy and the Dangerous Voyage to the Heart of Change', in *Arts Approaches to Conflict*, ed. Marian Liebmann, London, Jessica Kingsley Publishers, p.93
[5] Geese Theatre Company was initially founded in the US by John Bergman. In 1986 a UK company was set up by Clark Baim, a former US company member.
[6] Geese Theatre Company Programme 1993
[7] Godwin, W. (1946) *Enquiry Concerning Political Justice*, Toronto, University of Toronto Press; Godwin, W. (1966) *Four Early Pamphlets*, Gainsville, Florida, Scholer's Facsimilies and Reprints; Ferrer, F. (1913) *The Origins and Ideals of the Modern School*, London, Watts; Freire, P.(1972) *Pedagogy of the Oppressed*, London, Penguin; Freire, P. (1974) *Education For Critical Consciousness*, London, Sheed & Ward; Tolstoy, L. (1967) *Tolstoy on Education*, trans. Leo

practice is in their affirmation of a rational approach which is taught not through instruction and competition but through participation, co-operation and a non-coercive form of pedagogy.

Drama with offenders.

As discussed in Chapter One the rehabilitative or 'treatment' methods used with offenders are drawn from a complex theoretical context. In order to give some clarification to the different approaches to 'treatment' work, I will argue for an approach to drama-based offence-focused work which begins with the crime as a *reason* for society's interfering in the life and liberty of the offender. This view differs from the 'treatment' orientation in penology, which starts and ends with the personality of the offender, and which sees the offence as no more than a superficial symptom of some underlying disease or disorder.[8] In this view, the smallest and least serious offence could betoken the most profound psychological difficulty, and warrant the extensive incarceration of the individual offender for treatment purposes. The approach I will argue for starts with the offence behaviour as a practice which needs to be dealt with directly, openly and honestly with as many as possible of those offenders who wish to change what they do and in ways that will remove them from the 'uncomfortable grip' of the criminal law.[9] Some of the theoretical perspectives discussed in the previous chapter tended to deny the responsibility of the offender for his or her offence behaviour: the causes are held to lie beyond the individual in the wider environment - familial, social, cultural and political. The cures for these conditions, according to the theories, lay in social or political action. The approach in this monograph certainly does not deny the significance of many of the social and political factors reportedly associated with criminal behaviour, but it *does* assert the value and validity of

Wiener, Chicago, University of Chicago Press; Faure, S. (1914) *La Ruche: son but, son organization, sa portee sociale*, Rambouillet, La Ruche.
[8] McGuire, J. and Priestly, P. (1985) op.cit., p. 22
[9] ibid., p. 22

work with individual offenders, as part of an overall strategy to de ⸻ᴗᴗ ɹe and criminal behaviour.

One of the crucial arguments in this thesis is that drama with offenders may contribute to a change in understanding or attitude towards criminogenic behaviour. Change can not be talked about with ease, nor is it easy to measure in any meaningful way. Because the range and extent of motivational factors influencing an individual is complex, the elements which may influence a change in behaviour should also be viewed as multifarious.

Changing attitudes.

The argument of this thesis is for drama to be seen as a means of changing understanding, with an emphasis on affective/cognitive growth. From this perspective, the role of the practitioner is not to preach morality, or to instruct, or involve a 'client' in therapy, but to encourage personal growth, development and knowledge. How often this occurs is debatable. More often an arts practitioner in prison is confronted with a circle of guarded, resentful faces feeling threatened by yet another perceived 'treatment' for their 'bad' behaviour. There is no single way of bringing about change, and in my experience, no way of altering someone's attitudes or values against his or her will (at least in terms of liberal or humanist thinking). If change is to take place at all it has to be with the informed consent and active co-operation of the person concerned. Gaining that consent is one of the issues that has confronted the development of practical intervention work with offenders. Resistance, even in voluntary participants, is common and to be expected. Not every offender admits to creating victims. The following passage is the testimony of a murderer recounting the process he went through during his incarceration:

Prison's the only place in the world you can go where there's nothing else to do but think: and it took me the whole of the first seven years in there before I got my thinking straight, it really did. I wasn't going to let myself admit I'd really killed a guy, you know what I mean? I was all the time making excuses about it: it'd been an accident because I hadn't meant to do it, or he'd had a weak...artery, or he'd seen the punch coming and tried to duck out of it but he'd miscalculated and ducked into it instead. And anyway what if I hadn't hit him? Him and those guys with him, they'd have beaten my buddy to death. So what, if I killed one man I'd saved the life of another. On and on I went, every variation I could think of, trying to think of an escape. Like I say, for seven years I did that, but finally I stopped. I don't know why: perhaps because I ran out of excuses, that's all, but in the end I recognised them for what they were and accepted the fault was no one else's but mine. [10]

It is important to acknowledge an offender's justifications and rationalisation, because these are all aspects which feed into the overall picture. McGuire and Priestly identify three strategies which can help participants to acknowledge, recognise and develop attitudes linked to criminal behaviour, they involve: (a) the use of role-play and role-reversal techniques; (b) the direct challenging of anti-social attitudes; and (c) confrontation with the consequences of offending behaviour in the person of the victim. [11] I want to focus on how drama-based techniques are used in these strategies with offender groups. For drama to be effective in these terms there needs to be a shift in appraisal, an act of cognition which involves a change in feeling so that some aspect of a participant's perspective on life is questioned and (hopefully) deepened.

The social skills model.

Although there is considerable evidence to support the view that social skills training can be an effective means of helping people to improve interaction with others, it is important to ask whether offenders, in general, experience the kinds of

---

[10] Parker, Tony (1995) *The Violence of Our Lives*, London, Harper Collins, p.33
[11] McGuire, J. and Priestly, P. (1985) op.cit., p.47

social-skill impairments which this training is designed to redress. [12] Drawing from the literature on the subject there are no generalisations to be made about the social skills of offender groups, but some research does indicate that problems in this area are probably not uncommon. [13]

The nature of social skills training is based on a specific approach to human development known as 'social learning theory'.[14] Bandura's model ascribes importance to cognitive processes - and the way in which human beings may learn from observation and then develop through trying out different forms of behaviour. From this 'normal' development, Bandura highlights two key elements which may go wrong with the process. Firstly, individuals in childhood and youth may never have the opportunity to learn certain things; their social behaviour later in life may then show a 'deficit' of certain kinds of skill. Second, individuals may be exposed to behaviour which is maleadoptive, or out of adjustment with the 'norm' in some way; as adults they may then be likely to manifest these kinds of behaviour themselves.

The contention of the social learning model is that these kinds of damage can be repaired. By giving people training - social skills training - they can overcome the disadvantages of learnt behaviours. Argyle noted that the process of social skills training was like many other forms of learning, an instructor first explains what to

---

[12] There are a number of studies which indicate that social skills may be a valuable form of training, in psychiatry: with schizophrenics Herson, M. (1979) 'Modification of skill deficits in psychiatric patients', in A.S. Bellack and M. Herson (eds.) *Research and Practice in Social Skills Training*, New York, Plenum Press; patients with neuroses Falloon, I.R.H., Lindley, P., McDonald, R., and Marks, I.M. (1977) 'Social skills training of out-patient groups: a controlled study of rehearsal and home-work', *British Journal of Psychiatry*, 131, pp. 599-609; and mentally handicapped Wehman, P., and Schleien, S. (1980) 'Social skills development through leisure skills programming', in G. Cartledge and J.F. Milburn (eds.) *Teaching Social Skills to Children: Innovative Approaches*, New York, Pergamon..

[13] Freedman, L.W., Rosenthal, L., Donahoe, C.P., Schlundt, D.J., and McFall, R.M. (1978) 'A social-behavioural analysis of skill deficits in delinquent and non-delinquent children', *Journal of Consulting and Clinical Psychology*, 46, pp. 1448-1462. Freedman et al. compared two groups of male adolescents using an Adolescent Problems Inventory. The results indicated that the 'delinquent' group were significantly less socially competent than the other group - and that the 'delinquent' groups lack of social skills increased the risk of a young person 'getting into trouble'.

[14] Bandura, A. (1977) *Social Learning Theory*, Englewood Cliffs, N.J., Prentice Hall.

do; then demonstrates how to do it; asks one to try it out; and then gives some comments on how well the job was done. [15]

McGuire and Priestly present a useful social skills model, which consists of the following four elements: [16]

1. *Instructions* - individuals are given a basic understanding of a social encounter, and if necessary some suggestions of things to say or do that will help them cope with it satisfactorily.

2. *Modelling* - the social skill equivalent of demonstration; if instructions are not enough someone shows the individual what he or she would do in the encounter, i.e. supplies a concrete example of behaviour that can be copied.

3. *Role-play practice* - individuals then try this out for themselves in artificially set-up scenes (role-plays) in which they can try the new behaviour without fear or real-life 'disaster' if they get things wrong.

4. *Feedback* - by listening to the advice of others, viewing themselves on video, or preferably both, individuals try to make gradual improvements in how they handle an encounter, practising as much as necessary.

The relevance of this social inter-actionist model for offenders is made clear through a number of research studies. [17] In one study 37.2 % of adult male offenders cited 'people' and 'dealing with others' as a major problem linked to criminal behaviour, and many of the other difficulties noted clearly contained a social-skills element within them (family, marital problems, interacting with the police, dealing with authority). [18]

---

[15] Argyle, M. (1969) *Social Interaction*, London, Tavistock.
[16] McGuire, J. and Priestly, P. (1985) op.cit., p. 82
[17] Freedman et al. op cit.; Spence, S. (1979) 'Social skills training with adolescent offenders: a review', *Behavioual Psychotherapy*, 7, pp 49-56.
[18] Priestly, P., McGuire, J., Flegg, D., Hemsley, V., Welham, D., and Barnitt (1984) *Social Skills in Prisons and in the Community*, London, Routledge and Kegan Paul.

Re-enacting an offence.

In order to examine more closely the patterns of interaction that take place before, during and after the commission of an offence, both between co-offenders and between offenders and their victims, it is important to re-create as fully as possible an example of an actual offence. [19] The overall aim of using re-enactment is to help individuals learn from their own past experience, by asking them to do two things: first, to look closely at an offence and analyse it in as much detail as possible; and second, to think carefully about how the event chosen could be made to turn out differently next time around.

From the drama and probation point of view the moment of actual offence is of least interest. Of more relevance are the pressures, thoughts and feelings which led up to the incident, and those that followed. For example, in order for participants to build up an understanding, the role-play can be stopped at various points for the action to be explained - by asking questions such as 'What is really happening at this moment?' 'What is the person thinking/feeling?' 'Why did s/he say that?'

The point is not merely to *understand* what was going on; it is to use the role-play to search for alternative ways of dealing with similar situations which might arise in the future. Many of the re-enactment techniques are adapted from Boal's Forum Theatre, in which a problem is presented, analysed by stopping and starting the action, discussed, in an attempt to open up the concept of positive alternatives. [20] The aim of re-enactment and identifying positive alternatives (whether of things to say or do) is to provide, for the offender concerned, and for group members who share similar experiences, a glimpse of other possibilities,

---

[19] Depending on the nature of the participant group, offences can be (a) real stories or, (b) fictional scenarios created by the group. For example, The TIPP Centre's Blagg! workshop creates a fictional offender and crime created by group members. The advantage is that the focus is not on one group member but that issues of offending behaviour are generalised.

[20] Boal, A. (1979) *Theatre of the Oppressed*, London, Pluto Press.

other ways of acting and reacting which lead to different conclusions, i.e. *not* to the inevitable commission of an offence.

One of the crucial elements used in drama workshops with offenders is the notion of causality, against which is measured the efficacy of their rationalisations. As Esslin notes, drama provides a method by which we can 'translate abstract concepts' - a form of thought, a cognitive process - into 'concrete human terms' and by which 'we can set up a situation and work out its consequences'. [21] This links to Freire's assertion that the more accurately causality is linked to participants' own reality, the more critical their understanding will be; and that when causality is submitted to analysis, participants can reflect on the action to 'reveal its objectives, its means and its efficacy.' [22] It is a way of testing consequences and implications of a given situation. Bolton:

> It is this looking into the future because of what we do now, coupled with knowledge that what we do now belongs to what we and others did in the past that characterises the drama experience. [23]

If a drama practitioner can relate this aspect of drama to the participants' own lives, then a clearer understanding of how much the past and future informs the present can develop. And this is a key area for looking at the consequences of criminal actions.

Theatre and education in prisons and probation is about offering *reflection through a process of creative action*; reacting to the shifting complexity and multidimensionality of meaning in reality. According to George Kelly, a psychologist who used drama-based techniques in the 1950's, the problems that his clients have is, due to fear of the unknown, anxiety or deeply ingrained habit

---

[21] Esslin, M. (1978) *An Anatomy of Drama*, London, Abacus, p.23
[22] Freire, P. (1974) *Education For Critical Consciousness*, London, Sheed and Ward, p. 54
[23] Bolton, G. (1979) *Towards a Theory of Drama in Education*, London, Longman, p. 76

that they cling to rigid and inappropriate sets of interpretations about reality. He argues that human perceptions of the world are both free and determined, that 'we are free to construe events, but are bound by our constructions.' [24] His practical concern with clients was to encourage people 'to represent themselves in new ways, to behave in new ways, to construe themselves in new ways and thereby to become new people.' [25] Kelly used role play and re-enactment extensively to enable clients to rediscover 'a spirit of exploration' and establish construction of life as a creative process.

The purpose of a re-enactment, from an educational perspective, is to balance the critical analysis with the crucial emotional information which may be conveyed in a scene; to elaborate aspects of construing, to provide the means for experimentation within the safety of a group situation; and to protect participants from tackling more threatening issues in the 'real' world before they feel ready. The type of drama for understanding that I am arguing for is not about emotional catharsis, but about encouraging offenders to explore and question his/her ideas, attitudes and feelings and develop ways of making sense of, expressing and communicating them. Similarly, States argues for a: 'theatre that brings us into contact with what exists or with what it is possible to do, theatrically, with what exists'.[26]

Because drama focuses on the process of sharing experience in the development of a 'joint expressive act', there can be a negotiation of meaning in different ways, e.g. on the imagined, fictional social network, and in the real social network in the group. [27] The nature and quality of the latter network underlies and informs the involvement of the group, particularly in a prison where hierarchical and status-

---

[24] Fransella, F. & Dalton, P. (1990) *Personal Construct Counselling in Action*, London, Sage Publications, p. 218
[25] ibid., p.245
[26] States, Bert O. (1985) *Great Reckonings in Little Rooms*, California, University of California Press, p.37
[27] McGregor, L., Tate, M. and Robinson, K. (1977) *Learning Through Drama*, London, Heineman Educational Books, p. 17

orientated structures of personal motivation and impulses exist (as they do in all/most contexts). The play between the represented social network and the real one may produce positive elements. Aside from the sheer extrinsic social benefits of working together on anything creative which may in itself be socially productive, when participants act and 'reflexively develop action through interaction' they enter into dialogue with each other: [28]

> As each one moves and speaks, s/he affects and modifies the action and behaviour of the others. They change and challenge the contributions of each other; they modify and explore the symbols they are using so that they may be drawn nearer to understanding the problem of meaning with which they are concerned. [29]

I will discuss how these *ways of seeing* and construing are explored in drama workshops later, but in practical terms, what other distinctive and specific contributions can theatre make to this area of education for understanding?

Role reversal.

There is some evidence that role reversal can bring about changes in the views of those who engage in it; and specifically that extremist but unconsidered views can be moderated by having to take the role of someone who takes an opposing view. [30] Role reversal has several uses in the educational process - it enables other group members to get a complete picture of the protagonist's view of the important people in their life through their dramatisation of these individuals; it enables the protagonist to experience the world from the viewpoint of the other and in this position to receive the impact of him/herself. Role-reversal can also be used to encourage the protagonist to develop self-control by immediately putting him/her

---

[28] ibid., p. 17
[29] ibid., p.17

in an alternative role, and giving them the opportunity to experience him/herself viewed from a different perspective. Blatner and Blatner note that 'role reversal is a way of transcending the habitual limitations of egocentricity'. [31]

One of the potential effects of using role reversal is that those who watch or are involved in a role-play may feel a sense of alienation, or as Brecht termed it 'Verfremdung'; the principle of getting an actor to 'demonstrate' a part; viewing the drama from a socially critical angle, and not losing himself/herself in the action of the play. [32] From Brecht's point of view, the crucial point was that an active sceptical distance ought to be applied to our social surroundings, nothing should be taken for granted; in order that 'nothing may seem unalterable'. [33] Transferred to the context of group work the emphasis on the 'Verfremdungseffekt' - the need for critical detachment and scepticism - can lead to Freire's notion of 'critical consciousness' and promote a notion that reality is 'capable of alteration'.[34]

The ability to 'take the role of the other' is one of the foundations of moral maturity. McGuire and Priestly indicate that an inability to do so may be at the root of some offending behaviour. [35] Chandler's work with 'egocentric' offenders suggests that there are benefits to be gained by running role-play sessions in which the individual offender is required to play different parts in the same scene. [36] Chandler attempted to counter 'egocentrism' in young offenders, by employing a method of 'multi-role reversal' in which participants role-played all or most of the parts in the scenario. Significant reductions in recidivism were obtained when

---

[30] Culbertson, F.M. (1957) 'Modification of an emotionally held attitude through role playing', *Journal of Abnormal and Social Psychology*, **54**, pp 230-233.
[31] Blatner A. and Blatner, A. (1988) *The Foundations of Psychodrama. History, Theory and Practice*, New York, Springer Publishing, p. 96
[32] Willettt, J. (1977) *The Theatre of Bertolt Brecht*, London, Methuen, p. 177
[33] ibid, p.177
[34] ibid, p. 80
[35] McGuire, J. and Priestly, P. (1985) op.cit., p. 48
[36] Chandler, M.J. (1973) 'Egocentrism and anti-social behaviour: the assessment and training of social perspective-taking skills', *Developmental Psychology*, **46**, pp. 326-332

this method was used with groups of adolescents. [37] Spivack et al. also identified the significance of individuals being able to empathise with other people's points of view. In clinical psychology work this 'social cause-and-effect thinking' has been assessed using a *projective* test, i.e., in which individuals are asked to say what they think about pictures of an interpersonal situation of some kind; it is assumed that their comments indicate something about their own attitudes and preoccupations.[38] In drama-based work image theatre techniques may be used to explore scenarios, individuals may be asked to describe how the situation looks to each of the characters involved; the extent to which they can 'empathise' with different points of view can supply a rough measure of perspective-taking skills.

Perspective taking - developing ways of seeing.

Phenomenological concepts such as Husserl's 'epoche' and States' 'first four seconds' can be used to describe how theatre may engage in a critical discourse of meaning. An 'epoche' suggests a pause or suspension of pre-suppositions about the nature of an experience. The experience is 'bracketed' so that crucial qualities may be perceived. A similar concept is expressed by Bert O States as 'the first four seconds', which refers to a moment when the object or image establishes itself in our perception as something that connects and compels us to feel what we perceive.[39] Drama can do this, Phenomenologists suggest, by 'ingesting' the world of objects/signs and bringing them to life again.[40] Theatre and drama can create the illusion of 'bracketing' reality for an audience, so that willingly or involuntarily, a suspension of belief in the empirical world occurs, and members

[37] ibid.
[38] McGuire, J. and Priestly, P. (1985) op.cit., p. 176
[39] States, Bert O. (1985) op.cit.
[40] De Marinis, M (1993) *The Semiotics of Performance*, Bloomington and Indianapolis, Indiana University Press, p.141

of the audience may attune themselves to a reality 'reduced by parameters and the manipulations of the artist'. [41] States views theatre as:

> ...a process of mediation between artist and culture, speaker and listener; theatre becomes a passageway for a cargo of meanings being carried back to society (after artistic refinement) via the language of signs.[42]

However, in drama with offenders the emphasis is not on the mediation between an artist and an audience. It is about the process involved in creating drama, of selecting, manipulating and bracketing signs, and of constructing meanings from everyday experience. Therefore the playing process becomes the focus of the group, not the need to create a performance for an audience. What characterises drama work with offenders from other community groups, is that the playing will often be related to criminogenic or specific educational issues. The playing has an agenda.

Before an agenda is introduced though, the offenders must learn how to play with some of the theatrical 'toys' available to them. The 'bracketing' of reality that drama enables can help to reveal important elements, or ideas, that are 'embedded' in the dizzying multidimensionality of signs in reality; by condensing or shaping things like time and space, cause and effect, beginnings and endings. As Mario Vargas Llosa points out 'life can take on a meaning that can be perceived, because art gives us a perspective that real life, in which we are immersed, often denies us'. [43] And it is this invention of order which 'brackets' reality, reducing its scale and making it accessible. The participant can therefore judge it, understand it, and above all play with it with an impunity that real life does not allow.

---

[41] Reinelt, J.G. and Roach, J.R. (eds.) (1992) *Critical Theory and Performance*, Michigan, University of Michigan Press, p. 371
[42] States, Bert O. (1985) op.cit., p.6

These are important functions for drama because they are a link to everyday life skills. Goffman's (1959) hypothesis of 'daily life as performance' can be understood both in the metaphorical sense and the practical. He informs us that not only is daily life full of fiction, but that truth and lies, pretence and real acts, and display and concealment constitute the basic materials that theatrical interactions are made of. Goffman:

> A character staged in a theatre is not real in some ways, nor does it have the same kind of real consequences as does the thoroughly contrived character performed by the confidence man; but the successful staging of either of these types of false figures involves use of real techniques - the same techniques by which everyday persons sustain their real social situations. Those who conduct face-to-face interaction on a theatre's stage must meet the key requirement of real situations; they must expressively sustain a definition of the situation. [44]

However one may not use drama just to recount life, but to transform it. In the same way that dramatic time is an artifice fabricated to achieve certain psychological effects, dramatic reality is an invention that, whilst it might appear to recreate life, might be more accurately said to be amending it. Goffman's assertion that an actor must always sustain a definition of the situation is correct, but where theatre and daily life differ, is in the ability of art to turn realism inside out by creating expressionistic 'realities' or fantastical allegories which can represent and recreate internal states and emotional experiences which reach beyond everyday realities.

In other words drama is capable of making the *familiar unfamiliar*, and of making the *unfamiliar familiar* through the imaginative use of symbolisation, allegory, and metaphor. This principle links to Brecht's use of the term 'Verfremdung' to signal how theatre could show everything in a fresh and unfamiliar light, so that

---

[43] Llosa, M. V. (1996) *Making Waves*, John King (ed.) London, Faber and Faber, p. 323

[44] Goffman, E. (1959) *The Presentation of Self in Everyday Life*, Middlesex, Pelican, p.254-255

the spectator is 'brought to look critically even at what he has so far taken for granted': [45]

> It is a matter of (critical) detachment, of reorientation: exactly what Shelley meant when he wrote that poetry 'makes familiar objects to be as if they were not familiar', or Schopenhauer when he claimed that art must show 'common objects of experience in a light that is at once clear and unfamiliar'. [46]

The effectiveness of a symbol whether it is an action, object, or language, is dependent on its concreteness and on its power to stir deep feelings in the people concerned. The use of an object or action may start as something quite inconsequential or seemingly unlikely for use as symbolic representation. For example, in a TIPP Centre project at HMP Hindley the action of stealing some shoes off someone became strongly symbolic of the tensions within one of the character's the group had created. [47] The shoes represented a number of things: the characters desire for expensive clothes; the status that the shoes would bring among his friends; his impatience and lack of concern of how he obtained what he wanted; his broken promise to himself to stop stealing; his broken promise to his mother not to steal; his conscious ability to minimise and justify his crime. The action of stealing the shoes was also significant because this was the first crime he committed after being released from prison. The action was described by one participant as being like 'the first drink of an alcoholic who has been dry for several months'. The eye of the practitioner should be directed at always seeing beyond objects as objects (or situations as situations), otherwise s/he can unconsciously prevent participants from developing the potential of the material.

The use of symbolism and metaphor extends the suggestion that meaning is not fixed, that, as Derrida noted, there is a transmutability of all discourse; that

---

[45] Willettt, J. (1977) *The Theatre of Bertolt Brecht*, London, Methuen, p. 177
[46] ibid., p. 177

meaning is always deferred, elsewhere, multiple and shifting.[48] And thus, ironically, 'there is always a wealth of meaning and a simultaneous absence of meaning in circulation'.[49] The role of the drama practitioner then is twofold, to help the participant re-define subjectivity by clarification, but also set it in a multidimensional and complex context. And, as many writers suggest, (De Marinis, 1993; Derrida, 1978; Reinelt, 1992; Hawkes, 1977) the richness of the semiotic context means that it is virtually impossible to arrive at a final decoding of an aesthetic message,[50] because: '....ambiguity generates further cognate 'rule breaking' at other levels, and invites us to dismantle and reassemble what a work of art seems at any point to be saying'. [51]

In terms of work with offenders the 'works of art' are the images and signs which the offenders create in the process of playing with, and 'bracketing' reality. The role of the drama practitioner may be to draw attention to the reading skills, the dismantling and reassembling of signs, which are produced by a group. This can be directly or indirectly connected to criminogenic references. For example, West Yorkshire Probation Service has introduced drama workshops which explore representations and perceptions of masculinity. [52] These workshops aim to look at the way in which group members represent their masculinity, and how this affects their behaviour, before going on to generate and encourage new signs and readings. The representation of masculinity therefore becomes something for which there is a wealth of interpretations, as well as an absence.

---

[47] Greater Manchester Probation Service (1996) *The CLEVER Project Report and Evaluation*.

[48] Derrida, J. (1981) *Positions*, trans. Alan Bass, Chicago, University of Chicago Press.

[49] Reinelt, J.G. and Roach, J.R. (eds.) (1992) *Critical Theory and Performance*, Michigan, University of Michigan Press, p. 111

[50] See De Marinis, M. (1993) op.cit.; Derrida, J (1978) 'Structure, Sign and Play', in *Writing and Difference*, Chicago, University of Chicago Press; Reinelt, J.G. and Roach, J.R. (1992) op.cit.; Hawkes, T. (1977) *Structuralism and Semiotics*, London, Methuen.

[51] Hawkes, T. (1977) *Structuralism and Semiotics*, London, Methuen, p.141

[52] Tomalin, D. (1995) General report on drama work in Probation in *The NACRO Annual Report*, NACRO.

Offenders may have (by their own testimony and as appraised by others) problems with ineffective or inappropriate behaviour in personal encounters, with outcomes that may be damaging to themselves as well as others. Can drama-based techniques help to improve their capacities in this area? In general the response to this question appears to be 'yes'. Firstly, there is some evidence to suggest that a drama-based approach can enhance the general social performance of individuals, and even at this level can reduce the risk of recidivism. [53] Secondly, other evidence suggests that drama-based social skills training can be very specific, and can enable individuals to improve their interactions with certain other groups of people - such as partners, authority, parents.[54] Finally drama-based methods like re-enactments, role-play, and role-reversal appear to have an impact not only on social behaviour, but also on an individual's 'perspective taking' about themselves and others. [55]

The drama-based tools of re-enactment, role-reversal, the social skills model, 'perspective taking' form a basis from which companies like Geese Theatre have developed techniques and approaches to working with offenders. Geese Theatre, the longest established national touring theatre company to work exclusively in prisons and probation, provide an example of how performance and drama-based methods have been developed and adapted to rehabilitative work with offenders. A study of Geese Theatre provides an opportunity to identify potentially effective

---

[53] Chandler (1973) op. cit.

[54] Sarason, I.G. (1968) 'Verbal learning, modelling and juvenile delinquency', *American Psychologist*, **23**, pp.245-266; Sarason, I.G. (1978) 'A cognitive social learning approach to juvenile delinquency', in R.D. Hare and D. Schalling (eds.) *Psychopathic Behavior: Approaches to Research*, New York, Wiley; Sarason, I.G. and Ganzer, V.J. (1973) 'Modelling and group discussion in the rehabilitation of juvenile delinquents', *Journal of Counselling Psychology*, **20**, pp.442-449; Scopetta, M.A. (1972) A comparison of modelling approaches to the rehabilitation of institutionalised male adolescent offenders implemented by paraprofessionals, unpublished doctoral dissertation, University of Miami.

[55] Ollendick T.H. and Hersen, M. (1979) 'Social skills training for juvenile delinquents', *Behaviour Research and Therapy*, **17**, pp. 547-554; Spence,S., and Marzillier, J.S. (1979) 'Social skills training with adolescent male offenders: 1. Short term effects', *Behaviour Research and Therapy*, **17**, pp. 7-16

methods for practice. It also highlights difficulties with which arts practitioners may be confronted in the context of the criminal justice system.

Geese Theatre Company.

Geese Theatre Company was founded in the US in 1980 by John Bergman, an English actor and director. During the nineteen-eighties the company toured to over three hundred and fifty prisons in forty states and five countries, received two major awards from the American Correctional Association, and had its work profiled by The Wall Street Journal, CBS News, and Time Magazine. [56] In 1986 (shortly before the US company disbanded) a UK company was founded and in the last ten years it has built up a successful touring schedule, with regular performances and workshops in 175 prisons and probation centres in Britain and Ireland. [57] The UK company has been the subject of several television documentaries and made presentations at over twenty international criminal justice conferences. The company has pioneered TIPP practice in the US and the UK, and has been at the forefront of developing and extending drama and theatre practice in prisons and probation. Seventeen years after the company's original formation, Bergman and the company believe they have developed a way of working with offenders which is 'original, effective and significant' in helping offenders to change their criminal behaviour. [58]

There are two elements to Geese Theatre Company - a touring group which take plays and workshops to prisons throughout the country, and a team of programme workers who work with offender groups over a longer period of time. Geese Theatre UK states that their principle aim is to prevent crime. [59] The company, accept the notion of individual autonomy, and work from the premise that the offender is an individual who is responsible for making active choices. Whilst

---

[56] ibid.
[57] Geese Theatre Company Programme 1993
[58] Baim, C. (1993) Interview with author.
[59] Programme notes produced for the Geese Theatre show *Hooked On Empty*.

acknowledging socio-economic factors influencing crime, the company focus on the offender's own responsibility for criminal actions and for changing that behaviour.

Geese Theatre and the use of masks.

In both performance and drama-based group work programmes the company place great emphasis on visual imagery. The company believe that offenders often lack social and linguistic skills and that visual imagery can be an effective way of relating directly to the thinking of inmates:

> They [offenders] need pictures that reflect something inside their minds before their defences deny the pictures' reality....The hope we hold out to the inmates is that they can change when they catch sight of the dangerousness of their minds and beliefs. [60]

One of the key ways in which Geese Theatre have employed visual imagery is by using masks. A Geese mask is used to allow rapid changes in characterisation and as the sign of inner feelings. When a character has her/his mask on s/he is playing a role. When s/he 'lifts the mask' s/he must speak honestly about her/his feelings. This type of technique aims at: '...putting young offenders in touch with themselves: recognising the mask they wear in the world, and the excuses they continually make for themselves which 'permit' offending behaviour'. [61] In this way, the mask becomes a metaphor. Bergman comments: 'Our contribution to this kind of therapy has been the powerful theatrical metaphors we've created which represent these states of mind; and which resonate strongly with offenders'. [62] The metaphor of the mask, came directly from an inmate:

---

[60] Bergman, J. and Hewish, S. (1996) op.cit., p.98
[61] *The Times Educational Supplement.* 27.4.90, p.20

I got to get it (money) from my family, so I tell my mother I love her, that my life is dangerous and I need money. She gives it to me. When I lie like that, I just wear a mask...The truth is that for a lot of us, our ladies, even our family members, are a source of money, and money is survival...I turn to my lady...I put on a big smiling mask like I really love her...and then I ask her for $50 dollars...And if she doesn't give me the money, then I get rageful and she doesn't want that...But I got to use the mask to get what I need. [63]

The company were interested in the idea that offenders manipulated and distorted facts about their lives in prison. The use of mask as a method to represent inmates' manipulations was a crucial development in Geese Theatre's approach to creating relevant dramatic metaphors that offenders could use to 'make a difference' in their lives. [64] The company believe this can be achieved by using masks to represent the most extreme aspects of offenders' anti-social behaviour. By 'lifting the mask' an offender is given the opportunity to 'stand back' from his actions and explore alternative behavioural options, e.g. being honest.

The first Geese Theatre play to use masks was *The Plague Game* which also combined improvisation and audience participation to confront problems about families and visits. Throughout the play, families are portrayed as having to deal with pressures of visits, as well as problems in daily life - housing, debt, raising children, coping with being a single parent. *The Plague Game* is structured to challenge inmates' attitudes and to explore new strategies to maintain the survival of emotional links, between families and friends, whilst in prison.[65] To win the game, characters must learn to accept changes, listen, talk honestly about feelings, and plan effectively for release. At key points in the show, when the character has to make a decision, the actors turn to the audience for consultation. At these points the audience can direct the character in what action to take. This style of

---

[62] ibid, p.20
[63] Bergman, J. and Hewish, S. (1996) op.cit., p.96
[64] ibid., p.95
[65] Baim, C. (1993) op.cit.

interaction allows an analysis of positive and negative aspects of behaviour, and enables the audience to see the consequences of alternative behaviour.

> The underlying intention of the piece, from an actor's standpoint, is to push the most negative perception of an inmate into the cognition of the peer group, and to create a temporary rejection that will validate seeming pro-social responses. For example, when the audience is very aggressive, we meet this aggression by portraying an inmate whose violent and negative interactions with his girlfriend results in her finally leaving him....Prisoners are quick to see the pattern, and will interject vociferously, often with shouted comments like "raise your mask and tell her you love her" or "don't hit her". [66]

Lifting the Weight continued the successful formula of masks, improvisation and audience interaction. [67] Also played as a game, the actor-players must deal with a variety of situations which occur on release. The characters confront key issues in five main areas: survival; family; work; authority; free-time. Each area contains tokens which players must try to win in order to stop themselves from returning to prison. Tokens focus on issues such as relationships, personal responsibility, peer pressure, self control, alcohol and drug abuse, the potential to re-offend, and the repercussions of institutional life. In both *The Plague Game* and *Lifting the Weight,* the company has incorporated a compere games master, called The Fool. S/he is a character that stops and starts the game, sets out the rules and watches over the characters - sometimes testing the players with temptations, sometimes acting as mischief maker. If things are going too well for a character, the Fool will throw in what Geese call a fool factor, a seemingly random event that complicates

---

[66] Bergman, J. (1989) unpublished article, transcript available from the TIPP Centre, p.11
[67] Lifting the Weight also introduced a new mask into the Geese gallery, a large evil looking bird of prey, called Death Bird: a mask which stalks the characters in the performance. Baim: 'The Fool may roll down a car window and put a purse on the front seat, but it is Death Bird who will whisper over the shoulder of the character and say "Now. Now. Help yourself." He represents the temptation to re-offend. We are giving the audience visual metaphors to which thay can attach their own feelings and attitudes towards criminal behaviour'.

the character's struggle and makes them more likely to re-offend. The function of the Fool in Geese's work has clear similarities to the Joker in Forum Theatre, although the link to Boal is not acknowledged by the company. However, both figures preside over the proceedings and ensure the smooth running of the scenes, whilst interacting with the audience and setting out the guide-lines. The form and structure of Boal's democratic amphitheatre bear a strong resemblance to Bergman and Geese's aims: to empower the spectator to influence the action, contribute ideas and use the tools of theatre to affect everyday problems and find solutions. The idea of a 'rehearsal of reality' is one that informs and strongly links the work of both approaches.

The Fragment Masks.

The half mask that Geese use in *The Plague Game* and *Lifting the Weight* is raised when characters talk the truth or give voice to their true selves. The implication is that we all place a mask over our 'real selves' and play roles and that somewhere, inside of us, lurk our real selves. Supposedly this self is a static and formed reality; there are moments when it shines out, and others when it is camouflaged. This is one view of the self. Another would be that there is no fixed, true and real person inside of one, because being a person necessarily implies becoming a person, being in process; a process of change; not fully formed. This makes one's identity a far more complex matter, it is no longer simply a case of lifting *a* mask to discover *a* self. Instead there is a dynamic process which makes it hard to distinguish between what we really are at any given moment in our development as persons and what we pose as being. Erika Fischer-Lichte makes a similar definition of identity as something which is of itself, but variable; that takes shape only in the course of the communication process. [68]

---

[68] Fischer-Lichte, E. (1992) *The Semiotics of Theatre*, trans. Gains, J. and Jones D.C, Bloomington/Indianapolis, Indiana University Press.

To some extent Geese Theatre has addressed this over-simplification of identity by developing the Fragment Masks. Whereas the masks used in *The Plague Game* and *Lifting the Weight* were simple half-masks with neutral expressions, the Fragment masks represent 'roles' that participants act out, particularly in a group work environment, in order to avoid honest self-communication. The masks represent the magnification of an aspect of personality, deliberately manipulated to exaggerate a behavioural trait. The Fragment masks are used as a short cut for the facilitator in a group work situation. Clark Baim, from Geese:

> It's very useful for the facilitator to have the mask there and say: 'This is what you're doing right now'. We ask offenders 'who are these masks, what do they do?' They catch on very quickly. We have given them a language to talk about the group dynamic. Just as on the landing the guys will say 'lift the mask' as a metaphor for honesty, in the group guys will actually say 'he's wearing the Good Guy mask.' The masks don't even have to be there any more - we've given them a metaphor, a very visual thing to attach a certain kind of behaviour to. [69]

The point is central to understanding why Geese Theatre use masks; that by creating 'potent metaphors' that reflect an attitude and/or a set of beliefs that are palpable to the offender, the normal linguistic defences may be circumvented. [70] The company's belief is that the criminal deviousness, as represented by the half-masks, is 'the result of very conscious and very real pathological drives'. [71] The Fragment Masks are 'glimpses of the inmate's very hidden sub-consciousness', designed to visually represent manipulative and defensive attitudes used by offenders to deny and minimise the consequences of their crimes. [72]

---

[69] Baim, C. (1993) op.cit.
[70] Bergman, J. and Hewish, S. (1996) op.cit., p.97
[71] Bergman, J. (1989) op.cit., p.15
[72] ibid., p.17

Mr Fist is one of a series of 8 masks and shows an angry face, with a fist coming out of its forehead. The character who wears this mask acts extremely aggressively and violently, trying to unnerve others and make sure they do not come anywhere near him:

> In a group work setting what he's doing is basically trying to make the therapist or other group members back off. "Don't challenge me, because I will become really nasty and you will regret it". But it's really a manipulation, because what he's actually doing is trying not to deal with what he's there for.[73]

The other Fragment masks Geese Theatre has created include: [74]

- *The Bullshit Artist* (big blabbing mouth) who is likely to tell the group leader anything and everything that s/he thinks they want to hear - and will talk his way out of being confronted with serious personal issues.

- *The Good Guy* (a saintly looking mask with angelic wings). Geese identify the wearer of this mask as someone who explains his actions in terms of defending or helping another person. Baim: 'If the wearer is a violent offender he may only get into fights where he has to defend his friends from some other 'brute'. If he is a sex offender he may say': "What I had for my nephew was an excess of love, and the other thing I did was...well...he was 13 and young boys have to be shown how to perform sexually, therefore what I was doing was part of his education".

- *Victim Mask* (mask with a sad face and a target on its forehead). The wearer of this mask is asking the group to excuse him for what he has done, because he was a victim. This mask tends to deny his own personal responsibility, trying to put the group off course. Geese Theatre maintains that this is one of the most 'popular' and key masks with offenders.

- *Stone Wall* (a face with a forehead made to look like a brickwall). This mask represents someone who just sits in a session, if the facilitator asks him a question, his response is to ignore the question/facilitator all together.

- *Mr Cool* (prominent dark shades). A wearer of this mask uses 'cool' justifications for his actions. Baim: 'For example: "Yeah, I am violent, but

---

[73] Baim, C. (1993) op.cit.
[74] ibid

who isn't? Perfectly justifiable what I do, I am a big man I've got... my image". "Rapist? No I am not a rapist, I don't have to force myself on women. Women love me.'"

Geese workers use these masks to demonstrate that the need to seek refuge in roles, masks and games is the result of an almost natural reflex action to avoid the fears and the risk that self-revelation involves. The key development here is that the Fragment Masks are used to suggest a plurality of defensive roles and parts which are forever shifting and changing. This is a far more dynamic vision of identity than the simplistic 'lifting the mask' perception, and one which is shared by practitioners of Psychodrama:

> Not only are we, at any given moment when seen in cross-section, a complex and simultaneity of parts, but through time parts or roles we play evolve, mature, wane, go dormant, die out. We are in that sense not just a plurality but a community.....in short, to use one of his (Moreno's) favoured images, each of us may be thought of as a group. [75]

The work of Peter Pitzele, a psycho dramatist working in New York State with physically and mentally abused adolescents, is similar to Geese Theatre's work with Fragment Masks. Pitzele recognised that his clients, seriously disturbed adolescents, suffered from crippled self-esteem and had taken to assuming defensive roles or 'masks' to hide their perceived deficiencies. He observed a teenager who appeared 'world-weary and bored even when talking about (his) mother's suicide', another who was constantly angry, one who was always joking, lively, wore 'outlandish get-ups to distract from scarred arms', and others who intimidated, remained passive or lied to the group with 'all the skill of a con artist'. [76] Pitzele identifies these masks as characters who one had to acknowledge,

---

[75] Pitzele, Peter (1991) 'Adolescents inside out', in Holmes and Karp (ed.) *Psychodrama: Inspiration and Technique*, London, Routledge, p.16
[76] ibid, p. 18

but at the same time get past in order to get to the 'group' within. Pitzele regards these masks as resistance; and notes that the more disturbed an individual was, the stronger the persona of the mask. The process of meeting the mask is a Psychodynamic one, but it is important to recognise that the masks have been designed to help people cope, that breaking through a Fragment Mask is attempting to break through a 'coping mask'. Pitzele:

> They (the masks) have origins: they were created to serve a purpose: they have a story to tell all bound up with feelings too powerful to sustain, feelings that require the services of a mask to conceal, freeze, to split from. Thus the mask serves as a guardian and yet also a gateway to the complex, many-mooded, many-storied realm inside these troubled adolescents (or people). [77]

Geese Theatre argue that for offenders the culture of prison is riddled with games - games of survival; of gaining and maintaining status in an aggressive hierarchy; of playing the system for self gain; of avoiding guilt; of minimising the consequences of actions on others. [78] When working with men in prison these games can be little manoeuvres employed to avoid self-realisation and self-communication. They are 'shields which are designed to protect a person from being hurt and help him to win little victories or successes which bring protection or recognition'.[79] What Geese Theatre claim to be interested in is 'the discovery of patterns of behaviour that are encodable in metaphors or are already encoded by the inmates - in visual and verbal metaphors'. [80] The Fragment masks have been designed for a specific purpose - to generate a particular meaning that resonates with prisoners:

---

[77] ibid, p. 18
[78] Baim, C.(1993) op.cit.
[79] ibid.
[80] Bergman, J. (1989) op.cit., p.17

To make something that has value and meaning for
seeing who they are, as they are, without a poli
theatre of problem-solving, of changing, of memo
detail, decoding and understanding the special audiences real lives.

Working with violence.

One of the key developments for Geese Theatre Company in recent years has been *The Violent Illusion Trilogy,* which combined performance and drama-based workshops in an attempt to 'represent to an inmate his inner landscape of violence, in the hope that he will renounce what he sees and experiences'. [82] The trilogy is designed to run as a week-long programme, consisting of two plays, a series of drama-based workshops and at the end of the week a 'simulation' in which inmates' non-violent social skills are tested out. The structure of the week draws on a cognitive-behavioural treatment model, first suggested by Novaco.[83] Novaco's treatment of anger and aggression is designed to make individuals more aware of the 'anger' process and enable him/her to intervene in aggressive patterns of behaviour. *The Violent Illusion Trilogy* is an interesting example of the ways in which Geese Theatre has attempted to translate 'a non-arts objective into an arts based method'. [84] It is also a model which the TIPP Centre's Pump programme sought to build on and develop.

The premise of Geese Theatre's *Violent Illusion Trilogy* is to help offenders isolate patterns of thinking, feeling and behaviour and to introduce them to the notion of interventions. [85] In order to accomplish this, Geese Theatre attempt to raise an offender's awareness of the thinking and feeling process, and how these processes relate to behaviour. Performance and drama-based techniques are used to 'surface' feelings and thoughts which the company encourage offenders to

---

[81] Bergman, J. and Hewish, S. (1996) The Violent Illusion, Dramatherapy and the Dangerous Voyage to the Heart of Change, in *Arts Approaches to Conflict,* ed. Marian Liebmann, London, Jessica Kingsley Publishers, p. 95

[82] ibid., p.102

[83] Novaco R W. (1975) *Anger Control,* Massachusetts, Lexington Books.

[84] Thompson, J. (1996) op.cit., p. 74

identify. The premise is to raise self-awareness by encouraging offenders to identify their destructive behaviour. Geese Theatre argue that through using simple metaphors and translating behaviour directly into scenarios recognisable to offenders, behaviour and thinking patterns that are destructive to offenders and others may be named and the process of change begun. The first two parts are performed in full-mask and consequently the actors/characters do not speak. The intention of using full-face mask and mime is to create 'universal' characters, in the hope that inmates may project their own internal dialogue into the action:

> Violent Illusion (Part One and Two) works on the principle that the audience will create their own 'script' from watching the mime as the story unfolds, and will identify not only with being a victim themselves but also, more importantly, a perpetrator. [86]

Part One is the story of a child growing up in an increasingly hostile domestic environment. The play examines patterns of physical and sexual abuse in a family, and the consequences on the child victim. Part Two explores similar domestic themes: a husband recently released from prison returning home; a wife struggling to bring up children. However, the emphasis in Part Two, is not on violence or abuse, but on the methods family members use to deal, in a non-violent way, with difficult emotions such as anger, jealousy, and rejection. In other words, the first play is a demonstration of a negative model of family life - governed by violence as a principle solution to solve social conflicts. The second play presents similar problems, which are resolved through non-violent strategies. After the performances and in follow up workshops Geese Theatre performers work with the inmates to identify the main issues, underlining the examples and skills that the characters used to find non-violent solutions to moments of conflict. Geese report that inmates find self-control and behavioural change 'too difficult to even

---

[85] Geese Theatre Company (1994) *From Insult to Injury - Course Manual.*
[86] Geese Theatre Programme 1993, p.7

contemplate'. [87] While inmate/participants often strongly resist the non-violent position taken by Geese, the company attempt to re-assure the inmates that any small degree of change will benefit both individuals and their families. [88]

After four intensive days of performances and workshops exploring issues of violence, and alternative non-violent strategies, some of the inmate/participants can volunteer for *Violent Illusion 3 - the Corrida* . [89] The final part of the trilogy is designed as a test of inmates proficiency in managing provocative situations, and does so by creating simulations aimed at inducing anger or aggressive responses from the inmates. The premise, translated from Novaco's 'inoculation skills training', is that an individual is confronted with a simulation of a conflict that he is likely to encounter in real life. [90] In Novaco's model the client is exposed to a number of different scenarios, beginning with the mildest and progressing to the most anger arousing. As the client applies coping skills to these increasingly stressful simulations, the theory is that they begin to 'inoculate' themselves against real life provocations.[91] However, in Geese Theatre's *Corrida* there is only one simulation, and the process of the test is 'ritualised'.[92] The cognitive-behavioural coping skills that have been rehearsed with Geese Theatre Company

---

[87] Bergman, J. and Hewish, S. (1996) op.cit., p.105

[88] Evaluations from West Midland's Probation Service and the Scottish Prison Service indicate that offenders on Geese Theatre anger management courses find the work 'to be challenging, to have had a considerable impact on their thinking and behaviour'. It should be noted that these studies do not include any re-offending data or long-term follow up work. Information: Quinn, A. (1994) 'In defense of Geese', *The Probation Journal*, June, p.12

[89] Bergman, J. and Hewish, S. (1996) op.cit., p.106; Corrida - from the Spanish 'corrida de toros' - 'course of bulls'.

[90] Novaco, R W. (1983) *Stress Inoculation Therapy for Anger Control: A Manual for Therapists*, Irvine, University of California Press, p.18

[91] ibid., p.19

[92] The Corrida set represents a bull-ring, within which the simulation will take place. Around the side of the circle sit an audience and four judges (other inmates). The judges will vote on whether the person has passed or failed. There is also a victim box (in which an actor can represent the individual's victim) and an off-stage area from which an inmate emerges to do the test. If he succeeds he will walk out of an exit, if he fails he must exit from the circle from where he came (this entrance/exit is called the Wasteland). A Corrida master (a company member) is present to 'set up' the rules of the test and make sure everyone is clear about their rights and responsibilities.

during the past week can be applied to the simulation, and enable both inmates and Geese Theatre to gauge the inmates' proficiency: [93]

> Violent Illusion 3 is an astonishingly simple piece of theatre/theatre therapy. A man stands alone in a special space and agrees to use a new way to deal with an old problem. He does not know what will happen in this space or how his resolve will be challenged and he can ask for no help....There is only the stark reality that under great duress he either succeeds or fails. And he does this while being watched from outside the space by other inmates, company members, prison officers, teachers and maybe even family members. [94]

Bergman describes the approach to working with violent men as 'action medicine' and argue that in order for theatre to be effective with these men it must recognise and present 'psychological portraits' that combine both the 'ethos of the criminal culture' and a 'feasible recipe for pro-social change'.[95] Bergman claims that it is possible to teach inmates 'to catch sight of the dangerousness of their minds' and help them to 'interfere' with anti-social core beliefs about themselves and other people. [96] Using traditional drama-based techniques as a basis - role-play, empty chair, hot seating, role reversal and re-enactment - the company has developed innovative approaches to working with offenders. Geese Theatre has frequently translated complex cognitive-behavioural methods into drama-based methods. The semi-improvised plays, the Fragment mask group-work and the *Violent Illusion Trilogy* are all interesting attempts at creating 'relevant rehabilitative theatre'.

---

[93] The value of inoculation training has been emphasised by a variety of skills training approaches: D'Zurilla, T. and Goldfried, M. (1971) 'Problem solving and behaviour modification,'*Journal of Abnormal Psychology*, **78**, pp.107-126; Meichenbaum, D. (1975) 'Self-instructional methods', in F.H. Kanfer and A.P. Goldstein (eds.) *Helping People Change*, New York, Pergamon Press; Suinn, R. and Richardson, F.(1971) 'Anxiety management training: A non-specific behavior therapy program for anxiety control', *Behavioral Therapy*, **2**, pp. 498-510.
[94] Bergman, J. and Hewish, S. (1996) op.cit., p. 95
[95] Bergman, J. (1989) op.cit., p.2
[96] Bergman, J. and Hewish, S. (1996) op.cit., p.98

The 'therapeutic' needs of the offender.

Bergman and Geese Theatre have, over seventeen years, developed their ideas of the ways in which theatre can be effective with offenders. Primary to their concern is to 'accurately create and mirror an offender's special world' and to create metaphors of 'special meaning' that may 'make a difference' to an offender's life. [97] The experience gained from working in prisons has helped them to construct an understanding of the nature of prison and the 'interior landscape' of inmates. [98] For example the very first Geese Theatre US production was a 'didactic historical/political treatise' performed in Stateville Correctional Centre in 1980. [99] The premise of the show was that the right kind of political information could empower inmates 'enchained through ignorance': 'we made the classic mistake of seeing this special audience through our political 'leftness' rather than through their specialness'. [100]

The perspective of the offender as victim of socio-economic factors, and the corresponding notion that Geese Theatre were martyrs who were there to 'help the helpless' was short-lived. [101] The company's view of offenders has swung from an 'us-versus-them anti system politic' which reinforced the idea that theatre should covertly attack the institution, to a position in which the offender needs to be helped to 'recover their rageful inner landscape'. [102] Since the first production in 1980, Geese has increasingly moved towards 'a theory of behaviour based on what we saw, heard and also had collected from our many hundreds of workshop sessions'. [103] Bergman and the UK company have now gone their separate ways, but each continues to evolve and develop their own practice. Bergman's search for insight into the 'interior landscape' of the criminal mind has led him to the

---

[97] ibid., p. 95
[98] Bergman, J. (1989) op.cit., p.12
[99] Bergman, J. and Hewish, S. (1996) op.cit., p. 93
[100] ibid., p.94
[101] Bergman, J. (1986) op.cit., p.13
[102] Bergman, J. and Hewish, S. (1996) op.cit., p.98
[103] Bergman, J. (1986) op.cit., p.14

conclusion that offenders are people who are 'maladoptive to life, who must be nursed gradually against the odds to share a very small part of the social pie'. [104] Bergman also argues that offenders can be seen as people who have 'no self' and that the role of a theatre practitioner is to design drama-based approaches 'to aid inmates in the initiation of a constructed self'.[105] Bergman's rationale indicates an orientation to a 'treatment' model of practice, in which the crime is a symptom of an underlying disease or disorder. [106] It is not readily clear what is meant by Bergman's idea of treatment, or what treatment is attempting to alter: the 'underlying disorder'; the offending behaviour; or the link, if any, between the two?

The view that criminals may be suffering from psychological abnormality and that experiences in early development could cause an imbalance in their personality to develop was first suggested by Maudsley (1835-1918) and later in general terms by Freudian psychologists. [107] Bergman's position follows an argument that offenders suffer from some sort of personality disorder, they are damaged and limited in their control of primitive impulses and urges; they may suffer delusions and feel persecuted, worthless and alienated. [108] The argument extends to non-violent criminals, who may be motivated by a lack of insight and control caused by 'personality disorders'. [109] As a result, they seek immediate gratification of their needs without consideration of right and wrong or the needs of others.

The perspective of the offender as emotionally and/ or mentally 'sick' clearly has implications for the way in which treatment approaches to personal change are implemented. Bergman's emphasis is on the offender's situations and

---

[104] ibid., p. 7
[105] ibid., p.5
[106] This was briefly discussed in 'Drama with offenders' earlier in this chapter.
[107] See Scott, P. (1970) 'Henry Maudsley', in Hermann Mannheim (ed.) *Pioneers in Criminology*, Montclair, N.J., Patterson Smith, p.212; For analysis of Freud's influence on criminologists see Rathus, S. (1988) *Psychology*, New York, Holt, Rinehart and Winston, pp. 412-20.
[108] Aichorn, A. (1965) *Wayward Youth*, New York, Viking Press.

relationships, past and present. Present problems are related to each other and to past events, and the 'drama therapist' interprets the material in terms of certain motivational patterns or themes. Gahagan outlines the basic assumptions behind this type of approach:

> ...the inadequate or problematic social behaviour is caused by underlying fears and conflicts that are the manifest symptoms of present problems are caused by latent emotional processes; that changing behaviour will not be successful without modifying the latent process. [110]

Knight, an observer of Geese's work in the US noted the 'therapist' role which Bergman adopted in workshops:

> The role Bergman played in drama workshops was that of a 'therapist' who by virtue of his knowledge, training and special insight has access to truths above and beyond the capacity of the client. This role is about power. The 'therapist' interprets the 'client's' truth and attempts to tell him what it all really means. Hence, clients' behaviour responses are identified by a series of categorised responses. Bergman would say things like: "These are your defences. I see through them to what is beyond". The truth of the 'therapist' is stronger than the truth of the 'client'. The 'therapist' wears a mask that marks his separateness from the 'client,' he is never questioned in the same way the client is questioned. He is not held to account by the same reasoning and rationale that the 'clients' are...
>
> ...The questioning of defence systems through things like the Fragment Masks, is a confrontation of one person (the 'therapist') who thinks he/she is in possession of the truth and that the other person (the 'client') who is wrong, would be made to see the error of his/ her thinking. This power relationship is

[109] Halleck, S. (1967) *Psychiatry and the Dilemmas of Crime*, New York, Harper and Row, pp. 99-115

[110] Gahagan, J. (1994) 'The management of social relationships', in J. Anderson and M. Ricci (eds.) *Society and Social Science*, Milton Keynes, Open University Press, p.188

the right to have one definition of reality (the 'therapist') prevail over another ('the client'). [111]

However, as Prins has demonstrated, the relationship between mental and/or emotional ill-health and criminality is an uncertain one.[112] Prins summarises the principal psychiatric classifications of disorder and illustrates the forms of offending which may be associated with them - or indeed, be less likely to arise where individuals are suffering from particular disorders - concluding: 'Most psychiatric disorder are only very occasionally associated with criminality'. [113] Prins also illustrates well the difficulties in establishing cause and effect in this complex area: 'We are trying to make connections between very different phenomena, and these phenomena are the subject of much debate concerning both substance and definition'. [114]

To assume that the majority of offenders are 'sick' is to mislead and negate the transparent and frequently reiterated need for flexibility within the criminal justice agencies.[115] Flexibility is required in the conceptualisation of 'mentally/emotionally disordered offending' as a general theory, explanation and treatment of crime. To return to the dual image of the criminal as being *either* free-willed or pathologically 'sick' is to construct an abstract image of humanity, each a 'caricature of reality': [116]

---

[111] Knight, M. (1994) Interview with author. Malcolm Knight worked with the company in the US as a consultant mask maker and performer.
[112] Prins, H. (1990) 'Mental abnormality and criminality: an uncertain relationship', *Medicine, Science and Law*, 30/3, pp. 247-58.
[113] ibid., p.256
[114] ibid., p.247
[115] Peay, J. (1994) 'Mentally Disordered Offenders' in in McGuire, M., Morgan, R.and Reimer, R. (1994) *Oxford Handbook of Criminology*, New York, Clarendon Press, pp.1119-1160.
[116] Young, J. (1994) 'Incessant chatter: recent paradigm's in criminology', in McGuire, M., Morgan, R.and Reimer, R. (1994) *Oxford Handbook of Criminology*, New York, Clarendon Press, p.69

These two gross abstractions have shadow-boxed with each other throughout the history of our subject (criminology)...one abstract metaphysic is set up against an equally absurd 'scientific' datum. [117]

This relatively monological perspective of an offender may become problematic, particularly if a practitioner is always 'medicalising' the individual, and filtering responses through a paradigm of 'sickness'. The potential for an egalitarian dialogue, as argued for by Libertarian educationalists, is dramatically reduced. The following example highlights important issues about the role of a TIPP practitioner in challenging and motivating offenders to change.

The Vermont Treatment Program for Sexual Aggressors (VTPSA) was set up in 1981 to enhance offenders' empathy for abuse victims. [118] One element of the group-work required each offender to role-play the abuse he had perpetrated, first in his own role as the offender, then assuming the role of his victim while another group member played the abuser. Role play was also used to help offenders rehearse 'relapse prevention' strategies. [119] When two drama therapists joined the treatment team they were interested in extending the use of drama therapy to explore emotions associated with the offenders' own sexual abuse. Although the offenders on the programme admitted to being abused as children, they felt that the abuse was not directly connected to their offending behaviour. [120] The two workers viewed this as 'resistance' and began to implement techniques to overcome this 'denial and minimisation'. [121] Bergman:

---

[117] ibid., p.69
[118] Hildebran, D. and Pithers, W.D. (1989) 'Enhancing offender empathy for mental abuse victims', in D.R. Laws (ed.) *Relapse Prevention with Sex Offenders*, New York, Guilford, pp.236-243
[119] Pithers, W.D. (1997) 'Maintaining Treatment Integrity with Sexual Abusers', *Criminal Justice and Behaviour*, Vol. 24, No.1
[120] ibid., p.38
[121] ibid., p.38

He (the sex offender) is the master of real and psychological escape. He may be in your session but he really is not. His overriding need is to get you, the therapist, off his back. To do this he will lie, nod, smile, acquiesce, pretend and tell you whatever he can that he believes you want to hear. If you are smiling, nodding your head in therapist's listening mode then he is safe. He will neither be threatened, as he was possibly when he was very young, nor will his secret world of deviance be shaken loose into the PUBLIC eye. [122]

Bergman notes three major phases that are significant in work with sex offenders; the first phase is for the therapist to understand the 'hiding place' that the offender instinctively uses, and to make that 'public' by making an offender aware of 'the place', describing it and becoming conscious of its 'dangerousness'; the second phase involves getting an offender to experience the pain which their crime has caused and to re-experience abuse that might have occurred in childhood. [123] Bergman is adamant that this needs to be experiential work, which may be supported by cognitive behavioural therapy to help put experiences in context, but must be 'dramatic, affective and emotionally searing'; the third phase consists of high risk role-plays that test and re-test the coping skills, knowledge of cycle, and ability to intervene with the strength of the offender's cycle. [124]

However, the drama therapists ran into problems when several months into the programme the inmates raised complaints against the drama workers, at the same time contacting the American Civil Liberties Union (ACLU) who immediately requested an injunction to stop the use of drama therapy.[125] Sixteen out of forty (40%) of the offenders on the programme submitted signed affidavits asserting that they had personally experienced abusive conduct during drama therapy sessions. The main complaints were that during drama therapy sessions offenders were inappropriately touched, were placed in vulnerable physical postures and

---

[122] Bergman, J. (1996) *Drama Therapy and the Sex Offender*, unpublished article.
[123] ibid.
[124] ibid.
[125] Pithers, W.D. (1997) op.cit., p.38

had therapists shouting denigrations at them. [126] All of these actions, it was claimed, were taken without prior explanation and without the offenders' informed consent.

Several of the participants involved in the Program testified against drama therapy during the hearing. One of the testimonies described a session which was allegedly conducted to help Darrell (fictitious name) to open the door to unexpressed emotions associated with the sodomy his brother had performed on him when they were both children. The session involved drama practitioners directing Darren to:

> ...lay face down on the floor with his eyes closed, one drama therapist blindfolded him, as the second forcibly pulled Darrell's feet over his head so they touched the floor next to his head. The second drama therapist then pushed his knee into Darrell's buttocks and anus, slowly making circular motions with his knee, while screaming denigrations apparently intended to remind Darrell of his own abuse. [127]

The injunction hearing effectively put drama therapy with sex offenders on trial in the States. After the hearing guidelines were developed by the VDOC committee which recommended theatre practitioners gain 'informed consent' with respect to the potential risks and benefits of drama-based work and to offer offenders the 'right to refuse to engage in drama therapy' sessions.[128]

The Vermont case raises questions about the effectiveness of particular approaches to work with offenders. Kear-Colwell and Pollock indicate that intensely confrontational treatment methods tend to promote anger and distrust in clients, and argue that non-coercive motivational strategies are more likely to

---

[126] ibid., p.43
[127] ibid., p.39
[128] ibid., p.45

heighten an offender's active therapeutic involvement. [129] The same researchers argue that it is the client's 'sense of autonomy' in his/her own treatment that is the single most critical factor in 'effective personal change'. [130] As Freire also argues, it is the participant who is the agent of change, therefore the role of the facilitator would give the participant autonomy in the learning process. [131] The general efficacy of a programme can be, at least partially, reliant on individual motivation and/or the facilitator's ability to encourage motivation.

Drama with offenders may, at times, need to be challenging and confrontational, but this needs to be balanced against the rights and autonomy of the offenders as individuals. As Peay notes, even if one regards all offenders as mentally disordered in some way, it is still important to treat them as a person first, an offender second, and as mentally disordered third. [132]

In the final section of this chapter, I want to propose an alternative model to the one demonstrated by the last example. The model is based on egalitarian principles in which offenders can be challenged, but in which the facilitator-participant relationship is governed by rationality, respect and a reflexivity to group interaction.

The role of the theatre practitioner - a dialogical and egalitarian model.

Earlier I noted the link between Libertarian educational traditions and theatre practice.[133] The function of a Libertarian educator is to enter into a dialogue with

---

[129] Kear-Colwell, J. and Pollock, P. (1997) 'Motivation or confrontation: Which approach to the child sex offender?' *Criminal Justice and Behaviour*, **24**, No.1, pp.20-33
[130] ibid., p.23
[131] Freire, P. (1974) *Education For Critical Consciousness*, London, Sheed & Ward.
[132] Peay, J. (1994) op.cit., p.1123
[133] Godwin, W. (1946) *Enquiry Concerning Political Justice*, Toronto, University of Toronto Press; Godwin, W. (1966) *Four Early Pamphlets*, Gainsville, Florida, Scholer's Facsimilies and Reprints; Ferrer, F. (1913) *The Origins and Ideals of the Modern School*, London, Watts; Freire, P.(1972) *Pedagogy of the Oppressed*, London, Penguin; Freire, P. (1974) *Education For Critical Consciousness*, London, Sheed & Ward; Tolstoy, L. (1967) *Tolstoy on Education*, trans. Leo Wiener, Chicago, University of Chicago Press; Faure, S. (1914) *La Ruche: son but, son organization, sa portee sociale*, Rambouillet, La Ruche.

participants about concrete situations which relate to a shared reality, and to simply offer him/her instruments with which they learn to learn about knowledge. [134] The traditional authoritarian power position in which an educator transfers facts and knowledge to the passive student is a relationship which is an anathema to Libertarian educationalists. [135] The argument for dialogism in theatre and education may be reinforced by theorists attracted to Bakhtin's writings. [136] One of the key elements of Bakhtin's system is the utterance, the meeting point of a wide variety of different concerns:

> It is where…a new context provides an inevitable fresh perspective…where the speaker speaks in anticipation of and in response to the perceived or presumed activities of another person, and finally where the other, the recipient, (may) participate in all these activities from another perspective. [137]

The proposed relationship is one of 'unending refraction' in which the 'multiple perspectives' of the group are presented through the 'contrasting voices' of the educator and educatee.[138] With reference to education, Freire highlights a characteristic of anti-dialogical theory, which is the notion of a moral or cultural invader, whose own cultural-historical beliefs form a fixed construct of the world:

> He seeks to penetrate another cultural-historical situation and impose a system of values on its members. The relationship between invader and invaded are….relationships of authority….The invader thinks, at most, *about* the invaded, never *with* them; the latter have their thinking done for them by the former. [139]

---

[134] ibid.
[135] ibid.
[136] Carlson, M. (1992) 'Theater and Dialogism', in Janelle G. Reinelt and Joseph R. Roach (eds.) *Critical Theory and Performance*, Michigan, University of Michigan Press.
[137] ibid, p. 318
[138] ibid p. 314
[139] Freire, P. (1974) op.cit., p.113

This picture of a cultural invader is useful when considering the moral role that a theatre and education practitioner may be asked to play in prisons and probation. There is a danger that an educator may fall into the trap of preaching a fixed monologistic moral perspective. An educator must be able to justify his/her actions and arguments by giving reasons for them, and the participant should be prepared to accept these reasons if they are rationally compelling. In Freire's model of dialogism it is not the educator who is the agent of change, it is the participant. [140] In terms of working with offenders, values linked to criminogenic behaviour are subject to scrutiny in a systematic and rational process. Rationality, in these terms, is about looking for a beneficial mode of social behaviour created through comparing different courses of action in the same situation. Participants are encouraged to deduce principles from practice, to set up experimental role-plays, and to observe and test the results. Speculation about these principles arises out of a concrete situation and from being confronted with specific problems.

However, it would be wrong to assume that the facilitators of a programme addressing offending behaviour start from a neutral position. The structure of the workshop is set to emphasise the view that criminal behaviour is unacceptable, but the content is an exploration of the motivation and thinking of individuals who commit crimes. Erich Fromm:

> Knowledge means that the individual makes his own way, learning, feeling, experimenting......, observing others and finally coming to a conviction without having an 'irresponsible position'. [141]

The practitioner's function then with a group of offenders is not to instruct or impart knowledge, nor to attempt to impose morality or induce socialisation, nor

---

[140] ibid p.113
[141] Fromm, E. (1968) *The Heart of Man: Its Genius for Good and Evil*, Harper and Row, New York, p. 11

to think *about* the participants, but rather to think *with* them. The practitioner must first of all respect the values, experiences and principles of participants, but at the same time invite them to think critically about their behaviour and experiences systematically and collectively. This is achieved by drawing attention to points that are unclear and always looking at them problematically: Why does the person in the tableau seem threatening to the other? How does this make the other person feel? The question the co-ordinator is asking all the time is: 'Is this really so - and if it is, is it the best way?' The participant's situations are investigated by using facts, not judgements of the act - what happened, how did it happen - and by asking questions about the facts. The participants can then, as Freire maintains, 'reflect on the 'wherefore' of the fact and on its connection with other facts in an overall context'.[142] Freire argues for the development of an educational process that is founded on the philosophy of 'I wonder' instead of merely 'I do'. A process that moves away from what Whitehead has called 'inert ideas......that are merely received into the mind without being utilised, or tested, or thrown into fresh combinations'. [143] Or as Mannheim argues 'a frame of mind which can bear the burden of scepticism and which does not panic when many of the thought habits are doomed to vanish'. [144] This process invites participants to think critically about problems and develop interpretations of the facts.

The task of pedagogy in this context is to help learners realise and develop their own meanings. It is not a teaching initiative but a learner initiative. Instead of an active-passive relationship there is a concern to develop the capacity of individuals to reflect and act; to understand that the self exists in relationship to others; and to explore these factors in a safe environment that represents the interactions involved in the social world. The dialogical view of the client-participant is based on equality and respect for the autonomy of each individual

---

[142] Freire, P. (1974) op.cit., p. 124
[143] Whitehead, A.N. (1967) *The Aims of Education and Other Essays,* London, Ernest Benn, p. 106
[144] Mannheim, K. (1943) Diagnosis of Our Time, in P. Freire (1974) op.cit., p.23

and his/her value system. Faure took very seriously the libertarian tenet of the autonomy of the participant. The participant's dignity was to be seriously respected; the participant must be persuaded and not compelled; and as a guarantee of this the participant must have the right not to be persuaded.[145] Education, for libertarians is not a matter *just* of self-expression, but rather a matter of the self in relation to others. [146] In challenging values linked to criminal behaviour the dialogical relationship may present 'multiple perspectives through contrasting voices' by problematizing not just the participants' values, but also the facilitator's: 'Within dialogue and problem-posing educator-educatee and educatee-educator go forward together to develop a critical attitude'.[147]

Drama based on such principles is not about reproducing raw emotion or catharsis, but about filtering emotion through a critical self-awareness of what is happening. One of the principal purposes of affective educational drama is not catharsis, but encouraging offenders to question and explore their ideas, attitudes and feelings and so develop ways of making sense of, expressing and communicating them. The function of this approach to drama is to help participants elaborate aspects of construing, to provide the means for experimentation within safety of a group situation, and to enable participants to see themselves and their problems in another perspective.

Conclusion.

Drama, with affective learning goals, is not simply about modelling and rehearsing life skills, but about expanding and deepening the perception of the participants. The first step is to make public what is private, to objectify experience, to accept these attitudes and experiences of individuals. But the second step should seek to open up a debate about the validity of any one view of

---

[145] Faure, S. (1914) op.cit.
[146] Smith, M. (1983) *The Libertarians and Education*, London, Unwin.
[147] Freire, P. (1974) op.cit., p.127

reality. Drama can do this by 'bracketing' reality or realities, so that group members may analyse and understand how a number of conflicting and contrasting perspectives of reality can exist at the same time. The clarification which comes from this process of 'bracketing' reality involves much of the work I have been discussing; the exploration of attitudes; developing understanding of other perspectives and encouraging affective learning. All these aspects of TIPP work focus on questioning assumptions about the way in which individuals construct meaning from the world. The play element of the drama is used to explore and challenge criminogenic rationales for certain behaviours. The clarification of an issue is therefore, in a sense, loaded with an agenda. For example in drama workshops looking at the subject of domestic violence with men who batter, the 'bracket' highlights a very specific experience - violence in a relationship. It is important that facilitators, although respectful of the men's rationale, attempt to demonstrate that violence is not a positive behaviour, and therefore attempt to influence what is learnt from the playing. Drama is used to help show that meaning is negotiable.

In the next chapter I shall look at how the TIPP Centre has, in partnership with Greater Manchester Probation Service, built on the functions of drama discussed in this chapter in order to create The Pump Challenging Violence programme. The Pump programme aims to encourage critical problematisation and the questioning of habitual anti-social thinking. The starting point of the programme draws on Novaco's theories of anger, social skills training and Geese Theatre practice, but develops and extends this theory and practice in new ways. [148] I will also test out the libertarian notion which suggests that pedagogy is an important carrier of values. [149] If one teaches in a way that requires passivity and fixed reactions, then, one inculcates passivity and fixed reactions. The role of the theatre practitioner is, therefore, to be reflexive in the learning environment and to

---

[148] Novaco, R.W. (1975) op.cit.
[149] Smith, M. (1983) op.cit.

the needs of participants; to help create an egalitarian and dialogical relationship between facilitator-participant, and to suggest that 'there are no absolute truths since we all have our own unique way of looking at the world; this means it may be possible to change our ways of dealing with the world..' [150]

---

[150] Fransella, F. and Dalton, P. (1990) op.cit., p.27

Chapter Three

Testing theories in practice

- designing and implementing a drama-based cognitive-behavioural programme for violent offenders.

'Go on then - change me!'[1]

Introduction.

The above quotation came from a participant on a TIPP Centre Pump programme in HMP Manchester prison (Strangeways). I think it problematises the argument for an egalitarian, dialogical relationship discussed in the previous chapter. As a rationale for a theatre practitioner the egalitarian educator is a valid one, but for the participant - prison inmate or probationer - the arts practitioner is closely associated with the agencies operating within the criminal justice system. In the 'them and us' culture of prison, the arts practitioner will ultimately still be viewed by offenders as 'them' and not 'us', no matter how anti-authoritarian the artist may seem (no uniform, no keys). The relationship therefore, from the participant's point of view, may not be seen as egalitarian but as an extension of the authority of the system. This is particularly true of compulsory educational programmes with an explicit rehabilitation agenda, which participants may view with

---

[1] Quote from a participant on a Pump course, HMP Manchester prison, April 1995.

scepticism, suspicion and resistance. Given the 'treatment' methodologies of some TIPP practice, as described in the previous chapter, the natural and instinctive resistance which some participants adopt may be well advised. However, the 'go on then - change me' position may sit in opposition to the opportunity for positively exploring personal and experiential development; through the problems which have brought participants into contact with the criminal justice system. The TIPP Centre's Pump Challenging Violence programme serves as an example of a compulsory creative educational project which sought to provide a positive, egalitarian, dialogical model of practice; and it is through the analysis of this practical example that the model may be tested and its efficacy assessed.

Another reason I have chosen to look at the Pump programme is because it provides a useful example of how theatre in prisons and probation may incorporate criminological paradigms and agendas derived from criminal justice agencies. The process of collaboration between a criminal justice agency (in this case Greater Manchester Probation Service) and an arts organisation (the TIPP Centre) is of relevance because it may reflect the tensions and/or benefits which occur when devising a programme in partnership. Of particular interest is the extent to which practitioners from the different fields may traverse or transcend each other's methodological approach. For example, are criminal justice agencies only interested in using drama as pragmatic social skill training, or is it possible for theatre practitioners to develop a potentially broader approach within this remit (i.e. approaches discussed in previous chapter: developing attitudes and more flexible ways of seeing).

This chapter describes the design and application of a cognitive-behavioural approach to the treatment of anger problems. The treatment procedure utilised drama techniques, but also incorporated a variety of methods that were developed in the field of behaviour studies, and in particular cognitive and Pro-feminist theories on anger, aggression, and (male) violence. Extensive accounts of these various approaches to cognitive interventions can be found in Novaco, [2] Beck, Rush, Shaw and Emery, [3] Kendall and Hollon, [4] Meichenbaum, [5] Dobash and Dobash, [6] and Jack Bush. [7]

In the first section of the chapter I will discuss some general analyses about violent offenders before providing a theoretical and practical overview of Novaco and his contribution to a cognitive-behavioural approach to anger control. [8] I will also discuss why the pro-feminist perspective on anger and violence has been influential in the development of programmes that seek to contextualise male aggression. These two approaches were selected because programmes that include elements of cognitive-behaviour have proven to be more effective than other elements [9] e.g. in comparison with relaxation therapy or counselling. [10]

In the second section I will discuss how the TIPP Centre programme was developed from research into male aggression and violence before outlining the structure of the project itself. I will also describe and analyse my experiences of running the first two pilot programmes with offenders, in relation to Novaco's

---

[2] Novaco, R.W. (1975) *Anger Control*, Massachusetts, Lexicon Books.

[3] Beck, A.T., Rush, A.J., Shaw, B.F., and Emery, G. (1979) *Cognitive Therapy of Depression*, New York, Guildford Press.

[4] Kendall, P. and Hollon, S. (1979) *Cognitive Behavioural Interventions*, New York, Academic Press.

[5] Meichenbaum, D. (1977) *Cognitive Behaviour Modification*, New York, Plenum Press.

[6] Dobash, R.E. and Dobash, R.P. (1981) 'Community response to violence against wives: charivari, abstract justice and patriarchy', *Social Problems*, 28, 5, pp 563-581.

[7] Bush, J. (1995) Teaching Self Risk Management to Violent Offenders, in McGuire, J. (Ed.) *What Works: Reducing Reoffending*, Chichester, John Wiley and Sons.

[8] See footnotes 1-6.

[9] Gendreau, P. and Andrews, D.A. (1990) 'Tertiary prevention: What the meta-analysis of the offender treatment tells us about 'What Works'", *Canadian Journal of Criminology*, 32, pp.173-84.

[10] Novaco, R W. (1975) op.cit.; Novaco, R W. (1976) Treatment of Chronic Anger Through Cognitive and Relaxation Controls, *Journal of Consulting and Clinical Psychology*, 44, p 681; Lipsey, M.W. (in press) 'Juvenile delinquency treatment: A meta-analytical inquiry into the variability of effects', in K.W. Wachter and M.L. Straf (Eds) *Meta-Analysis for Explanation: A Casebook*, New York, Russell Sage Foundation.

three phases of anger treatment: cognitive preparation; skills acquisition; and application training. [11]

It is important to note, at this stage, that cognitive behaviour is only one of a number of different theories that explain the causes of anger and aggression; i.e. to what degrees it may be the result of learned, biological, or socially constructed factors as indicated in Chapter One. The incorporation of a cognitive-behavioural and pro-feminist approach to anger/aggression into a programme for violent men reflects a belief that the causes of anger and aggression are a combination of individual pathological and socio-political contextual factors. I would, briefly, like to set out why cognitive-behaviour, in particular, was chosen as a relevant theoretical approach to the design of the TIPP project.

Analytical Perspectives.

The starting point of devising an educational course for violent offenders has to be that the possibility for change exists, and one of the main principles of the cognitive-behavioural model is that we have this ability to bring about change in ourselves and other people. The implication of this assumption is that we all have a choice in how we perceive, interpret and ultimately respond to our experiences of the world; that through thinking we have 'the capacity to be aware of ourselves as being a particular person distinct from all others and to reflect on the experience of being that person and who that person is'. [12] This links to Freire's perception of the individual as relating to the world in a critical way, 'apprehending objective data through reflection - not by reflex as in animals'.[13]

---

[11] Novaco, R.W. (1983) *Stress Inoculation Therapy for Anger Control: A Manual for Therapists*, Irvine, University of California Press.

[12] Stevens, R. (1985) 'Personal Worlds', Block 4 of D307, *Social Psychology: Development, Experience and Behaviour in a Social World*, Milton Keynes, The Open University Press, p76

[13] Freire, P. (1974) *Education for Critical Consciousness*, London, Sheed and Ward, p.3

The issue of the self-efficacy of the individual is also prominent in Libertarian education, as well as phenomenology.[14] While cognitive behaviourists are concerned with enabling the cognitive management of emotions, pro-feminist researchers concentrate on the underlying motivation for behaviour. The beliefs and expectations of some men about some women are not only learnt from their early social environment, but can be actively reinforced by their present social environment.[15] The personal construction of the world becomes more than something that is learnt and unlearnt, it is something influenced by common ideologies held by different groups of people determined by social formations like class, gender, race, and age. The emphasis on identity being informed by the social environment is similar to Erikson's concept that the individual is influenced by an intrinsically *psychosocial* process: 'We deal with a process 'located' in the core of the individual and yet also in the core of his [or her] communal culture'.[16] This relationship between the individual and the social environment, and how the one influences the other, is a key area which distinguishes cognitive-behaviourists from social learning theorists, e.g. the pro-feminists.

However, in criminal law the notion of individual agency is a cornerstone. Because 'if offenders are forged in the crucible of societal action, then it logically follows that crime can be eradicated by the treatment and eventual elimination of the responsible social elements'.[17] The assumption is based on the fact that, with a few exceptions (certifiably insane; under a certain 'legally responsible' age), we are responsible and accountable for our actions. The cognitive-behavioural view then is part of a mainstream view of ourselves as having autonomy over our actions. From this perspective it is unacceptable for a person to plead that a crime

---

[14] In Libertarian education Ferrer, F. (1976) *The Origins and Ideals of the Modern School*, Madrid, Zyx; see also Smith, M. (1983) *The Libertarians and Education*, London, Unwin. For phenomenology see last chapter or reference section at end.
[15] Dobash, R.E. and Dobash, R.P. (1990) *The CHANGE Project Annual Report 1990*, University of Stirling, p.11.
[16] Erikson, E.H. (1968) *Identity: Youth and Crisis*, London, Faber, p. 22.
[17] Siegal, L.J. and Senna, J.J. (1990) *Introduction to Criminal Justice* (5th ed.) St. Paul, MN, West Publishing, p.85.

is a result of an unconscious impulse, or the result of a hormonal imbalance, or even that he/she comes from a disadvantaged background.

These fundamental arguments about the nature of identity, in what ways it is a social and/or private construct, have all influenced the development of educational courses for violent offenders. In the next section I will detail how Novaco's cognitive-behavioural and pro-feminist perspectives were taken into account in devising a course for violent offenders. Principally the section will view the work of Novaco, George Kelly and Dobash and Dobash as practitioners who have worked from different theoretical perspectives to create practical methods of working with angry and/or violent people.

General research on violence.

Drawing from the vast amount of research on violent criminal behaviour, Dobash has sought to make some generalisations about the 'typical' profile of a violent offender: Criminal violence is primarily gendered; it is not always men who are violent, but it usually is; criminal violence has no single cause and cannot be cured with any single treatment; some dangerously violent men use violence frequently, others very rarely; some men are mentally ill, others show no sign of emotional disturbance at all; and many have experienced abuse themselves as children, but others have grown up in seemingly normal environments. [18]

Bush also draws on the extensive criminological literature on violent men, to identify three points which support the case for a cognitive-behavioural approach to treatment: [19]

- Violence is not an isolated form of criminal behaviour.

  Studies suggest that a burglar is as likely to be reconvicted for a violent offence as would someone who has existing violent convictions. [20]

---

[18] Dobash, R.E. (1994) *'What Works?'* Conference presentation, Salford University.
[19] Bush, J.(1995) op.cit.

- Patterns of violence and criminal behaviour are embedded in habits of thinking.

Attitudes, beliefs and thinking patterns in the minds of violent individuals support and promote their violent behaviour. Violent people may truly believe, for instance, that if they abandon violence the world will overwhelm them. They may form the habit of thinking of themselves as victims. They may nurture underlying feelings of righteous anger and resentment toward the world. They may believe they are entitled to hurt others because of the hurt they have suffered. These kinds of attitudes, beliefs and thinking patterns can make violence seem to be a normal, justified, and necessary behaviour. [21]

- Violence is a learned behaviour.

Violent people learn to use violence as a coping response to a wide range of stressful experiences. It is often their most familiar and, from their point of view, their most effective means of responding to threatening or stressful circumstances. Violence may be experienced as their only reliable means of experiencing their own power and efficacy. Violence for these people is rewarding. Non-violence is not. [22]

The latter point underlines a central tenet of cognitive behavioural theory: that in all cases the gains for the client must outweigh the losses or else he/she would not behave in that way. The question for people working with violent offenders is: what is being validated for the client by behaving as he does? One explanation links aggression with the desire to achieve self-recognition and suggests that a sense of devaluation fuels a great deal of aggressive behaviour. [23] The point being that those who have been neglected and disparaged develop a strong need to assert

[20] Beck, A.J., (1987). *Recidivism of Young Parolees*, Washington D.C., Bureau of Justice Statistics Special Report.
[21] Andrews, D. (1990). 'The Role of Antisocial Attitudes in the Psychology of Crime', Paper presented to the *Canadian Psychological Association*, Ottawa.
[22] Bandura, A. (1973). *Aggression: A Social Learning Analysis*, Englewood Cliffs, N.J., Prentice Hall; Goldstein, A. (1988) *The Prepare Curriculum*, Champaign, Research Press.
[23] Siann, G. (1985) *Accounting for Aggression: perspectives on aggression and violence*, London, Allen and Unwin, pp. 165-6

themselves and so behave violently. In short, violence is the only way an offender may know that will gain him a position in intimate social relationships.

The notion of thought processes having an influence on emotions and behaviour is a recent development in behaviour theory. One of the first to explore this area was George Kelly; through his Personal Construct Theory (PCT) developed in 1955. [24] Kelly explained an individual's current behaviour in terms of the ways in which he anticipates events. For instance, a red traffic light signals to one driver that he must stop, otherwise an accident may occur. However, to another driver a red light might signify a challenge and s/he might accelerate the car.

One of Kelly's propositions is that an individual's behaviour makes sense to him/her. He noted that other factors, such as social, cultural, biological sources contribute to the way humans behaved. However he believed in 'constructive alternativism', the ability that individuals possess to reconstruct their way of perceiving the world: [25]

> ....all our present perceptions are open to question and reconsideration and [this] does broadly suggest that even the most obvious occurrences of everyday life might appear utterly transformed if we were inventive enough to construe them differently...[26]
>
> It is we, as individuals, who do what we do, nobody else does it to us. Neither past nor future events in themselves can be regarded as basic determinants of the course of our actions - not even the events of childhood. It is what we make of them which forms the basis of our subsequent anticipation of events. [27]

---

[24] Kelly, G.A. (1986) *A Brief Introduction to Personal Construct Theory*, London, Centre for Personal Construct Psychology.
[25] ibid., p. 3
[26] ibid., p. 4
[27] Fransella, F. and Dalton, P. (1992) *Personal Construct Counselling in Action*, London, Sage Publications, p.7

Kelly is of particular interest to theatre practitioners because of his affirmation that the process of questioning the way in which we perceive the world is a creative one. In Kelly's model behaviour itself becomes a playful experiment. He incorporates role play and drama to demonstrate to his clients that behaviour is part of a process rather than an end product.

Social behaviourists, like the phenomenologists, have attempted to examine and explore the process of perception. In phenomenology, as outlined by Husserl, the process involves a mental operation of placing aspects of experience in 'brackets' thereby 'suspending efficacy of these aspects as determinative of the course and content of conscious experience'. [28] Social behaviourists, like Dodge, have set out perception in terms of steps in the effective processing of social information: [29]

1. Encoding social cues.
2. The cognitive representation and interpretation of these social cues.
3. Searching for appropriate ways to respond.
4. Deciding on the best way to respond.

Kelly believes that we all develop 'core' constructs by which we maintain our identity, and that these constructs or beliefs about the world are learnt from a social environment. His view of his clients was that they were prone to becoming 'psychologically stuck', and became unable to conduct alternative experiments and so continue to develop their perception in reaction to a problem. [30] In terms of Dodge's steps (set out above) individuals in crisis search for and perceive fewer social cues than other, more 'stable' individuals. Dodge and Newman suggest that aggressive people not only search for and perceive fewer social cues than

---

[28] Dufrenne, M. (1973) *Phenomenology of Aesthetic Experience*, Evanston, N. Western University Press, p.xvii
[29] Dodge, K.A. (1986) 'A Social-information processing model of social competence in children', in M. Permutter (Ed.) *Minnesota Symposium on Child Psychology*, Hillsdale, N.J., Erlbaum, p.18
[30] Kelly, G.A. (1986) op.cit., p.7

non-violent people, but they are more likely to interpret cues in a hostile fashion. [31] In Aaron Beck's model of emotional disorders he suggests that:

> Individuals affected characteristically misinterpret their daily experiences in a self defeating fashion. Adverse experiences are over selected and attributed to personal deficiencies. Standards (and expectations) are set too high........difficulties are seen as disasters, the worst is expected. [32]

Hence the emphasis of cognitive-behaviour is on the idea that the interpretation of events can have an important effect on an individual's emotional state and behaviour.

An outline of Novaco's work.

Novaco's proposition of anger assumes a notion of 'agency' in individual behaviour which is in line with other cognitive-behaviour practitioners. [33] Importantly Novaco and Kelly believe that the human capacity for agency, can help people realise that they do have a choice in the way that they construct and respond to the world, as Kelly suggests: 'No-one needs to be the victim of his biography'. [34]

Novaco's general psychological model of anger is that of a cognitively mediated emotional state that is reciprocally related to cognitions and to behaviour.[35] A central proposition is that there is no direct relationship between external events

---

[31] Dodge, K.A., and Newman, J.P. (1981) 'Biased decision-making processes in aggressive boys', *Journal of Abnormal Psychology.*, **90**, pp. 375-9; see also Slaby, R.G. and Guerra, N.G. (1988) 'Cognitive mediators of aggression in adolescent offenders: 1. Assessment', *Developmental Psychology*, pp. 580-8.

[32] Beck, A.T. (1976) Cognitive Therapy and the Emotional Disorders, reprinted in M. Scott (1993*) A Cognitive-Behavioural Approach to Clients' Problems*, London and New York, Tavistock/Routledge, p.2

[33] Kelly, G.A. (1955) op.cit.; Beck, A.T. (1976) op.cit.; Scott, M. (1993) op.cit.

[34] Kelly, G.A. (1955) op.cit., p.15

[35] Novaco, R W. (1979) 'The Cognitive Regulation of Anger and Stress', in P. Kendall and S. Hollon (Eds.) *Cognitive-behavioural Interventions: Theory, research and Procedures*, New York, Academic Press.

and anger. That is to say, that the arousal of anger is a cognitively mediated emotional process. Implicit in the cognitive labelling is some impulse to action. The cognitive labelling process inherently involves an inclination on the part of the person to act in an antagonistic or confrontational manner towards the source of the provocation. The urge to attack, injure, or destroy by real or symbolic actions is part of what differentiates the emotional state of anger, as opposed to something else like 'being upset' or 'tense'.

From this perspective arguments for different treatment interventions are resolved by definition. For example a psycho-analytical perspective on violence may suggest that violent offenders suffer from repressed anger. The view of violence may be that clients react to situations because of difficult or abusive past relationships with their parents and as a result carry the baggage of their experience in terms of anger and resentment towards people in their present day lives. [36] The implication is that people are indeed, in response to Kelly's suggestion, prisoners of their own biography and therefore only partially accountable for their behaviour. The solution then to violent criminal activity is not punishment or imprisonment but long term psychodynamic therapy. For these reasons the concept of repressed anger is not meaningful in the present context.

Prior to Novaco, anger received little attention in psychological literature, certainly far less than anxiety and depression. [37] The treatment approach to anger disorders, or what Novaco referred to as 'chronic anger problems' or 'proneness to provocation', was informed by the belief that it was possible to clinically intervene in maladoptive thoughts and emotions and formulate a procedure that could be systematically applied to the management of anger. [38] Novaco found

---

[36] Stevens, R. (1985) op.cit.
[37] Novaco, R.W. (1983) op.cit., p.2
[38] ibid., p.2

that cognitive treatment interventions were an effective means of reducing anger and facilitating constructive coping mechanisms in response to provocation. [39]

Novaco's model identifies a complex arrangement of feedback that includes the following components. A provocation instigates a physiological arousal that is labelled anger. [40] This 'anger' is then translated into one of several behaviours, one of which may be aggression. The consequences of aggressive behaviour often serve to provoke more arousal and the anger intensifies. The view taken here is that anger is an emotional state defined by the presence of physiological arousal and cognitive labelling. [41] The cognitive label does not define anger precisely, but rather it is an approximation used to cover varying intensities of feeling, such as annoyed, irritated, enraged, provoked, etc. Novaco refers to this labelling as the 'subjective affect' dimension of emotional states. [42]

Novaco's use of cognitive psychology implies that our emotions can be modified as we become more aware of associated cognitive processes. In other words, he suggests that by recognising thoughts which lie behind emotions like anger, the emotions can be changed.

The causes of anger and aggression.

It is important to recognise the multiple functions of anger, that as an emotional state it has adaptive as well as maladaptive functions. It should not automatically be viewed as a negative condition. Anger may energise coping activity, act as a discriminative cue for problem-solving efforts, or serve as a vehicle for expressive communication of negative sentiments. However it may also disrupt information processing and task performance, instigate aggressive actions, or promote a desire

---

[39] Novaco, R W. (1975) op.cit.; *and* Novaco, R.W. (1976) op.cit.

[40] Novaco, R W. (1975) op.cit.

[41] ibid.; *and* Konecni, V.J. (1975) 'The mediation of aggressive behaviour: Arousal level vs. anger and cognitive labelling' , *Journal of Personality and Social Psychology*, **32**, pp 706-712.

[42] Novaco, R.W. (1983) op.cit., p.3

for control over others. The cognitive-behavioural approach to anger problems aims to maximise the positive functions and minimise the maladoptive.

Novaco's proposition was that anger is neither necessary nor sufficient for aggression, yet it can be a significant precursor of aggression and has a mutually influenced relationship with aggression:

> This bi-directional causality postulate means that the level of anger influences the level of aggression and vice-versa. Whether or not aggression occurs following provocation is thought to be a function of various social learning factors other than anger, such as reinforcement contingencies, expected outcomes, and modelling influences. These same social learning factors can also influence the occurrence of aggression independent of anger arousal. Thus, it is possible for someone to aggress without becoming angry, as when the infliction of injury or damage is expected to produce personal gain or when the aggressive act is a well-learned behaviour. [43]

Therefore 'treatment' of anger and aggression is designed to make the individual more aware of the 'anger' process and enable him/her to intervene in aggressive patterns of behaviour. Basically, anger control techniques attempt to enhance specific cognitive and behavioural skills. This is achieved by using *attention* and *restructuring* skills. The *attention* skills include the ability to recognise provocation cues and physiological signs of arousal; anger 'diaries' are often used to promote this awareness. The *restructuring* skills include adjusting expectations and reappraisal of the circumstances that provoke arousal.

Determinants of anger.

An offender's anger experiences can be examined in terms of the events that happen in their lives, how they interpret and experience those events, and how they behave when and after these events occur. Three defining factors that

---

[43] ibid., p.5

Novaco identifies are external circumstances, internal processes and behavioural reactions. [44]

The external circumstances relate to the cluster of events that routinely provoke anger; these may be similar in nature (frustrations, annoyances, insults etc.) or may vary widely. Novaco asserts that the events are not provocative in themselves but depend on a number of factors internal to a client. Furthermore:

> ...cumulative exposure to aversive environmental elements progressively shapes a disposition for anger...it may well be that the anger was in large measure due to ambient, distal circumstances, rather than an acute, proximate event. [45]

The identification of internal processes refers to two basic factors that are thought to influence anger arousal: expectations and appraisals. Novaco defines appraisals as a concept pertaining to the interpretation or 'meaning analysis' of present and past events, as well as to the person's judgement about his/her ability to cope with the threat or demand. Expectations are the subjective probabilities that a person has concerning future events. These pertain both to the anticipated event and to one's behaviour in response to the event.

Novaco uses the term 'private speech' to define an act that may work as a self-arousal mechanism. 'Private speech' is a form of antagonistic self-statement which 'pumps up' or inflames anger. These anger instigative thoughts provide information about the client's cognitive structuring of the provocation situations. The idea is rather like the concept of a soliloquy delivered by an actor which allows an audience an insight into the internal frame of mind of a character. Novaco's treatment basis is to make the client aware of these 'private' thoughts

---

[44] ibid., p.10
[45] ibid., p.11

which maintain and heighten the arousal of anger, and to short-circuit them through self-calming statements or other such methods.

The third determinant that Novaco defined pertained to <u>behavioural reactions</u> to provocation incidents. For example an antagonistic response to an event results in the definition of one's emotional state as anger. Furthermore, aggressive behaviour in an interpersonal context may often result in others behaving antagonistically, which increases the probability for anger in the subject. Toch showed that provocation sequences escalate from minor annoyances to serious injury as each person in the interaction responds antagonistically. [46]

Novaco's proposition is that these factors that cause anger are all 'transactionally' related. [47] He believes that it is not a matter of thoughts causing emotions or emotions causing behaviour or environmental influences causing everything else: 'Transactionality means that there exist processes of mutual influence between elements in the system'. [48]

I will come back to Novaco's application of cognitive-behavioural theories later. But first I would like to consider a different way of understanding anger, aggression and violence. This perspective is based on the arguments of pro-feminist writers and researchers who believe that (male) violence needs to be viewed in the context of a patriarchal society. The pro-feminists prefer to look at male violence on a much broader scale, and place greater theoretical emphasis on the influences that social factors have on individuals. The feminist viewpoint, as Morash has pointed out, is one that criticises but is not necessarily antithetical to cognitive-behavioural explanations, despite the use of different paradigms for theory building. [49] She states that both are eclectic methods, although feminist writers place greater store on historical and anthropological analysis whilst

---

[46] Toch, H. (1969) *Violent Men*, Chicago, Aldine Publishing Co.
[47] Novaco, R.W. (1983) op.cit., p.14
[48] ibid., p.14
[49] Morash, M. (1986) 'Wife Battering', Criminal Justice Abstracts, June 1986, pp 252-271

cognitive-behaviourists prefer survey methods and analysis of contemporary social structures. In fact, as I shall discuss later, both these theoretical viewpoints may positively contribute to practical approaches to working with violent men.

The pro-feminist perspective.

A number of pro-feminist writers have criticised Novaco's theories for failing to place male behaviour in a wider socio-political context of sexism and patriarchy. [50] The pro-feminist approach, particularly concerned with domestic violence, disregards the notion that it is anger that causes men to be violent, but more the consequence of a socially imposed 'need' to control women. [51] Therefore anger control programmes may teach new communication and social skills, but without challenging the underlying misogyny of abusive men. Consequently men who control their anger are not necessarily less likely to be abusers.

The concern about abusive males' controlling behaviour and need for dominance in relationships emerged in the early 1980's from researchers' working with battered women. The wives and partners of men who had been on an anger control course in Pittsburgh reported that whilst in some cases the physical abuse was lessening, the psychological abuse intensified. [52] The men concerned were using the programme the same way they used violence - to manipulate and control their wives. Anger programmes, it appeared, had the potential to create what Gondolf termed 'non violent terrorists'. [53]

---

[50] Holmes, M. and Lundy, C. (1990) 'Group Work For Abusive Men: A Profeminist Response', *Canada's Mental Health*, **Vol. 38**, December 1990; *and* Dobash, R.E. and Dobash, R.P. (1981) 'Community response to violence against wives: charivari, abstract justice and patriarchy', *Social Problems*, **28**, 5, pp 563-581; *and* Dobash, R.E. and Dobash, R.P. (1990/91) *The CHANGE Project Annual report 1990 and 1991*, University of Stirling.

[51] Scheter, S. (1982) *Women and Male Violence*, London, Pluto Press.

[52] Gondolf, E (1984) 'How Some Men Stop Battering: An Evaluation of a Group Counselling Program.' Paper presented at the second *National Conference for Family Violence Researchers*, Durham, NH.

[53] Gondolf, E and Russell, D. (1986) 'The Case Against Anger Control Treatment Programs for Batterers', *Response*, **Vol. 9**, No 3.

Dobash and Dobash have studied the socio-historical roots of domestic violence and maintain that for centuries husbands have used violence both systematically and severely to dominate, punish and control their wives simply as a husband's prerogative. [54] This prerogative of the man over his wife was sanctioned by the church (devotion and submission) and articulated in English common law; a husband was allowed to "give his wife a severe beating with whips and clubs for some offences".[55] Thus Dobash and Dobash argue that physical force in domestic situations was both legally and socially acceptable.

Although laws and social views of wife battering are now changing, at the heart of the pro-feminist argument is the belief that domestic violence reflects an unequal power relationship between men and women in society and therefore within personal relationships. Strauss:

> The most fundamental set of factors bringing about wife beating are those connected with the sexist structure of the family and society...The cultural norms and values permitting and sometimes encouraging husband-to-wife violence reflect the hierarchical and male-dominant type of society which characterises the Western world. [56]

Anger and violence are viewed as a method men use to secure control within the relationship:

> Men's abuse of and violence towards women is seen as a learned and intentional behaviour rather than the consequence of individual pathology, stress, alcohol abuse or the fact that he lives in a 'dysfunctional relationship' [57]

---

[54] Dobash, R.E. and Dobash, R.P. (1981) op.cit., pp 563-581
[55] Hecker, E.A. (1910) A Short History of Women's Rights: From the Days of Augustus to the Present Time, reprinted in L. Smith (1989) *Domestic Violence: An Overview of the literature*, London, HMSO.
[56] Strauss, M.A. (1977) 'A sociological perspective on the prevention and treatment of wife-beating', in M. Roy (ed.) *Battered Women*, New York, Van Nostrand Reinhold, pp 194-239.
[57] Dobash, R.E. and Dobash, R.P. (1990) op.cit., p.11

Holmes and Lundy argue that men abuse women because of what they believe, not what they feel, so the approach to working with men is to uncover beliefs and intentions of abusers, and the effects of their violence. [58] Wilson has argued that domestic violence is an extreme form of 'normalisation' - an exaggeration of how society expects men to behave as authority figures in the family. [59] Thus, pro-feminist researchers disagree with the use of terms such as 'anger' or 'stress' to define motivational factors behind violence and/or aggression. For example Gondolf and Russell argue that violence is often a premeditated system of debilitating control. [60] This argument is illustrated by a number of other writers who have drawn attention to the economic dependency of women. [61] Pahl's empirical study shows that more than three quarters of the women in her study had husbands who seemed to use money as a more general attempt to control and subordinate their wives. [62] This finding is consistent with other studies; for example the Dobashs' found that the majority of arguments preceding violence focused on three subject areas: the husband's jealousy; differing expectations regarding the wife's domestic duties; and the allocation of money. [63] Evason found that those groups of women (in her sample) who had experienced violence were more likely to have had husbands who kept control over finances and who gave their wives money as and when they saw fit. [64] Non-violent husbands were more likely to have opted for joint management of money.

---

[58] Holmes, M. and Lundy, C. (1990) op.cit.
[59] Wilson, E (1983) *What Is To Be Done About Violence Against Women*, Harmondsworth, Penguin.
[60] Gondolf, E and Russell, D. (1986) op.cit.
[61] Chapman, J.R. & Gates, M. (Eds.) (1978) *The Victimization of Women*, Beverly Hills, California, Sage; Homer, M. *et al* (1985) 'The burden of dependency', in N. Johnson (Ed.) *Marital Violence*, Sociological Review Monograph, London, Routledge and Kegan Paul; Kalmuss, D.S., & Strauss, M.A. (1981) 'A wife's marital dependency and wife abuse', *Journal of Marriage and the Family*, (May), pp. 277-286.
[62] Pahl, J. (1985) *Private Violence and Public Policy*, London, Routledge
[63] Dobash, R.E. and Dobash, R.P. (1981) op.cit., pp 563-581
[64] Evason, E (1982) *Hidden Violence*, Belfast: Farset Press.

Along with the many elements identified as contributing to domestic violence (alcohol; allocation of money; sexual problems; unemployment), pro-feminists argue that abusive men tend to be emotionally insecure and have fixed expectations of their own authority and the role of women in the relationship. [65] Gayford, for example, concluded that men who abused their partners were more likely to be jealous than other, non-abusive males; abusive males also tended to apply strict rules and forms of conduct within the marriage or relationship. [66] Campbell supports this view with testimonies from women who describe becoming emotionally isolated by their partners' vague suspicions which crystallize into obsessions about their imminent infidelity: "We were two miles from the village. He allowed me half an hour to walk there and back and ten minutes to get what I needed at the shops....If I was not back inside that hour and ten minutes I got met at the door (by him) saying where the f----ing hell have you been?". [67] From my own observations with working with violent offenders, I have found a notable presence of possessiveness, jealousy and/or insecurity. One of the many examples was a man who prevented his wife from working or getting further education by insisting that she stay at home. He would phone her at odd times of the day, and arrive at the house unexpectedly just to 'keep track of her'.[68] When his wife insisted on getting out of the house he decided to get her pregnant; this he saw as the best way to keep her away from other people and occupied. This is an example of how a husband's domination over his wife had to be complete, there had to be no possibility of her forming alliances that might curtail his ability to control her.

Campbell views the central problem for abusive men as the interplay between the need for both intimacy and control; the abusive male finds it hard to relinquish the

---

[65] Roy, M (1977) *Battered Women*, New York, Van Nostrand Reinhold

[66] Gayford, J.J. (1975) 'Wife battering: a preliminary survey of 100 cases', *British Medical Journal*, (January), pp. 194-197

[67] Campbell, A. (1993) *Out of Control: Men, Women and Aggression*, New York, Pandora, p.104

[68] Personal notes, unpublished.

nagging doubt that his dependence makes him vulnerable, and he uses aggression to regain control. Campbell believes that aggression, whether verbal or physical, has a twofold advantage for men:

> First it (aggression) distances the parties involved; instead of partners there are now antagonists. Empathy is disregarded instead of competition, and thus the relationship shifts from the emotional minefield of dependency to the more familiar landscape of struggle for dominance. The second effect is the man's almost certain ability to win in any physical confrontation. No longer at a woman's mercy, thrown from power by the perceived weakness of emotions, a man can take control and 'seize power' in the relationship. [69]

The shortcomings of anger control.

The pro-feminists identify a number of shortcomings in the use of anger control with perpetrators of domestic violence. [70]

First, one of the initial steps toward conventional anger control is to identify personal provocation cues, which in the case of domestic violence includes annoying behaviours of the wife or partner. Schechter argues that such a process implies that the victim provokes the anger and precipitates the abuse.[71] The pro-feminist view suggests an oppressor/oppressed interpretation of domestic violence. That is, the violence is a result of a more powerful and dominating man relentlessly using abuse to control a woman.

Second, the denial of abuse by violent men, as a number of clinical reports suggest, is particularly acute. [72] Gondolf and Russell have therefore argued that batterers may use anger as another excuse for their abuse, much as they blame alcohol, stress, or other individuals. Anger control may feed the batterer's

---

[69] Campbell, A. (1993) op.cit., p.107
[70] *In particular*: Gondolf, E and Russell, D. (1986) op.cit.
[71] Scheter, S. (1982) *Women and Male Violence,* London, Pluto Press.
[72] Bernard. J.L., & Bernard, M.L. (1984) 'The Abusive Male Seeking Treatment; Jakyll and Hyde', *Family Relations,* **33**, pp. 543-547

tendency toward self-pity and self-deception and may lead him to self-justification and victim-blaming. [73]

Third, some men may accept anger control as an expedient way to profess being cured and lure their partners back. Gondolf and Russell cite research which demonstrates that some men use programmes in the same way they use their violence - to manipulate and control their wives. After learning a few anger control techniques, many batterers claim the problem is 'under control' in order to get back with their partners. [74]

The New Directions group is one of several re-education programmes for abusive men which base their approach on a pro-feminist position. [75] Based in Ottawa, Canada, the programme further develops the assumptions and strategies of group practice based on a feminist analysis. The focus of pro-feminist groups for abusive men promotes men to confront patriarchy in themselves and others. [76] Programmes study the benefits and privileges that accrue to men from their use of violence, such as having their needs met, gaining control and feeling powerful. Central to the practical approach to working with violent offenders, for example, is the identification of the various mechanisms of control and domination, the effects of violence on partners, an examination of the beliefs underlying sexist and violent behaviour, and the introduction of alternative ways of thinking about relationships. [77] Motivation to change is based on the realisation that relinquishing power and privileges offers its own rewards in terms of better relationships with their partners.

Like Novaco, the pro-feminists separate out anger and aggression, specifying that violence is an intentional and learned behaviour. Pro-feminist programmes also look into the determining factors of antagonistic behaviour, but select factors by

[73] Gondolf, E and Russell, D. (1986) op.cit.
[74] ibid.
[75] Holmes, M. and Lundy, C. (1990) op.cit.; see also The Change Project, Stirling
[76] See also Pence and Paymar, 1986; Holmes and Lundy, 1990; Dobash and Dobash, 1990.
[77] Holmes, M. and Lundy, C. (1990) op.cit.

looking at violence within the context of a patriarchal society. So, for example, Novaco's internal processes are viewed not simply as inflaming anger thoughts but as a way of justifying and rationalising the maintenance of power and control within relationships with women. The character soliloquy is now not an insight into anger, but a revelation of a desire to subordinate women.

Pro-feminist programmes for violent men also share common ground with Novaco's work in respect to exploring expectations and appraisals. In the Change programme men's expectations and 'meaning analysis' are explored by careful attention to what underpins their behaviour. [78]

> If the violence is seen initially by the man as an explosion of anger, a detailed breakdown of the incident can reveal that it most often occurs when his partner defies his expectations of authority and denies him the services he expects in certain situations. These expectations may conform to his appraisal of what denotes proper male and female behaviour. Given this appraisal of roles within the family the challenge which he experiences to his authority when his partner behaves out of role by not obeying him or contradicting him or by acting without his consent may cause a sudden crisis of confidence in himself and in the integrity of his role. His 'anger' or 'temper' which results in violence is his way of restoring order and authority to any threatening situation. [79]

Therefore, pro-feminist programmes such as Change, Duluth, or New Directions add another factor to Novaco's behaviour reactions. As well as antagonism or avoidance/displacement of provocation there is control and manipulation through intimidation. This clearly is not about emotion, but about the benefits and privileges that accrue to men from their use of violence, such as having their needs met, gaining control and feeling powerful.

---

[78] Dobash, R.E. and Dobash, R.P. (1990) op.cit.
[79] ibid., p.9

The anger management and pro-feminist theories do share common ground, but choose to emphasis' different factors involved with anger, aggression and violence. Novaco suggests that chronic anger reactions (including aggression and violence) can be understood as a learned way of coping with life demands. [80] The pro-feminists take this further by proposing that as well as being learned the benefits of violence for the man outweigh the costs.[81] Therefore treatment must not merely concentrate on cognitively controlling intense emotions but on challenging the man's cost-benefit assessment of his behaviour.

Some feminist researchers do not reject the relevance of other factors, such as social stresses, individual pathology, or theories of chronic anger problems, but argue that their explanatory power is not sufficient. [82] But if Novaco's blame on individual cognition fails to be sufficient, so, too, it can be argued, can the blaming of a patriarchal society. It seems to me that each theory is only partially effective in explaining the causes and possible interventions that can be made. There is a need to continue to link socio-structural and cultural factors with personality development, cognitive-behaviour and situational factors. The ultimate goal must be to move towards a society in which domestic violence is not tolerated: a society in which social, cultural, legal and economic influences inhibit its development. This involves confronting how as a society we construct and define behaviour termed 'masculine' and 'feminine'; how we ascribe roles within marriage; and how those processes regulate the position of women.

The development of The Pump programme.

In 1994 the Theatre in Prisons and Probation (TIPP) Centre was approached by Greater Manchester Probation Service to work on a project aimed at helping violent offenders deal positively with their aggressive behaviour. The project, funded by the Home Office, took two years to complete from initiation through to

---

[80] Novaco, R.W. (1983) op.cit.
[81] Holmes, M. and Lundy, C. (1990) op.cit.
[82] Dobash, R.E. and Dobash, R.P. (1979) *Violence Against Wives*, New York, The Free Press.

a finished course structure. The role of the TIPP Centre in the new programme was to create a drama-based approach to anger management work. TIPP's director, James Thompson, stage designer Jocelyn Meall and myself formed the main TIPP team.

The theories of Novaco, Kelly, and pro-feminist researchers like Dobash and Dobash were very influential in the development of the TIPP Centre programme. The TIPP Challenging Violence project was not an attempt to 'reinvent the wheel', but an opportunity to create a drama-based approach to standard methods of presenting anger management and/or pro-feminist interventions to violence. The concepts that have been developed were directly related to the theories and procedures of researchers and practitioners who were already well established in this field (Novaco, Dobash and Dobash, Kelly etc). One important note is that anger management programmes may work with offenders with a wide range of violent offences, from street affray, arson, aggravated burglary to domestic partner or physical child abuse. In recent years, specific domestic violence courses have been developed aside from anger management programmes in recognition of pro-feminist arguments. [83] However, it is very common to find participants who have been arrested for non-domestic offences, who, during a 'general' anger management course reveal domestic incidents. Therefore it is important that both the facilitator and the course have a clear rationale and ability to deal with such issues. As one participant said: 'If I could control my violence at home, I could control my violence outside'. [84]

Background.

The project was devised over a two year period and consisted of the following stages:

---

[83] In the North West of England Greater Manchester, Cheshire and Merseyside Probation Service have developed or are developing specific domestic violence programmes aside from anger management courses.
[84] Personal notes.

Research and consultation (duration: 3 months). The TIPP Centre looked at existing course components, and studied relevant research. A liaison committee of Probation practitioners met regularly to offer advice about running anger management groups and help with the devising process as it progressed.

Trials (duration: 4 months). Once an outline of the programme and some techniques had been established, the TIPP Centre demonstrated its initial ideas to a number of different groups; clients who had completed an anger management course, a group of probation officers, theatre practitioners. The many useful comments and criticisms from these groups fed into the completion of the structure of an 8 week pilot course.

Pilot programmes and evaluation (5 pilot schemes run over 16 month period). Five courses were run in five different probation centres in the Greater Manchester area. The first two courses were run simultaneously, one in Salford, another in Bury.[85] The other centres were Rochdale, Stretford, Bolton and Hyde/Oldham. Again feedback from all the people concerned - participants, probation staff, TIPP staff, and outside observers (some of the courses were recorded on video) developed the ideas, techniques and structure of the programme.

The aims which guided the project through the practical devising stage were:

- To examine the links between anger, aggression and lack of self control with offending behaviour.
- To help participants to understand causes of their anger and raise awareness of the consequences of violent behaviour.

---

[85] The location of the pilot programmes has been altered to protect the identity of participants.

- To improve participants' abilities to behave and respond more appropriately. In particular to learn techniques of anger control and develop other skills, such as communication skills, to avoid confrontational situations.
- To develop victim awareness.
- To examine, in instances of domestic abuse, how anger may only be one explanation for violence.

The TIPP team wanted to create a programme utilising a combination of image theatre, role play, role reversal, Forum theatre, metaphors and visual stimuli, that would communicate in a straight-forward way difficult anger management concepts. The basic premise of the programme was simple - to help offenders isolate patterns of thinking, feeling and behaviour linked to anger and/or violent behaviour and to introduce them to the notion of interventions. Similar to other probation/theatre projects the underlying process was based on an egalitarian, dialogical model of practice. The contribution of the facilitator was not, in Freirian terms, a moral or 'cultural invader' who went to groups to impose and instruct, but to find ways in which the men could take a new stance toward their problems of violence - that of intimacy with their problems, one orientated toward research instead of repeating 'destructive' behavioural patterns.[86] As discussed previously (in Chapter Two), the programme needed to be open in its anti-violence values, but responsive and reflexive to the rationalisations of the men. In drama terms, the playing had an agenda, but the agenda was explicit to the group.

However, what was distinctive about this particular project was that some participants attended the programme as a condition of their Probation order under 1A of the 1991 Criminal Justice Act (there were also a few volunteers on each course). On the one hand this meant that drama techniques were an accepted approach, validated by the Probation Service, within criminal justice work. On the

---

[86] Freire, P. (1974) *Education for Critical Consciousness*, London, Sheed and Ward, p.113

other hand the conditional element meant that some participants felt 'forced' into the programme, and as a result the resistance and suspicion of the dramatic techniques was palpably more intense than in other projects with a voluntary requirement. I will return to this point later on.

The eight week programme was divided into four sections: The Pump (x 3); The Jack (x 2); The Behaviour Box (x 2) and a feedback and evaluation session. A full description of the programme can be found in appendix 3.

The next section will outline how the methodology of the TIPP programme was developed. I will then discuss how the various elements of the Pump programme fit in with the three phases or steps of an anger management type programme; cognitive preparation, skill acquisition and application training; before considering some of the practical problems associated with cognitive behavioural work.

The Behaviour Box.

The Probation Liaison committee advising the TIPP Centre made it clear that conventional machismo attitudes were often used by clients to manipulate their position within a relationship in order to get their own way - no matter what. The question was how would the course promote a pro-feminist approach in a men's group who found the idea of equality in a male-female relationship absolutely foreign. Furthermore, to challenge this type of behaviour was far more difficult than questioning an act of violence because the aggression was indirect and often invisible. The characteristics of the indirect aggression mode of behaviour were more complex than anger/aggression and avoidance/displacement behaviour.

Informed by pro-feminist arguments, the aim of the Behaviour Box section was to make clients aware that physical aggression was not the only form of behaviour that could be identified as violent. The course aimed to demonstrate that violence was not only physical, but that intimidation and coercion were also forms of violence. The session would also need to show how certain types of behaviour had certain short and long term consequences - both for the perpetrator and for those on the receiving end. The idea was that the client makes an appraisal of the cost-benefit ratio of acting violently or being aggressive. The short term goals of restoration of authority are balanced with the loss of love, respect, companionship, intimacy and trust resulting in a relationship that is based on fear or else the departure of the woman whom the man has been so concerned to keep under his control. If it can be demonstrated that certain kinds of behaviour will, in the long term, have certain kinds of effect, then one may be able to appeal directly to the client's self interest to change.

In dramatic terms, the TIPP team wanted to find a way to represent these ideas as straight-forwardly as possible. The techniques would combine image work and thinking reports, as well as role-play and role reversal in order to problematise the men's perceptions and justifications for coercive behaviour. But the team also wanted to visually represent the various types of behaviour associated with violent or coercive actions, in order to support the dramatic approaches to the work. The TIPP team explored ways of looking at male power and control in relationships. The team drew two lines on the floor, one that represented 'control', the other a 'power' scale. Diagram a.

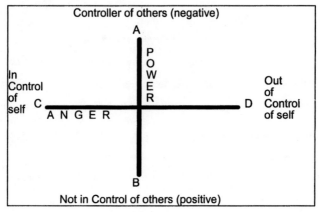

The power and control lines (diagram a.) indicate a scale for anger (the control axis) and a scale for manipulative/intimidating behaviour (the power axis). The purpose of the diagram was to pin-point incidents by mapping a character's progression through a story. The second diagram illustrates a fictional incident involving a drunken man coming home late. The man enters his house to discover his wife waiting for him in the kitchen. She is cross with him for being out late. A ferocious argument ensues and ends up with the man beating up his wife.

Diagram b:

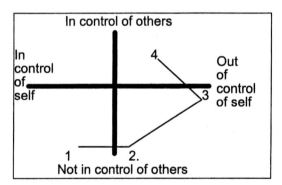

The graph was a rough way to map and record a (fictional) client's progress through an incident. However the probation advisory group thought that the idea was not wholly workable; it was hard to grasp; it would be complicated to explain, especially to a group without much experience of graphs; and the mapping of a single incident was not particularly 'theatrical'.

However, what the TIPP team and advisory group did think useful was that the quarters of the graph seemed to tie in with the behaviour reactions that Novaco and Pro-feminists noted, for example antagonism, aversion/diversion, and indirect aggression. From these behaviour characteristics, the TIPP designer wanted to find pictorial representations, and so created a collection of painted images, sketches and collages from magazine cuttings. One of the images for the indirect aggression box, was of a malevolent puppeteer (dressed like a gangster), who skilfully manipulated and controlled his puppet (a woman). The image of the antagonistic behaviour reaction was represented by a large fisted boxing-glove, with a face on it, leaping out of a box. The assertive behaviour reaction was represented by a person meditating. It was these images that led the TIPP team to developing four character types or archetypes which existed at the extreme of each polarity.

The Godfather represented someone totally in control of himself and others. For example, a psychological torturer who with the slightest look can manipulate others would be at the far edge of the space and towards the centre one gets less dominant. In other words this section represented 'getting people to do what you want' behaviour.

The Jack in the Box is, at its extreme, a character out of control of himself/herself but whose aggression and violence has power over others. From this archetype the TIPP team got the idea of someone 'thinking with his fist', and the image of the fist-face coming out of the box.

Self Mutilator was someone who avoided confrontation, but displaced the anger, taking it out on inanimate objects or turning anger inwards. The TIPP team thought that the archetype of the Self Mutilator was not as effective as the others. Self mutilation is a characteristic not a character like Jack in the Box or the Godfather. It also did not conjure up the right image of anger displacement that Novaco writes about. More effective representations were sought, like Punchbag, but no archetype for this type of behaviour reaction was ever successfully found.

Buddha represented the far extreme of our aspirations. This archetype practices assertiveness. Buddha manages his anger without hurting other people, he does not seek to control others; he shares and negotiates.

Diagram c:

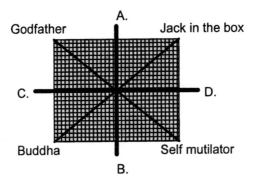

The Probation liaison committee and ex-offenders who were involved with the trials of the TIPP programme were concerned with the use of archetypes. The feed-back from these two groups indicated that using archetypes in offence focused work could 'glamorise' or promote the very behaviour that the programme was attempting to discourage. Probation officers, in particular, felt that although the archetypes were very effective, they represented almost gladiatorial figures of good and evil forces struggling to take over the spirit of a normal human being. The aesthetic argument for the archetypes was to present visual representations which dramatically heightened awareness of general and specific modes of behaviour. As Landy notes:

...the more the drama therapist chooses theatrically stylized devices for treatment (i.e. masks, puppets, epic theatre techniques) the more he over-distances the client. In choosing more realistic devices, such as psychodrama and documentary techniques, the therapist will create less distance. [87]

---

[87] Landy, R. J. (1986) *Drama Therapy: Concepts and Practices*, Springfield, Illinois, Charles C. Thomas, p. 103

In educational terms, the reference to over-distancing is the extent to which the facilitator focuses attention on fictional scenarios/techniques or personal stories. The aim of creative arts educational work, I think, is to find a balance between the dramatisation of 'general' experience and the link to personal documentary work. The advantage of 'over-distancing' techniques, for example asking an offender group to create a fictional offender which in some way represents a composite picture of the individuals in the group, is that it allows for greater 'therapeutic' movement and a safer structure for self disclosure. Individuals can project their feelings and experiences onto the fictional character, in a way that is not so threatening as being asked to reveal their own feelings. This approach has been particularly effective in work with women offenders, who have been able to discuss physically and mentally abusive situations by creating fictional women characters that undergo painful and violent experiences:

> By creating fictional female characters who suffered extreme incidents of physical and sexual violence and mental cruelty, the women in the group were able to discuss their own personal experiences by proxy. More importantly after the workshop several of the women came to me asking for one-to-one counselling, a service that up until then had been offered but for which there had been few volunteers. [88]

Therefore paradoxically the fictionalisation of experience may bring participants closer to themselves. This is possible through the dramatic/theatrical structure and the resonance of dramatic archetypes, symbols, metaphors and characters. As Jennings notes: 'the character is more than a role, a character has a totality, a wholeness', which if created by participants can reflect and refract the multifarious experiences of the individuals within the group. [89] The proposed

---

[88] Interview with author; Patricia Holmes, Rape Crisis Counsellor in HMP Styal, on using the TIPP Centre programme: Blagg!

[89] Jennings, S. (1990) *Dramatherapy with Families, Groups and Individuals: Waiting in the Wings*, London, Jessica Kingsley Publishers, p.21

archetypes in The Pump programme were, potentially, a way to explore violent and coercive behaviour with the men without destroying any defence systems of rationalisation, denial and minimisation as noted by pro-feminist researchers. [90]

However from one of the early feed-back sessions with probation officers, in which the idea of the archetypes was presented, there was concern that in order to define each of the archetypes the programme would have to explore the 'powers' of each of the characters; and thoughtless demonstrations of, say, the 'Godfather' behaviour, could inform the men in an unhealthy way. This criticism links to the pro-feminist research which showed that anger management projects could actually 'teach' coercive and manipulative skills to violent men, and create 'non-violent terrorists'. [91] For example, one exercise that was proposed involved two participants, one person telling a story about him/herself, the other going through three stages of listening - interested, indifferent, ignoring. The power that the listener started to have over the other was obvious. The talker became offended, often felt diminished and boring. As a demonstration this was an effective and clear example. However, it was realised that such an exercise might educate participants to use new techniques to advance their power base. Probation feed-back also indicated a concern that the names might be misinterpreted, for example the Godfather might be associated with the glamour and power of the Mafia as depicted in gangster films; the Buddha might bring a certain amount of baggage with it, or might just seem alien to users.

For the ex-offenders involved with the trials there were two concerns about the archetypes. First the terms confused them, and they found them hard to relate back to their own emotional and cognitive experiences. Second, 'the Godfather' in particular could be seen either as an attractive role model, or conversely was so abhorrent and 'evil' that offenders would be reluctant to identify with him.

---

[90] Dobash, R.E. and Dobash, R.P. (1990) op.cit., p.10
[91] Gondolf, E and Russell, D. (1986) op.cit.

So although the archetypes were resonant images and had obvious dramatic potential for exploring behaviour reactions in an almost gladiatorial arena, they were discouraged by the trials with Probation Officers and ex-offenders.

The debate about the archetypes highlights the process in which the aesthetic and probation agendas are negotiated and developed. The negotiation process can be positive and beneficial, setting up a dialogue informed by different methodologies, or as Carlson phrases it 'multiple perspectives through contrasting voices'. [92] But the concern expressed by probation officers was that the creation of a parallel and fictional world of archetypes meant that the programme would not be able to investigate the personal stories of offenders in detail. I think there are a number of explanations for this response, firstly, that the probation agenda revolves around personal disclosure and working with offenders to take responsibility for their actions, therefore 'over-distancing' techniques suggest a generalisation of experience, and thus a move away from the recognition of personal cycles of violence, triggers and high risk situations so inherent to anger management practice. Secondly, the probation service is sensitised to the political perception and reception of its practice. The Pump programme was funded through the Home Office, and developed during Michael Howard's reign as Home Secretary (under which the probation service was constantly being 'reviewed'). There was, and is, a constant necessity to discuss probation work in 'acceptable' language and terms. In my view, the aesthetic language and the proposed archetypal techniques were difficult to reconcile with the need to explain and promote the programme to a wider, more political context. Thirdly, in pragmatic terms, the Pump was designed so that the TIPP Centre would eventually be training probation officers to run the programme by themselves, and that by using 'safer', more acceptable and familiar terms of cognitive-behaviour the programme might be more 'transferable'.

---

[92] Carlson, M. (1992) 'Theater and Dialogism', in Janelle G. Reinelt and Joseph R. Roach (eds.) *Critical Theory and Performance*, Michigan, University of Michigan Press, p.314

The concern expressed by probation, and to a lesser degree by ex-offenders, had crucial implications for the aesthetic elements of the programme. The dramatic process and techniques became more concerned with the 'actual' experience of participants, rather than the 'symbolic' or 'fictional', leading to a greater emphasis on personal disclosure. I will discuss this issue later, when I look at the practical problems experienced as a result of applying a cognitive approach to violence.

As a result of the trials with probation officers and ex-offenders the TIPP Centre team re-developed the idea of archetypes as behaviour types or characteristics that are within us all; that someone who shows Jack behaviour is someone who is violent, or that someone who shows Godfather behaviour is someone who intimidates and threatens. Another result from the trials was that most of the names were changed; Godfather became Indirect Aggression, Self Mutilator became 'Bottle it up' behaviour, and Buddha became Assertiveness. However the 'Jack' image was kept as the clients giving us feed-back felt that it was an effective metaphor that summed up a particular way of responding to a situation. Furthermore, because the 'Jack' referred explicitly to violent behaviour, the TIPP Centre team decided to extend its use in the programme; so the 'Jack' concept was developed and adapted to help structure two sessions focusing on men's rationalisations of violence and victim empathy.

The Jack.

The purpose of the Jack session is to explore the thoughts and feelings that lead up to an offender's violent incident, looking at the violent incident in detail to show what the trigger factors might be. The two Jack sessions are informed by pro-feminist theories that anger can be used as excuse and explanation for violence which gives the perpetrator greater power and control within a relationship. The focus is on the attitudes, beliefs and habits of thinking that are a factor in offenders committing violent crimes. This is a way to challenge the 'I flew into a blind rage and it just happened' excuse that offenders may use to justify their actions. The aim is to teach an offender to uncover the historical connections between his thoughts and his acts of criminal violence. As the Change Project states:

> He (the man) must learn something about the way he feels and acts in situations where he has been violent and abusive in the past. He must focus on his cues or signals, patterns in his behaviour, and past violent situations in order to take responsibility for making himself safe to be around. Developing this skill means that he can learn to avoid using violence. [93]

The Jack in the Box prop was developed to link the process of detailing incidents of violence into trigger factors. Included in the design was a clock with a hand and several coloured segments. When the pointer was at the top of the dial the Jack would spring out. This represented a moment of violence. The other segments signified the moments leading up to the angry outburst. The actual design of the Jack in the Box deliberately moved away from the notion of a childhood toy. The designer's idea was that the Jack would be a combination of a boxing glove and a face. The effect of the gloved face leaping out of the box was intended to shock as well as demonstrate clearly what a 'Jack' moment represented.

Tableau work in particular would enable groups to visualise stories. The segments would be used to break down an incident into a series of still images, from which a report of the offender's thoughts and feelings could be compiled. As well as this detailed analysis of an incident, the facilitator would seek to find the triggers which moved the client from one segment to the next. These triggers are often the attitudes that cause the client to respond violently. If these motivations can be identified by the client group, then the preventative strategies will be found with greater ease. Clients can then see for themselves how violence does not occur 'out

---

[93] Dobash, R.E. and Dobash, R.P. (1990) op.cit., p.10

of the blue' but is a response to particular trigger situations, thought patterns or attitudes.

An important aspect of these sessions is gathering offence-related information in a systematic way. The two 'Jack' sessions deal with personal stories of violence, with the aim of identifying patterns of thoughts, feelings and behaviour which lead to offending. The offender acts out the build up to the incident in slow motion, but is stopped by the group members at key points and asked what he is thinking and feeling. These thoughts/feelings are written up on a flip chart or board. The 'thinking reports' display how each phase of thinking and feeling gives rise to the next in an escalating rationale for violence. [94] Walking through the stages of the incident also provides a visual reference for the group. It is possible to then identify the key steps by going back through the story and establishing a tableau for each developmental stage combined with the material from the thinking report. The information produced from this process needs to motivate the group members into identifying specific value-based expectations and appraisals that are linked to violent, angry or coercive behaviour. The information derived from the tableaux and thinking reports is subject to investigation and dialogue. Thus a fact cannot be recounted in details of dates, times, places, people, and reduced to something static and fixed. The fact itself must be stated problematically. In dramatic terms the re-orientation of the facts may be achieved by looking at the event from the victim's perspective or 'a significant other', by using a similar process of tableau-thinking report or role-reversal. The purpose of this process is not to castigate the offender's version of the story, but to enable the individual and the group to 'reflect on the "wherefore" of the fact and on its connection with other facts in an overall context'. [95] The process is an attempt to demonstrate a plurality of experience, by exploring not the authenticities of thinking, feeling and action responses, but the multifarious

---

[94] Bush, J. (1995) op.cit.
[95] Freire, P. (1974) op.cit., p.124

meanings which can be chosen to give to the context. This can serve as an encouragement to participants to bear in mind the objective of reviewing responses in a situation before determining what action will be taken. This links to phenomenological concepts, as Derrida emphasises, that meaning is always deferred, elsewhere, multiple and shifting and therefore a process but not a product. [96] The strength of this suggestion for a violent offender group is dependent on the extent to which they view their perceptions and actions as being fixed. If the premise is accepted by individual participants, perceptions and behaviour may become the subject of experimentation, behaviour can be seen as a part of a process rather than an end product. However, it is just as likely that participants' rationalisation for violent action will be justified, and the concept for thinking creatively and critically about perception/action rejected. Often it is the intransigence and fixed constructs which have created the violent conflict, and continue to be rationalised in the group work situation. This is particularly true when violence is endorsed by the rest of the group members and/or the socio-cultural environment as being 'the only way to deal with the problem'. The relevancy of the social environment echoes the pro-feminist concerns that 'sexist structures of family and society...' create 'cultural norms and values which permit and sometimes encourage...' domestic violence. [97] I will discuss these issues of resistance and contextual justification in more depth later on in the chapter.

The Pump.

The Pump section of the course deals with the processing of social information; from the encoding of social cues, their interpretation, and the choice of response. This section links in with Novaco's identification of <u>external</u> provocations and <u>internal</u> <u>processes</u> as factors which determine anger response. From the research

---

[96] Reinelt, J.G. and Roach, J.R. (1992) *Critical Theory and Performance*, Michigan, University of Michigan Press, p.111
[97] Strauss, M.A. (1977) 'A sociological perspective on the prevention and treatment of wife-beating', in M. Roy (ed.) *Battered Women*, New York, Van Nostrand Reinhold, pp 194-239.

on violent offenders and the experiences of Probation officers working in the field the TIPP team identified that some offenders are more likely to interpret social cues in a hostile fashion. [98] The Probation officers had worked with men who interpreted many situations as 'a wind-up', even when this clearly was not the case.

The 'wind up' term was an obvious starting point. It was decided to define 'wind-up' as meaning a deliberate action aimed at causing annoyance or aggravation. A 'wind up' could be a way of looking at someone, a word, an action etc. But it could not be a given fact - like receiving a Council Tax demand, or the non-arrival of a Giro. After all, everyone receives bills and the disorganisation at the D.H.S.S. is usually not a premeditated act. This type of given situation was defined as a 'Knock', as in a 'knock on effect', because it suggests that the person delivering the knock is not necessarily to blame. The idea was to try and distinguish between provocations that were intentional, and ones that were circumstantial and not deliberate. Of course a 'Knock' and a 'Wind up' can occur together - a postman delivering a bill and then laughing at you - but the skill of interpretation is still as important, there is still a need to separate out what is intentional and what is not.

An additional factor in the cause of anger is what Novaco defined as 'private speech'; internal cognitions which inflame or 'pump up' antagonistic thoughts and feelings.[99] Pumping thoughts were therefore defined by the TIPP team as internal 'wind-ups', thoughts that nag away inside and increase anger. For example 'he's not going to talk to me like that....who does she think she is.....I'm not going to let him get away with that...etc.'

The prop designer added visual aids to reinforce the 'Pump', 'Knock' and 'Wind up' terms. A client's anger would be measured by a simple thermometer device which used a red tape to move up and down a six foot pole. The red tape could be

[98] Beck, A.T. (1987) op.cit.
[99] Novaco, R,W. (1975) op.cit.

used to signify increases or decreases in the intensity of angry reactions. The designer added to this a door knocker (the Knock) a winch handle (a wind up) and a foot pump (a pumping thought).

The reason for simplifying the language was that the Probation Officers advising the project talked about how specialist words or jargon of anger management theories were often confusing and ill-defined for clients. The idea behind simplifying the linguistic 'register' was to provide a preliminary structure for the group members' learning. The metaphors ('pumping thoughts' 'wind-up') can act as a conceptual bridge between cognitive-behavioural jargon and every day language. [100]

The metaphors in the language ('antagonistic thoughts are like a pump blowing up your anger...') are used in conjunction with the prop. The two are designed to complement each other. The prop short-cuts an explanation of the representation, and the Pump terms focus the learner's attention on the key aspects of the prop. It is important then to have a careful process of understanding through mutual definition of the metaphors and their meaning. In terms of the Pump Programme this is an attempt to avoid the mismatch between what the facilitator means when s/he uses a term, what the group understand when s/he uses it and probably what they think s/he *means* when s/he uses it. For example in the first Pump session the facilitator gives complete explanations, and clearly refers to the prop. However after the first few exchanges where the Pump prop and terms are discussed fairly explicitly, the facilitator can taper off his/her contribution so that in the end s/he is providing more attenuated cues. If there is someone who needs further help, the facilitator can shift back to more extensive cueing and then work forward again, reducing cueing once more.

The nature of individuals in groups for angry and violent men will be characterised by people who are prone to provocation. Therefore, people who

---

[100] Barnes, D. (1969) *Language, the Learner and the School*, London, Penguin.

have angry, antagonistic dispositions or response styles are inclined to become frustrated and impatient, which can emerge in relation to the learning process itself. If the learning is indirect or overly complicated the offender can become disengaged from the session. In this regard it is advantageous for the programme's language to be clearly defined and explained so as to minimise ambiguity and frustration that might result in vague expectations regarding learning outcomes.

The three sections, the Box, Jack and Pump were designed to work both as an eight week course and/or as individual sessions that could be integrated into other anger management programmes. Novaco outlines the three basic phases involved with anger control: cognitive preparation, which looks at awareness of cognitive and behavioural patterns; skills acquisition, learning to make new cognitive and behavioural interventions; and skills rehearsal, practising new skills through simulations. [101] The TIPP programme also integrated into these phases pro-feminist concerns which may be explored if these issues arise with a particular participant. The Jack, and the Behaviour Box, are particularly useful for exploring pro-feminist issues.

Cognitive Preparation.

In terms of the Pump Programme the cognitive preparation phase is designed to raise awareness of personal anger patterns. In the Pump programme this is a cumulative process that is developed at the beginning of each of the different sections. The overall programme content begins with a general awareness stage, in which violence and anger is discussed in non-specific terms. As the programme progresses the emphasis shifts from non-specific to specific examples related to the participants' own life experience. To illustrate how the Pump programme approached this phase, I would like to focus on how the course set out to identify high risk situations and personal cues that trigger anger/violence; describing what

---

[101] Novaco, R.W. (1983) op.cit.

154

this involves and giving a couple of examples of how individual's motivational triggers were analysed.

High risk situations and triggers.

Henderson conducted an analysis of the narratives given by adult male violent offenders about the types of situation in which they behaved in a violent manner. [102] This study is of particular interest because it gives an indication of the settings in which violent incidents, at least those involving adult males, are most likely to occur. Henderson's analysis revealed four broad categories of violent situations: 1) violence in conjunction with another crime - sometimes intentionally, sometimes in panic as when discovered committing another non-violent offence such as burglary; 2) family violence directed towards both women and children; 3) violence in public places such as bars, street incidents, road rage. 4) violence in institutions - police stations, prisons, etc.

From my experience with violent offenders the most common of these categories are family violence and violence in public places. It is an important process for the programme and for the men in the group to identify at an early stage where they perceive their anger or violence problems to lie. In order to get an indication of this, the group are asked to list situations in which anger and/or violence occurs. From this list group members prioritise areas in which anger/violence occurs most frequently and with the most intensity. In the Pump programme continuum lines are used to start discussion on this issue. The group members are asked to stand at a point of the line where they think they are in relation to a high risk situation. Very often people are not willing to admit to situations in which their real problems lie, this can be for a number of reasons: they are anxious about revealing themselves to the group; they have no trust in the programme yet; it is part of their denial and minimisation of their behaviour; they are unconscious of

---

[102] Henderson, M. (1986) 'An empirical typology of violent incidents reported by prison inmates with convictions for violence', *Aggressive Behaviour*, **12**.

specific 'at risk' situations; they do not want to disclose information about themselves, etc. As the course progresses it is possible to refer back to the results of this exercise, and at the end of the course the exercise is re-done to see if offenders' self awareness or motivation to admit to certain actions has changed. For the facilitator the exercise is a way of gathering initial information about the group members, and getting a feeling for the context in which the offenders' violence occurs.

The facilitator does have some influence over how much group members invest in this process. In the initial pilot programmes, participants were allowed to set their own levels of engagement. What I found was that unless there was one person particularly motivated to offer detailed information about himself, the group members would suggest ridiculously 'low risk' material about their situations. For example, when asked to fill-in anger diaries, the information would relate to instances like 'when I tripped over a wire in the pub'. The selection of this type of 'low risk' material allowed for the minimum investment in the process. Sometimes this low investment was dispersed as the course progressed and a more trusting environment was established, at other times this type of selection was maintained throughout. In order to address this situation, the facilitator needs to help set the 'level' of group investment, by setting out more specifically what type of material is required. For example, in the first session, the offences participants have committed are recorded, so that from the very beginning, the discussion of anger and violence is connected to real events.

Johnnie's story.

When it comes to exploring the personal cues in detail, as the Jack section does, the objective is to look at the complex motivational reasons for violence, and the specific thinking that leads to violent actions. One of the members on the first pilot course was Johnnie (see appendix 4 for background). His story was a good example of how intricate and complex the reasons for violence can be. His partner, Gill, did not like his family and accused him of 'clinging to his mother's apron strings'. Johnnie told the group that on the day of the incident he and Gill were in a pub at about 3 p.m. A member of Johnnie's family had come in and started talking to Johnnie at which point Gill walked away and, in Johnnie's view, had started chatting up another man. At about 7 p.m. Gill left the pub and said that she was going to another bar to meet up with some friends. Later, he found her dancing in a pub and became irritated at seeing her enjoying herself without him. When Johnnie approached Gill, she told him that she did not want him in her house any more. Johnnie, who had already been drinking since 3 p.m., decided to have a few more pints and consider his position. As he sat drinking at the bar he watched Gill and became very angry. At about 1 a.m. he tried to talk with Gill again and asked her to go home with him. She refused. He pulled her by the arm out of the bar and started to 'escort' her home. She argued vociferously with him, insulting him and his family. As the couple stood arguing Johnnie said he reached for her handbag to get the house keys, she resisted and he 'lost it' and head-butted her.

Johnnie seemed stuck in his perception of why he had head-butted his girlfriend. He felt guilt, but he wanted her to understand his side of the story. He felt frustration and some justification in his anger. The head-butt was his way of 'getting through to her' - of making her see his way of thinking. After discussing the facts of the story, the group were asked to look at 5 key incidents in the story in chronological terms. They analysed the story by doing a tableau for each segment on the dial (representing a key point in the story). For each tableau a thinking report was recorded on Johnnie's thoughts/feelings. One of the Probation co-workers played Johnnie's girlfriend in some of the scenes and was good at feeding back how she felt in the situation. For example, minutes before the violent incident, Johnnie had grabbed his girlfriend's arm and insisted that they go back home. Johnnie had not realised that this action was threatening to his girlfriend, but the tableau of Johnnie holding onto her arm was immediately something we could analyse using the Probation worker's discomfort at being grabbed and led away.

From the five tableau and thinking reports the group were asked what they thought were the main triggers that caused the incident of violence. The group came up with four triggers and we worked at converting them into statements or attitudes/rules:

I don't like feeling embarrassed by my girlfriend when it affects me or my family;

I cannot stand constant criticism of my family;

I do not like to be rejected by my girlfriend or friends;

Alcohol prevents me from maintaining control of my actions.

Of these 4 triggers the group and Johnnie thought that rejection and alcohol were the main contributing factors in this violent incident. The group began to discuss ways that Johnnie could have avoided the violent incidents, and what specific strategies could have been used to prevent these triggers occurring again.

What is important when dealing with someone's story is the placing of emphasis on finding information about the incident. The aim is to show the powerful influence that thinking has on actions by teaching offenders to observe their own thinking, to recognise the consequences of that thinking, and to learn specific skills for controlling that thinking.

However, underlying the process is a moral imperative that alternatives to violence should be sought. The facilitator's aim is to employ the information gathered in a session to demonstrate that, ultimately, violence has negative consequences both for the perpetrator and the victim. The strength of this information gathering process is that the group have much more knowledge and understanding of what happened in the situation, both the external and internal processes having been recorded. But ultimately, if there is going to be a shift in attitude and behaviour, then the processes need to be questioned and challenged. In theory the information generated in the Jack session should weigh in favour of finding alternatives, however in practice arguing for moral and behavioural alternatives is a complex and difficult process. For example, during a recent course, an offender discussed how he had knifed his mother's boyfriend after a drinking session. Using the information gathering process a detailed record of thoughts and feelings was created. Feelings of jealousy, possessiveness, being isolated and excluded, anger, and resentment were identified and discussed. Many alternatives and consequences were explored, and several useful strategies identified and role-played. But at the end of the session the participant, with the support of the other group members, maintained that he was justified in further attacks on this other person. The sense was that once directly or indirectly hurt, violent revenge was the only applicable recompense. Even though the consequences of violence (for victim and perpetrator) and/or imprisonment were likely, the determination and desire to physically damage and hurt were so strong as to wipe out the benefits of other coping strategies. It is not easy to challenge the resolve of those who believe in the powerful sense of efficacy that violence appears to offer them.

The extent to which participants are willing or able to reflect on their perceptions and experiment with alternative behavioural reactions governs the efficacy of the work. As previously noted, it is the participant who is the agent of change, and not the facilitator. The compulsory nature of the Pump programme for participants may set an oppositional agenda from the very beginning. Some participants can take up a deliberately resistant position of folded arms, non-compliance and a 'go on then - change me' attitude. Others may be, as Kelly suggests, 'psychologically stuck', meaning that a participant's 'construing has become circular so that they keep testing the same hypothesis over and over again'.[103] The hypothesis of violence may also be something that is endorsed by the social-cultural context. This makes looking at anger problems or consequences seemingly irrelevant. The justification of aggression in a particular situation directly opposes the maladoptive emotional model or the concern for the effect on others or self. And it is the strength of this justification in some men which makes applying cognitive behavioural models extremely difficult. Because very often members in a group will not be at the stage of accepting that violence is somehow 'wrong', and without that acceptance the demonstration that changing aggressive thoughts, feelings and beliefs may affect behaviour is little less than redundant.

These elements of resistance to the programme's aim to elaborate aspects of construing may be evidenced in the general reluctance to 'play' and engage in creative drama exercises to the same extent as similar groups of offenders. This interesting point has emerged through the TIPP Centre running a variety of Pump programmes in different settings, facilitated by different theatre practitioners, who were all very experienced in prison/probation work. Traditional drama warm up games, exercises to encourage imagination and concentration, creative playing all have a tendency to work less well with groups of violent offenders than in other groups of a similar age range and background (and in context of prison/probation). The Pump groups, in general, have demonstrated less tolerance for creative arts work. This might be explained by the compulsory nature of the group, but in my view, relatively few participants adopt this position. A far more common oppositional position is the participant who has fixed constructs and rationalisations about his violence, 'I've been brought up this way, it's been bred into me'. Such behaviour is reinforced by peer group attitudes that it is part of an expected 'masculine' behaviour. The dialogical, egalitarian model is still applicable in this context; the principle of behaviour being governed by

---

[103] Fransella, F. and Dalton, P. (1992) op.cit., p.12

rationality, a theory of action and causality are perfectly valid; but the practice of running the Pump is that its anti-violence agenda is often in direct and intense opposition to the context of the group. This does not discount the dialogical model, it just highlights the intensity of the process. It highlights the problematic of creating, as Freire described it, an education of 'I wonder' rather than merely 'I do'.[104]

Pete's story.

Pete's case (see appendix 4) demonstrated that the dialogical approach can be efficacious in developing an interaction with the justifications of a participant.

Pete was bailed to a hostel for an offence he said he had not committed. He 'discovered' that his room mate, Simon, was a sex offender and beat him up twice in two days. Pete said he was already very angry and frustrated at having to stay at the Hostel. When Pete first met Simon he threatened him, even though he had no idea at this stage of his room mate's offences.

Tableau 1:

Situation: In kitchen threatening Simon.

Thoughts	*Feelings*
I don't like being here.	Anger
I want to kick the shit out of you.	Resentment
I want to show off.	Hate. Annoyance. Frustration.

The second tableau was of Simon's telling Pete of his offence. Pete set up the situation. Simon was lying on his bed as Pete and another friend stood over him asking questions. From this tableau it was immediately obvious that Pete, as Johnnie noticed, 'had an advantage' over Simon. The tableau showed that Pete

---

[104] Freire, P. (1974) op.cit., p.36

had not merely asked Simon about his offence but had been intimidating and pressuring him to 'confess'. Pete told us that it took him a week to get the confession from Simon. Pete's thinking report included the statement that 'we were laughing at him and winding him up'.

Tableau 3.

Situation: Outside room, 'deciding what to do with Simon.'

Thoughts	Feelings
I want to use him, degrade him.	Anger.
Just want him out.	Resentment/Disgust.
I just had to do it.	Revolted/Felt sick.
I wish I'd never been told.	Head done in.

Pete decided to 'make Simon hold out his hands and burn them with a lighter'. Pete then punched Simon, dragged him downstairs, made him tell the other Hostel lads 'what he was', then over the next two hours continued to punch and kick him.

Next day Simon was moved to another Hostel. A member of staff took him to a bus stop and returned shortly. Pete then got a group together and went to the bus stop with the intention of 'shelving him again'. Pete admitted to feeling sorry this time but insisted that 'it wasn't right that someone like that should stay in the same Hostel as me'.

Throughout the re-telling of the story Pete continued to feel justified in his actions, as the 'street law' for sex offenders dictates that they should be punished. He did say that the incident had caused him long term consequences which he had not considered at the time. In the short term Pete felt better about beating him up, though by the second incident he admitted to going beyond his duty to punish. In the long term Pete had been taken into court and given a Probation Order, only adding to his problems. Investigating the consequences for Simon, Pete recognised that the violence had not achieved anything. Simon probably felt more

162

scared, bitter, and angry. Pete's actions had hardly turned Simon into a model citizen. Johnnie reinforced this by saying 'you can't beat these things out of people'.

Having established trigger factors for an offender it is also important for the facilitator to point out that there are a number of interpretations to any one story. Tableau work, as well as Forum Theatre and role play, can be a powerful way of an offender viewing the incident from a perspective different from a personal one. An exercise that involves a man having to respond as his partner or having to hear her side of the story (as interpreted by another group member) can help to raise the man's awareness of another person's thoughts and feelings on the matter. It can demonstrate to clients that in a potentially violent situation there can be a number of interpretations and motivations for people's behaviour that are worth considering before hitting out. This is of course only a beginning. A course can appeal to the self interest of the man by showing that although violence may have short term gains it also has long term losses. And this self interest in change is integral to the cognitive preparation phase and can lead directly on to the motivation to acquire new skills.

Skills acquisition.

The intervention attempts to promote cognitive, arousal reduction, and behavioural coping skills, consistent with the analysis of anger determinants. At the cognitive level, the offender is taught to alternatively view provocation events and to modify the exaggerated importance often attached to events.[105] In the TIPP Centre programme this is achieved by distinguishing between different kinds of provocation; 'Knocks' (external events that are not deliberate antagonistic cues, but are nonetheless provoking) 'Wind ups' (external events that are deliberate provocations) and 'Pumps' (internal antagonistic self-statements). A basic goal is

---

[105] Kelly, G.A. (1955) op.cit.; Ellis, A. (1973) *Humanistic Psychology: The Rational-Emotive Approach*, New York, Julian Press.

to promote flexibility in one's cognitive structuring of situations. In this regard expectations and appraisals linked with anger arousal are targets for modification. The acquisition of the skill to question and appraisal of situations, before getting angry or acting impulsively, is important. In the Pump section of the TIPP programme particular attention is paid to inordinately high expectations of other's behaviour and to the appraisal of events as personal 'wind-ups'. The ability to "not take things personally" is a fundamental skill. This is accomplished by fostering a task orientation to provocation, which involves focus on a number of alternative behavioural choices and the implementation of pragmatic strategies to achieve the best outcome for everyone involved.

In the Pump programme it was discovered that although standard self-calming anger management techniques were useful, it was far more effective for the strategies to be individualised by the offender with regard to particular situations or provocations. Traditional anger management techniques such as taking a 'time out' (going into another room to calm down; walking round the block to cool off etc.); calming statements (thinking calming thoughts); and relaxation were demonstrated. In dramatic terms these were 'modelled' by a combination of techniques - image theatre, role-play and scenario. The facilitator sets up a problematised scenario in which a protagonist (played by a probation officer) becomes increasingly angry. A number of self-control strategies are introduced and their efficacy tested in the scene. At key points in the scene the group members may 'freeze' the action, and ask characters what they are thinking and feeling. Group members are also encouraged to interpret the 'frozen' still image by looking for signs of aggressive body language, gestures, facial expressions. Once the self-control strategies have been demonstrated the workshop moves on to applying these and other suggested strategies to personal stories from the group. Once a 'real-life' anger scenario is agreed upon between the group and the facilitator, the protagonist walks through the story describing the physical setting and lay out of the place or room where it occurred. Detailed props are not required, everything can be indicated verbally or by the use of a chair or table. This slow-motion rehearsal of the scene is crucial, not only in technically helping to set the scene and cast other group members, but in establishing thoughts, feelings, and outlining a rough script of what happened. Once this is done the role-play is performed, ending at a crucial point in the story - which may be violence or someone angrily storming out, depending on what actually happened. The group members performing and watching the role-play are then asked to select at least three alternative ways of resolving the situation. These may be self-control anger management strategies, or pragmatic resolutions which may be inherent in the relationships and interactions in the scene. Each one of these strategies, including violence if relevant, are tested out - both short and long term consequences. It was important to establish a task-oriented process which was concerned primarily with problem-solving. This process set up personal anger/violence stories as problems of behaviour reactions which all the group members had to solve.

The purpose of the skills acquisition stage was to identify and extend the repertoire of group members in dealing with a range of anger-related situations. The focus on behavioural coping skills was concerned with the effective communication of feelings, assertiveness, and problem-solving skills. The offender is helped to maximise the adaptive functions of anger and to minimise its maladaptive functions. When the anger is being 'pumped up' the offender is taught to use the thermometer (part of the prop) to record the intensity. The offender is also taught how to distinguish between internal and external cues and to then either communicate anger in a non-hostile form or to use it to energise problem-solving action, keeping the arousal at moderate levels of intensity. The distinguishing of external and internal cues also helps an offender to identify specific strategies applicable to the situation. For example in the Bury pilot of the programme, the group members came up with a list of strategies and rules for the different cues:

Knocks	Wind-Ups	Pumps
Accept it	Try and ignore it	Thought stop
Laugh it off	Count to ten	Blank it out
Be positive	Calm yourself	Think of something else
Calm yourself		Watch T.V.
Rule:	Rule:	Rule:
Can't blame	Ignore it/deal with	Relax/stop it.
anyone else	it positively	

The Pump section in particular involves a strategic confrontation whereby the offender learns to focus on issues and objectives, as well as identifying behaviour instrumental to achieving them. This prevents the accumulation of anger and prevents an aggressive over-reaction by imposing critical thought between impulse and action.

The pragmatic emphasis on helping participants to think through their problems, and to examine behavioural responses and alternatives in a rational and systematic way was, for the participants, one of the most positive elements of the programme. [106] However, with a few of the participants there were signs that the programme was encouraging new communication skills, without challenging the underlying motivations of the abusive men. As previously discussed in relation to pro-feminist arguments, this has the potential that participants learn strategies of minimising their physical violence, but of intensifying psychological abuse. [107] For example, Johnnie talked about the fact that as a result of the programme he 'felt more in control' during arguments with his girlfriend. And he had even told his girlfriend that he 'no longer had an anger problem' and that perhaps it was 'her turn to see a counsellor or psychiatrist'. This statement was made after attending three sessions. Clearly, whilst wanting to encourage 'control' and 'management' the facilitators have to be sensitive to how these strategies and

---

[106] Details of the feedback are included in the next chapter or see appendix 6.
[107] Gondolf, E (1984) 'How Some Men Stop Battering: An Evaluation of a Group Counselling Program.' Paper presented at the second *National Conference for Family Violence Researchers*, Durham, NH.

skills are contextualised by participants. This issue, in particular, highlights the relevance of pro-feminist arguments, and their significance in being incorporated into a programme. The issue of underlying motivation for men, is something which the course addresses both in the cognitive preparation (looking at belief systems in the Jack session) and in the skills rehearsal stage (the behaviour box). It is also something that is explored at a personal level at the skills acquisition stage, for example if non-violent, but coercive behaviour is suggested as a solution to a problem (and it quite often was), then this will be examined and problematised in the same rational and systematic way as other suggestions.

Skills rehearsal.

The value of rehearsing skills is aimed at building personal competence, and therefore involves developing offenders' ability to manage provocative situations and in some cases testing their proficiency. There are a number of different 'theatrical' approaches to this phase. For example, like Novaco Geese Theatre Company's approach to rehearsing skills with violent offenders is conducted be means of imaginary and role playing inductions of anger.[108] The company set up 'provocation simulations' in the style of a 'corrida' (a bull-fighting ring). [109] The offender enters the ring to be confronted by a realistic situation that he is likely to be provoked by. The offender must then employ coping skills (which have been pre-rehearsed) to deal with his anger. In this way the offender and facilitators can gauge the proficiency of his acquired skills.

Although the TIPP Centre was keen to enable the offenders to rehearse new skills, the simulation of provocation was used as a starting point for problem-solving, rather than as an absolute test of proficiency. In the TIPP programme the emphasis is on training offenders to view the problem analytically, applying a number of behaviour strategies, and reviewing critically which option is the most

---

[108] Novaco, R.W. (1983) op.cit.
[109] ibid., p.11

workable. The rehearsal is not an attempt to instigate real or simulated emotions, but an exploration and demonstration of different social outcomes through role-play. For example, the 'pressure cooker' is an exercise which asks participants to identify three or four personal 'pressure points' which may in real-life incite anger or violence. A protagonist stands in the middle of a room, whilst other group members approach and using his personal 'pressure points' try to provoke him into losing his temper. The pressure builds up as more participants join in and attempt to provoke the protagonist. The protagonist or any observer may stop the action at any point in order to isolate a particularly provoking participant. The protagonist or other group members can suggest strategies to 'combat' the provocation, either drawing on skills learnt earlier in the programme, or identifying new ones. Therefore, the provocations are either resolved and dealt with in one intense role-play, or if there are problems the provocations, as represented by participants, can be resolved one by one over a number of role-plays. The provocations may either take the form of external pressures or internal 'pump' thoughts.

In the Pump programme Novaco's principle of skills rehearsal is extended to incorporate pro-feminist concerns about the underlying context of situations involving anger. Because in practice, participants often identified that conflicts were used as a deliberate way to control the relationship. For example Pete told the group that he and his partner had been having frequent rows and that he often caused arguments if he wanted to go out for the night alone; because he knew that 'after a couple of hours' shouting' his girlfriend would tell him to 'get lost' and he would not have to feel guilty. When asked what he did when his girlfriend wanted to go out, he replied: 'Sometimes I let her go, other times I stand in front of the door and stop her'. The programme explored this situation by asking Pete to identify what things about himself provoked his girlfriend into anger. Pete was then asked to be the protagonist, representing his girlfriend, and the 'pressure points' were all the various provoking strategies that he used in the relationship.

Similarly, when other group members suggested 'my wife nagging' as a potential 'pressure point' this was investigated, as was the misapplication of anger control techniques like 'time out' when participants used it repeatedly, simply as a way of avoiding a situation which needed to be confronted and resolved at some point.

The pro-feminist perspective, I think correctly, problematises Novaco's more straight forward model of cognitive preparation, skills acquisition and rehearsal by highlighting the underlying context in which violence occurs. This concern for the misapplication of skills was evidenced in the practical application of the Pump programme, and was one of several problematics which the TIPP team encountered.

Problems encountered with the application of cognitive theories.

The Pump programme is a particular kind of cognitive-behavioural approach to working with violent offenders. It emphasises Novaco's model of coping skills to develop competence in response to provoking cues and to prevent and regulate maladaptive responses to emotions. Through a process of cognitive preparation, (which examines and challenges expectations and appraisals of situations) and acquisition/rehearsal of coping skills, the offender (it is hoped) develops cognitive and behavioural proficiencies for dealing with maladoptive anger and aggression problems. The programme also incorporates pro-feminist theories on male violence reflecting a belief that the causes of aggression are a combination of individual pathology and socio-political contextual factors.

It is not clear from the Novaco model how programmes may challenge participants who advocate that in certain situations violence is necessary. The weakness in applying Novaco's model to work with violent men lies in two key areas, namely, the unbalanced emphasis on anger as a significant precursor to aggression, and the lack of socio-cultural context it provides. The relationship between anger and aggression needs to be carefully assessed on an individual basis, because for some men attending probation groups - in my view the majority - aggression may occur as a function of various social learning factors other than anger, such as reinforcement contingencies, expected outcomes and modelling influences. As Novaco, himself, writes:

> ....social learning factors can also influence the occurrence of aggression independent of anger arousal. Thus, it is possible for someone to aggress without becoming angry, as when the infliction of injury or damage is expected to produce personal gain or when the aggressive act is a well-learned behaviour. [110]

In the last two years of running the Pump programme it has been a constant feature that groups of men agree amongst themselves that violence in a range of situations is necessary. The 'rules' of when and where it is applicable vary from group to group. For some hitting a woman is forbidden, although the same men admit to intimidation and threats; for others violence is the only way to establish or maintain a reputation or respect in their community - therefore justifying a whole range of negative actions; other participants apply the notion of threats, arguing that it is important to hit before being hit, so are always on the alert for perceived 'dangers'.

Particularly in groups where there are young men, stories of street/pub violence are told in an exuberant, even playful recounting. The fighting is about heroism in the face of adversity, about winning against superior odds. The protagonists are often the forces of good; the forces of evil are strangers who provoke, or accuse, or challenge. To avoid the situation would mean not avenging the insult, and in most cases it is believed that 'real men' must go forward against even suicidal odds when their reputation is under attack. If the perceptions of these orientations are not explored phenomenologically, then a role-play or role-reversal may

---

[110] ibid., p. 5

demonstrate causality and harsh consequences (for perpetrator and victim) to no great effect. Because fighting among young men is often perceived as a form of recreation; and in groups the description of the fight is punctuated with laughter and knowing looks. If a man were to exercise self control during a fight, particularly a fight that was not going well for him, it might be mistaken for cowardice. Instead he must depend on others to break it up, and even then must make it clear that he is being forced to quit. [111] Therefore, in this context the dramatic process needs to progress not by concentrating on causality as a deterrent (at least not initially) but on theatricalising and exploring the abstract concepts of masculinity and the function, the need, and the desire, for violence. This links to the phenomenological concept in which experience may be placed in metaphorical 'brackets', so that crucial qualities may be apprehended and reviewed in a limitless 'plurality of meaning'. [112] The phenomenological approach is not reliant on 'direct, empirical inspection' but on the 'imaginative intuition' of experience. [113] The process is an attempt to enable a group to constantly move beyond each established level of meaning connected with 'masculinity', to be reflexive and responsive to a meaning that is 'always deferred, elsewhere, multiple and shifting...and therefore a process but not a product'.[114] In practical terms the fixed constructs about masculinity may trap some men in a 'male expectation prison' and educational programmes can help identify the nature and extent of these expectations, as well as some possible 'escape routes'. One exercise which the TIPP Centre has been developing for the Pump programme, draws on group members' expectations associated with masculinity, these may include: [115]

---

[111] Fox, R. (1977) 'The Inherent Rules of Violence', in *Social Rules and Social Behaviour*, ed. P. Collett, Oxford, Basil Blackwell. Fox studied a remote community on an island off Ireland and reported that at Saturday night dances, where a brawl was an expected side-show, young men would wait for their friends to grab their arms and then would struggle wildly and shout, "Hold me back or I'll kill him".
[112] Reinelt, J.G. and Roach, J.R. (1992) op.cit., p.111
[113] ibid., p. 354
[114] ibid., p.111
[115] Moore, P. (1997) *Acting Out: Therapy for Groups*, Aldershot, Arena, p.19

- protecting the family
- not showing emotion
- being in control
- taking 'no crap off anybody' (that is, verbal abuse or physical threats)
- making and keeping reputations
- being aggressive and competitive
- talking negatively about women

If these are expectations or masculine constructs which form aspects of a participant's 'rule-book', then each one needs to be explored and its efficacy tested out. It may be that in one context 'being in control' is positive, yet in another it may be negative, if not for the participant then for his partner or family. The theatre tool-kit of image theatre, role-play, role-reversal, Forum theatre may be used to investigate these expectations with the purpose of both extending the range of the expectations, as well as applying them to a systematic and rational process of experimentation. It may also be valid to explore where these expectations and beliefs are derived from, for example the existence of sexist or racist structures in society.

The crucial aspect of the Pump programme has been the facilitator's responsiveness and reflexivity to the experience of working with violent men. Novaco's theories have provided a useful basis from which the programme team have had to develop and adapt its methodology. But Novaco's anger management model, without the pro-feminist perspective, would have been dangerously flawed. Perhaps it would be more accurate to suggest that Novaco has been misapplied to the problems of violent men. Anger is often present in incidents of aggression (as is alcohol or to a lesser degree drugs), but it is not, in my view, the driving motivation underlying the majority of violent crimes. The consequences of developing a course around the 'maladoptive emotion' model is that the practical work does not engage with the question that for some people anger is a means to an end - a violent encounter. In many of the stories recounted and role-played during Pump workshops men have demonstrated that in order to become violent they actively need to incite their own anger by looking for the least provocation. In terms of the Pump course this calls for a re-orientation which is reflexive to the stage at which a large majority of young offenders seem to be - namely that before addressing self control issues what is needed is an exploration of the continued desire and need for violence. Novaco's model tends to present a man at the mercy of his emotions, whereas, from the experience of working with violent men, emotions are used with skill as a method to gain or regain power and control in a situation.

Drawing from the experience of running the Pump programme, it is the pro-feminist model, primarily concerned with domestic abuse, that may be more usefully extended to address men's rationalisations for violence outside of relationships. The pro-feminist argument is that domestic violence occurs when expectations of authority are defied, that the male offender experiences a threat to his security and thus resorts to violence as his way of restoring order and control to a threatening situation. [116] The explanation of the violent man in a relationship as needing to secure power and control, and of his violence being a learned and intentional behaviour, in my view, may reflect more accurately the use of violence in other contexts. In the groups that I ran, men would talk of losing and winning (and not just younger men), aggression for the men was what aggression achieved socially. It imposes control over other people, and in so doing creates winners and losers. It publicly affirms the masculine hierarchy. For most of the men on the Pump course, to be at the mercy of another person, whether physically or symbolically, was to be denied respect; and without respect there can be no self-esteem. [117] Thus it seems that violent men aggress to prove to others (and so to themselves) that they merit respect. But this does not mean that their aggressive

---

[116] Dobash, R.E. and Dobash, R.P. (1990) op.cit.
[117] Felson, R. (1978) 'Aggression as Impression Management,' *Social Psychology Quarterly,* **41,** p. 245-54

acts are devoid of emotion. When their reputation is under attack, men get angry. Their aggression is not a calculated decision to win back their personal integrity; it is an almost automatic and well practised response to challenge, and it is accompanied by righteous fury.[118] The anger they feel is at the impertinence of another person's attempt to devalue or humiliate them. For example, a recent participant on a course was convicted of A.B.H. on a housing officer dealing with his girlfriend's case (they were not living together). Although the participant talked of increasing levels of anger, this appeared to be more from a sense of frustration, and lack of control and self-efficacy in the situation. The only response he could think of was to hit out; he therefore felt a great sense of achievement in having 'taken control of the situation', even though he was arrested for the assault, and his girlfriend's case seriously delayed, he maintained that it was important for him to have 'taken control'. The other case studies used earlier in this chapter (Johnnie and Pete especially) also, I think, reflect that frustration, the lack of self-efficacy, the need for control and authority when constrained by a limited range of behaviour strategies may be significant factors in violent incidents.

As the Pump programme has developed, there has been an increasing emphasis on the interaction between belief systems, the need for power and control, and the extension of a behaviour repertoire in threatening situations. There has therefore been a corresponding move away from 'anger management' as a suitable or applicable model. The Novaco model, however, is not redundant, as it points to methods of exploring cognitive perceptions, social representations and teaching awareness of internal and external provocation triggers. For example, the Pump sessions, although derived from the 'anger management' model, have been developed to encompass cognitive representations of aggression, including the way in which an aggressive incident is interpreted, what emotional and moral

---

[118] Katz, J. (1988) *Seductions of Crime: Moral and Sensual Attractions of Doing Evil*, New York, Basic Books.

responses to it may be, what action is taken as a result of becoming angry. In the Jack sessions, Novaco's principles are used to look at how hostile actions are more likely to be in response to being challenged, humiliated or demeaned. For some men this sort of situation will mean that violence is simply necessary. If everyone else gave up their aggression then men would give up theirs. But that day is never going to come, they argue, because aggression is part of male nature.

Where the main limitation of the TIPP course lies, having identified 'problematic' patterns and responses to situations with individuals (i.e. beliefs and attitudes which have, or are likely to, endorse violent behaviour), is how to challenge beliefs/values which are embedded in the orthodoxy of a socio-cultural structure. For example in domestic violence, the pro-feminists argue that the most fundamental set of factors is connected with the sexist structure of the family and society. Similarly, racist violence is connected with the racist structure of the society or immediate community. However, even in violent incidents which may not be directly attributed to sexism or racism, there is, in some social groupings, a certain regard and reinforcement of violence being an acceptable strategy. Novaco mentions socio-cultural factors but suggests no practical interventions; the pro-feminists clearly identify patriarchy as a source of legitimised violence, but focus on the individual's own use (or more accurately misuse) of these structures to rationalise domestic abuse. In my experience none of these challenges in practice are particularly effective. What is important is to accept that in certain social groups violence may well be more prevalent as a means to solve disputes. Aiding and abetting this individual process are subcultures of violence whose members legitimate, even encourage, physical aggression as a response to conflict. [119] Violence becomes normalized as a routine part of everyday life and of achieving rough justice, and this normalization forms a subculture of violence. The concept

---

[119] Wolfgang, M. and Ferracuti, F. (1967) *The Subculture of Violence*, New York, Barnes and Noble; Bernard, T.J. (1990) 'Angry aggression among the truly disadvantaged', *Criminology*, **28**, pp. 73-95.

of 'an eye for an eye' is still a strongly held belief for many of the men who attended the TIPP programme. However, the concept of 'fair fighting' is very often used to justify all manner of behaviour, it becomes a license for the wide spread use of violence. For example, a recent participant described how he and a group of friends had beaten up a man (the man was put into a coma for 2 months) accused of hitting an old woman in a pub (none of the group had been in the pub at the time), later it was discovered that they had 'got the wrong man'.

Perhaps it is not so much a subculture of violence as one of masculinity. By building a reputation for toughness men may feel pride and a clear status in their identity, for some of the men the social groupings and the norms they support make violence a viable way to construct an identity for themselves. This is what makes a great deal of the theoretical work questionable in this context, because anger and aggression are perceived by the men in the groups as positives and not uncontrollable negatives.

Therefore, the critical factor for the Pump programme is that either it needs to focus more explicitly on these issues of identity and masculinity, or the criteria of selecting participants needs to be targeted at those men who admit to having 'a problem' and express a willingness to change. To some extent these are systemic problems, because either a new or adapted course needs to be designed or the process of contracting and selecting group members needs to be reassessed.

From the perspective of the theatre practitioner facilitating these types of groups there has been a constant need to adapt material to engage the men whilst trying to stick within a very clear probation agenda. This reflexivity to the practical work stands in opposition to the issue of programme integrity as set out by the What Works debate. But rather than this being a polarised issue, the solution lies in negotiating between the need for structured group work objectives and the need of the group and facilitator to 'improvise' and respond to one another as the material demands. This balances a Freirian model of education with a probation policy of accountability, that is to say creative reflexivity within a sound theoretical agenda.

The weaknesses in the Pump programme, I think, challenge some of the theories with which we constructed the practice. The practice has served to question the validity of Novaco's 'anger' model in this context, and extended some of the principles of the pro-feminist approach. Through the process of actually working with violent men it has been necessary to re-negotiate and re-focus some of the original aims and objectives of the programme. Significantly, this has meant that through the response to role-plays and the dramatic material generated by groups, the probation service and the TIPP team have had to re-assess the methodologies underlying work with violent men. The fact that this developmental response to creative work is accepted is a mark of the strength, reflexivity and influential nature of a working partnership which can and does exist between a criminal justice agency and an arts organisation.

Chapter Four

Indicating outcomes

- evaluating The Pump programme.

Introduction.

The evaluation of probation and prison projects, whether they be arts based or not, has a crucial contribution to make to the development of effective practice and methodologies of working with offenders. Without such evaluation there would be little evidence and no substance to the arguments for creative rehabilitative solutions to offending behaviour. In the current climate of economic restraint and public accountability, it is no longer acceptable to be unclear how groups and educational programmes may help people, in what circumstances and for how long. Practitioners, whether probation or theatre, cannot remain unresponsive to the demands for evidence and the need to combat a general climate of scepticism that creative work in probation is at best unproven and at worst ineffective. Theatre practitioners working in the criminal justice system have a responsibility to specify what they can do and how, to adopt a consciously evaluative attitude to their work. The purpose for a theatre practitioner is to ascertain to what extent the problems a client brings to a programme were remedied, and whether the remediation could be ascribed to the educational content and creative style of delivery. Demonstrable links between relatively permanent change and particular programme activities require further examination, whilst those changes that can be attributed to the programme need to be illuminated.

The outcome and process research into two pilot Pump programmes suggest that in terms of client improvement the programme can be efficacious. The efficacy is ascribed to several factors which I would like to describe in the first of three sections in this chapter. In the first section, after a brief introduction to the theories and structures of evaluation in the criminal justice system, I will assess the outcome of Pump courses piloted in the Greater Manchester area in 1994. To do this I will examine the findings of the Pump programme evaluation, before attempting to make comparative conclusions about the programme's overall impact. However, it must be noted that these conclusions are drawn from a low number of case studies, and that further research is necessary to confirm such findings.

The purpose of the second section is to highlight concerns and criticisms about an overtly positivistic approach to evaluation. I explore how the notion of evaluation fallacies becomes evident in the discussion of the validity of cognitive assessment techniques and the relationship between cognitive methods and cognitive change. With respect to assessment, an understanding of the similarities and differences among measures, and their relative strengths and weaknesses, is crucial to select an approach that is consistent with goals, needs, and theory.

In my view one of the main failings in social research applied to the criminal justice field is the lack of debate about the efficacy (or lack of it) of the evaluation tools used to promote notions of programme success and failure. The problem of monitoring and assessing 'change' in behaviour, particularly when emphasising positivistic methods (i.e. psychometric questionnaires), is that these evaluative tools are relatively unsophisticated. In the second section I will argue for a more balanced emphasis on what constitutes evidence, whilst remaining critical of the scope and range of any form of evaluation which intends to present evidence or indications of change in human behaviour.

To conclude the chapter I will discuss how the evaluation findings affected the aims and agendas of the project team, both from a probation and a theatre perspective. In particular I will look at how the programme has developed in response to evaluation, and in some cases had to re-assess theories which originally informed the project.

Evaluation theories.

The evaluation of prison/probation education programmes is characterised by its use of methods drawn from the social sciences. At times, the application of such research methods to drama practice can appear to be vaguely unethical. For example, in the positivistic tradition, effectiveness is normally assessed through the use of a control group, where individuals are randomly allocated to 'treatment' groups or 'no treatment' groups; alternatively there are two different types of 'treatment' group. Transferring this tradition into a criminal justice field can present both ethical and practical problems. Probation and arts practitioners may be more at ease with the notion of qualitative methods of research such as observation, interviews and anecdotal reports rather than quantitative data.

It can be difficult to reconcile the aims and assumptions of quantitative and qualitative approaches. Quantitative measures used in the criminal justice system tend to rely on numerical tables, statistics, calculable behavioural trends. The Reconviction Predictor Scales is one such method, which uses categories such as 'type of offence', 'age at offence', 'employment status at date of offence', 'marital status', 'number of previous convictions' etc. in an attempt to predict, numerically, the percentage risk of whether an individual offender is likely to re-offend. Another widely used method is the 'objectives' model; the advantage of this model is that it is straight-forward and seemingly scientific and impartial. The premise is that a project team agree on a set of objectives, and then devise and operate a programme that tries to achieve these objectives. The evaluation then consists of understanding to what extent the objectives have been met. The model was set down in a paper by Ralph Taylor, who argued that, since educational objectives aim 'to produce certain desirable changes in the behaviour pattern of the student, then evaluation is the process of determining the degree to which these changes in behaviour are actually taking place'. [1] The principle of the model is that if the objectives are clear then the changes in behaviour can be measured and the project can be judged effectively. Standardised tests of skills learnt and changes in attitudes, it is argued, can be statistically analysed to help substantiate 'scientifically' whether or not the project has 'worked'.

The qualitative (or 'interpretative') stand-point takes issue with the idea of objective and calculable research, disagreeing with the view of human beings as 'things' whose actions can be quantified, predicted and objectively investigated.[2] Therefore a social scientist, working with qualitative information, is interested not only in the actions of individuals but in discerning the context and subtexts for those actions. Action is viewed as a result of many forms of stimuli; thought; interpretation; analysis; and feelings. A human being can act on and change the social world in line with his/her own interests, needs, concerns, perceptions, aspirations. And it is these motivating aspects, what people say and do, which social research needs to confront in order to comprehend the nature of the social world. As a result the information that such a scientist is interested in is qualitative, subjective, concerned with individual testimonies, and often open-ended. Typically the work will seek to reconstruct the perspective of its subject, using description first, and explanation second. [3]

The debate currently under way in the field attempts to create a discourse between the polarised perspectives of quantitative and qualitative approaches; combining

---

[1] Tyler, R.W. (1949) Basic Principles of Curriculum and Instruction, Chicago, University of Chicago Press, reprinted in D. Hamilton, D. Jenkins, C. King, B. Macdonald and M. Parlett (eds.) Beyond the Numbers Game, London, Macmillan Education.
[2] Cohen, L. and Manion, L. (1994) Research Methods in Education, London and New York, Routledge, p. 32
[3] ibid., p. 30

methodologies and practice in order to present a composite picture of a given social subject. As Kerlinger argues 'subjective belief must be checked against objective reality' (objective referring to quantitative measures). [4] Researchers now tend to avoid conclusive arguments for and against quantitative or qualitative data, preferring to concern themselves with a 'combination of both which makes use of the most valuable of each'. [5]

Regardless of which combination of techniques is used there are certain criteria which I think any form of educational evaluation must acknowledge, and these are that the evaluation is:

- systematic; the methodology should be agreed at the outset of the programme, with the assurance that it is applied consistently and continuously.
- describable; the methodology should be describable to other researchers or practitioners in a way which is understandable and meaningful.
- objective led; that it is possible to say what the evaluation is trying to achieve prior to the start of the evaluation process.

However, I would also like to suggest that this characterisation of evaluation is an ideal rather than a reality. The process of understanding the value of something like drama and the effect has on participants is a complex and difficult one. The instruments available for the measurement of 'value' are still fairly rudimentary, even if applied systematically and carefully; the best results will only ever give approximate indications of outcome.

Structures of evaluation.

One of the key characteristics of learning is that the process is often invisible. Evaluation and research is an attempt at picking up clues from a number of areas

---

[4] Kerlinger, F.N. (1970) *Foundations of Behavioural Research*, Holt, Rinehart and Winston, New York, p.4
[5] Merton, R.K. and Kendall, P.L. (1946) 'The Focussed Interview', *American Journal of Sociology*, 51, pp 541-57

none of which on their own provide conclusive evidence. In attempting to measure the learning outcomes of participants on an anger management course one is looking for the match between what is said and what is done. This is a factor in most evaluation reports on educational based programmes; one must ascertain what the participant <u>thinks</u> s/he has learnt, discover what <u>has</u> been learnt and monitor what s/he <u>applies</u> in practice. For example the evaluation of a participant attending a course to up-grade his/her skills will ask for his/her reaction to the course, test his/her knowledge (an exam/essay) and then try to monitor if what has been learnt can be transferred into the work place. Similarly the measurement of a life-style impact of a challenging violence course on a participant will consist of the following four stages:

1. Reaction to programme: feedback from participants involved in learning.
2. Learning: assessment of participants' cognitive grasp of the programme 'tools'.
3. Skills transference; monitoring of participants' ability to talk about key concepts and transfer learning to an environment outside of the group.
4. Results: reports by peer group, family, independent observer (probation officer) of identifiable changes in behaviour; reconviction reports may also be used.

Feedback from participants can be gained in numerous ways. From informal discussions to structured interviews. Questionnaires or feedback forms are also useful, as are follow-up feed-back sessions with an independent (of the programme team) interviewer. The assessment of behaviour changes, of skills transference, and of learning outcomes is difficult. This is unfortunate as this is the area in which evaluation information becomes far more relevant for Probation researchers.

Learning, transference, and results.

The question of transference of skills from the learning environment to another (similar) situation is one that concerns many educational researchers. Goldstein's 'stimulus generalisation' concept informs us that the more similar the stimuli are to those originally used in training, the greater the strength of the response. [6] This suggests that the use of role play in simulating other situations and environments can be an extremely valuable training tool. The concept of rehearsing social and life skills, evaluating and re-evaluating participant's skills, seems then to have a high educational and training value when it comes to the transfer of these skills into other environments. However it must be noted that a researcher should avoid assumptions based on initial results. It has been shown that learning methods which achieve an initially high result immediately after a session, often prove to have less of an effect in the mid to long term.[7] So clearly it is important to measure the transfer of skills over a period of time. Probation evaluation of skills transference is usually monitored by systematically appraising the individual, both before, during and after the programme. The appraisal is normally undertaken by the individual's own probation officer; this has the advantage of using the experience of someone who knows the person and the programme, but is not necessarily involved in the learning process (a degree of objectivity). The officer can also undertake a long term appraisal of the individual.

The learning environment.

These areas of evaluation need to be supplemented with an appreciation that different groups will create different outcomes even if the programme remains fundamentally the same. Two obvious factors are relevant here, the individual/dynamics within a group, and the environment in which the group members are working.

The effect of the learning environment in which a programme takes place is also an important consideration in evaluating the outcome to a programme. Much research now points to higher motivation and success rates with programmes done

---

[6] Goldstein, A. (1988) *The Prepare Curriculum*, Champaign, Research Press.
[7] Garvey, D.M. (1971) 'A catalogue of judgements, findings and hunches', in *Educational Aspects of Evaluation*, P.J. Tansey (ed.), London, McGraw Hill p.218

in a 'community' setting. [8] One of the reasons given for this is that prison provides less of a stable environment; inmates are often far more anxious and prone to depression. The prison environment also tends to be one which is predominantly aggressive and frustrating, governed as it is not only by the rules of the institution but also by the informal 'rules' or 'laws' which exist between inmates. For example, informal rules exist if someone steals from another cell, the 'pad thief' needs to be dealt with and physically punished or else the owner of the cell opens himself up to being 'walked over' by everyone else on the wing. To a large extent these punishments are settled in private in someone's cell, out of sight of guards but not necessarily out of mind. Prison guards will often turn a blind eye to this violence, seeing it as a practical form of 'rough justice'. In such a way the institution endorses violence at an informal level. And perhaps it is asking too much for it to be significantly different. But certainly one can see that the environment of prison will affect the transference of essentially non-violent interventions as learnt on a challenging violence course. The prison environment also presents a researcher with many practical problems in designing evaluation procedures. For example the movement of offenders within the system disrupts studies; once re-released some offenders are hard to trace unless they return to the system. Therefore long term evaluation can be problematic.

Constraints of evaluation.

Evaluation in the criminal justice system is a process which aims to be systematic in its form of inquiry. It is also a process that attempts to gather both qualitative and quantitative data in order to understand a project's outcomes. As already mentioned some outcomes such as participant reaction and the cognitive grasp of the course's learning tools, can be assessed fairly confidently. Other outcomes, such as skills transference and changes in behaviour are much more difficult to

---

[8] Hollin, C. (1992) *Criminal Behaviour: A Psychological Approach to Explanation and Prevention*, London and Washington D.C., Falmer Press, p132

estimate. The key problem in evaluating these latter stages is that, to a large degree, assessment is dependent on the motivation of the participant and what sort of information he decides to offer. For example, some participants on the TIPP programme attended as part of a compulsory order. Failure to turn up for a session, or concerns about the offender's motivation on the course, could result in a breach and a return to court. For one participant, involved with physical child abuse, the programme was one more hurdle to jump through before he could see his family again. For others it was the alternative to a custodial sentence. Already the 'environment' of evaluation is far from neutral territory. The offenders were very conscious that their behaviour on the course had serious repercussions. This kind of threat hanging over the learning process can have a number of effects, such as influencing participants to stop and think about their lives, or encouraging them to 'play' the system, such as talking about how the course has changed them; paying lip service to the rationale of anti-violence; manipulating the evaluation process to suit themselves. The problem with the available techniques is that it is very hard to counter these kinds of strategies from an offender. The techniques for assessing 'objectively' if a participant's attitudes to violence were affected are fairly transparent to anyone who wants to manipulate the data to their advantage. The questionnaires (see appendix 7a), although extensively tested in psychological trials, are still rather unsophisticated in their ability to identify discrepancies between information given and information sought. The only data which can contradict this sort of manipulation is the observation of facilitators, reports from the family, probation officers, and objective evidence from a video of the session.

The science of quantitative data and the use of numbers and graphs to plot something as invisible and subtle as an individual's attitude need to be viewed with scepticism. There has been evaluation from anger management projects that document an increase in negative behaviour of clients. [9] This result can be misleading; the course has not necessarily failed, for it can be the case that clients have finished the course with a better awareness and definition of their behaviour. Also information about the clients' current situation can affect the interpretation. One of the Pump participants in Salford became increasingly stressed by life events; his wife left him, he was summoned to court, and so unsurprisingly when he came to fill out the post questionnaire he registered higher degrees of aggression and anger than recorded in the pre-test. To an 'objective' eye this might signify that the course is teaching an offender to become more aggressive, but in context one can understand the reasons behind the answers. Furthermore, when this single offender was excluded from the analysis, statistically significant differences were obtained.

Evaluation that puts no interpretation on the information gathered from questionnaires, can result in presumptions about the 'true value' of the responses to the questions. Putting aside the difficulties of literacy for the moment, I have witnessed 'combative' reactions to filling out questionnaires. For example, another of the offenders on the Salford course when asked if his crimes had ever harmed anyone, answered 'no' - and qualified that by saying 'but my wife would say I had'. The same offender had a record of hospitalising his partner on two occasions, including a punctured lung and severe bruising. There is a very real danger that information from a questionnaire is gathered in a social vacuum and that the results can be presented as a true representation of reality.

I am not suggesting that all offenders are capable of carrying out such manipulation, but in the cases of compulsory attendance, most offenders will attempt to 'play the game' to some extent because it reaps them obvious benefits. This sophistication in pretending to be good learners begs the question of whether

---

[9] Howells, K. (1989) 'Anger-Management Methods in Relation to the Prevention of Violent Behaviour', in J. Archer and K. Browne (eds.) *Human Aggression*, London, Routledge, pp.153-181

social skills simulation is the appropriate medium for learning. And as mentioned in the previous chapter, some researchers are extremely concerned that anger management courses may lead to a greater subtlety of violence.

The question of learner motivation is, undoubtedly, a complex one. The problem is that evaluation techniques, at best, can only provide very rough indications of outcomes in these areas. And the only way to counter manipulation of the process, is to have as many contrasting evaluation techniques as possible, which may provide a researcher with trends which can be compared, analysed, and interpreted.

Evaluating the long term results of a programme can also be problematic. As mentioned earlier, one must be aware of the discrepancies between discourse/utterances and behaviour/actions. For example positive testimonies from men who have finished an anger management programme often contradict the testimonies of their wives or partners living with them. One way to test outcomes in a 'clinical' environment is to set up simulated events which test reactions; Novaco's practice of 'inoculating' participants to 'high risk' situations by exposing them to increasingly provoking simulations is one example. [10] However this is still not conclusive evidence. If one has the resources, the family, partner or peer group can contribute to the evaluation of the participant, although this too has its problems - for example, men who threaten their partners to write up a 'good' evaluation. On the other hand without this feedback one relies totally on the individual's perspective on his behaviour. Particularly in anger management groups this type of evaluation has to be handled with discretion and care. The researcher is dealing with extremely personal issues, and ones that greatly affect individuals, peers, partners and (often) children.

---

[10] *See* Novaco R W. (1975) *Anger Control*, Massachusetts, Lexington Books.

A summary of the Pump programme evaluation.

In this section I will be discussing the findings of an evaluation report of two pilot Pump programmes authored by researchers from the Greater Manchester Probation Service.[11] The report focuses on three main areas: participant feedback, trainer feedback and observation, and the results from psychometric pre-and post-questionnaires. I have included a detailed presentation of supporting accounts and graphs in numbers 5-8 of the appendix.

As the Pump programme was funded by the Home Office, and devised in partnership with the Practice Development Unit (the research section of Greater Manchester Probation Service) it benefited from a high level of research and evaluation expertise. Because of the Home Office and Probation links to the project, the evaluation was governed by criteria set down by these organisations, and therefore mainly made use of positivistic and quantitative techniques. Before discussing some of the findings of this research, I would like to outline the general structure that the evaluation process followed.

The first step involved a careful and clear definition of what areas the evaluation process should cover. The evaluation questions influence the nature of information collected and as a consequence the conclusions that can be drawn, therefore it was crucial that the purpose of the evaluation was clearly defined from the outset.

The evaluation plan for the project was designed to assess three areas:

- Process evaluation; recording and assessing developmental stages (this was extensively covered in previous chapter) of the programme. This included minutes from meetings with TIPP and Probation Liaison Committee, writing regular reports about creative developments, and recording feed-back from trial workshops with different groups (Probation trainers and ex-offenders).

---

[11] GMPS (1995) *Evaluation of the Pump Programme*, available from GMPS.

- System evaluation; assessment/feedback from staff and participants running and/or observing programme in situation. This included full reports from Probation Officers involved with the first pilot groups, recording staff feedback after each of the eight pilot sessions, and comments made by independent observer reviewing the recorded video evidence from the sessions.

- Affective learning outcomes; did participants understand concepts used in the course and were they able to transfer them into another environment? The learning outcomes were monitored from client feed-back (structured interview), results from pre-and-post psychometric questionnaires, some drama-based evaluation, and 3 month follow-up 'progress' reports from each of the participants' probation officers.

Participant feed-back.

Two forms of gathering participants' feedback comments were used. The first asked participants to score a number of different elements of the course (the course's use of props, drama exercises, and to what degree participants had felt practical intervention strategies had been learnt). The second form of information gathering was post-course interviews conducted by participants' probation officers. From this a table of positive and negative elements of the course was devised.

In the two pilot anger management courses run by the TIPP Centre in Salford and Bury, responses from individuals varied considerably. For example one individual (on the course as a condition of his court sentence) sat for long periods with his arms folded and would answer monosyllabically when questions were put to him. There were serious concerns that this individual was still offending during the course. At the other extreme there was another individual on the same course who was an excellent contributor and who took an active part in the learning process. The fact that some participants were volunteers, while others were attending as a condition of their sentence, did not seem the primary factor in determining motivation.

Participants' scoring of the Pump course

The participants on the two TIPP Centre pilot programmes were asked at the end to give an appraisal of the 8 week course. The group members were given the following questions about the three different sections of the course and asked to respond by giving a rating between 1 - 5. 1 being low, 5 being high. The term 'effective' was defined as the relative usefulness of the props/exercises in helping the participants to achieve the learning objectives of the session.

1. How effective did you find *the props* used in these sessions?
2. How effective did you find *the exercises* used in these sessions?
3. How much do you feel you have learnt about practical intervention strategies (for avoiding angry or violent situations) from this section of the course?

From the results (see appendix 5) one can see a far higher degree of criticism from the Salford group, even though the courses were run at the same time, and with the same TIPP Centre facilitator. It is rather difficult to evaluate the Bury scores, as the responses were predominantly 5 out of 5 - which statistically is a little unrealistic and over-enthusiastic. There may be a number of obvious but relevant contributing factors for this difference: Salford was more critical and/or resistant to the style of programme; Bury less critical; better individual motivation within Bury.

Some participants (a. and b.) rated the programme below the average scoring of other participants on the same course. In his later evaluation comments, a. explained that he had not enjoyed the drama form of the course, and had felt that there was not enough space for simply talking about problems. Participant b. also felt uncomfortable at times with the drama element, although he had found the course, in general, to be useful.

There seemed to be a general trend that indicated the impact of the props was not as strong as other elements of the course. This can be shown in the difference between what participants thought about the props and what they thought they had learnt from the sessions, and also in the generally lower totals given to the props. There are a couple of factors which might explain this, first, that the props were genuinely seen to be less significant than other elements of the course, second, that the props were designed as learning aids to be used as a reference at selected points of the course, and therefore were not created to have a major impact. In many ways the props are embellishments to the course, that add a little bit of interest and focus for the learning aims of different sections, rather than being a central focus.

Participant feedback comments collected by Probation officers.

The second part of the feedback from offenders consisted of recording their verbal comments about the course. The participants were asked by their probation officers in one-to-one interviews about their general reactions (both positive and negative) to the course. Their responses were tabled into percentages so that it was possible to identify which aspects the participants felt were working more or less well. The sample size was again 7, consisting of the participants from both pilot groups. The group members were asked to assess in what way each section of the course had helped them, and also to comment critically on aspects which they did not find helpful. More than one response could be given by the same person, which is why in the tables the number of comments may be greater than the number of participants taking part.

Table of participants' positive feed-back on the course.

n = 7	No.	%
Thinking a problem through	10	48%
Thinking before acting, speaking or offending	5	24%
Applying strategies to life	4	19%
Thinking of others	1	4%

The positive table is an indication of which elements of the course were most beneficial. The participants on the two pilot courses felt that being able to 'think a problem through' was a very important part of the course content. Some of the recorded comments (see appendix 6) indicate that participants felt able to explore, through discussion and drama, situations in which they felt confused, angry, hurt, and vulnerable. Importantly, some of the course exercises were able to help 'break down' stressful and/or difficult situations and help participants come to a better understanding of those situations.

The second most beneficial element of the course, according to the participants, was its demonstration that cognitive interventions made before acting out, allowed time for a degree of reflection, and sometimes a change of behaviour. The simple message of 'stop and think' exercises in which participants looked at a number of different ways of behaving in difficult situations and observed very different outcomes seemed to be very useful. Some comments indicated the usefulness of the Pump props:

> The prop explains things very well. When I am in a situation now I see the prop in my head and ask myself - am I being wound up, is it a Knock, am I pumping myself up?

In general, participants felt that the drama exercises demonstrated in a very 'real' way that how an individual behaves can change situations 'if you think about what you say and how you say it':

> It helps you to see that there are different ways of seeing things. you don't have to be frightened about saying things - you can say it but in a certain way that calms the situation down instead of making it boil up, or you realise when not to say something - that it's sometimes better to leave it be.

Nineteen percent of the comments indicated that participants felt more control in dealing with their own practical problems. The aspect of the course which dealt in depth with participants' specific situations was important and useful. In particular the rehearsal of skills and strategies which could be tried out externally of the course were mentioned:

> I've tried to apply new strategies every day. First thing I do when I get in the house is sit down and have a brew and think about how I am going to play the situation. Then I go and do it. Not like before when I'd go straight in and shout at the kids to get up. I don't lose my temper half as much.

The 'thinking of others' score is low in consideration of the power of drama to promote empathy. This identifies an imbalance in the pilot programmes towards focusing on the men's thoughts and feelings, and the consequences of their actions. The victim perspective is explored in the second Jack session, but, as the probation staff also noted, there needed to be much more reference and awareness of another person's perspectives, feelings and thoughts.

Table of participants' critical feed-back on the course.

n = 7	No.	%
Irrelevant scenarios	5	24%
More personal scenarios	3	14%
More time/longer course	3	14%
Found drama element uncomfortable at times/more time for talk	2	9%

The critical table is an indication of which aspects of the course the participants felt needed changing most. Twenty four percent of comments were about the fact that group members felt the scenarios did not relate to their own personal situations. Scenarios were used in two ways, first to illustrate a general point, skill or strategy, and second, to work on specific problems of individuals. From the comments of the group members it was clear that most of their concerns were with the demonstration scenarios, rather than stories from within the group. This makes the point that it is unwise to assume things about the background of a group. For example, in Bury, all three of the offenders were in, or had recently been in, employment; whereas in Salford all the group were unemployed. So scenarios demonstrating strategies set in dole offices were relevant to some members but not all. The effect of dealing with personal stories within the group seemed a successful aspect of the course, and participants clearly felt that more time could have been spent on this area.

Nine percent of the comments from participants were concerned with their feelings that the form of the course did not suit them. The majority of the comments came from the two participants in Salford, already identified in the findings of the other feedback. These two group members expressed a need for more discussion in the group. A perfectly legitimate request, but from the organisational perspective, it is worth being clear that a discussion group might have different aims and objectives than an educational, social skills group. The function of 'discussion' groups tends to be more often connected to counselling and support work, which these individuals identified as a need for themselves. I think the feedback raises the necessity to identify individual needs at an earlier stage, and to make more explicit the purpose of the course, so that participants are clear about the reasoning behind organising the group.

Staff feedback and observation.

In this section I will summarise the feedback from staff involved with the project. The evaluation report draws from three sources; staff (TIPP and Probation facilitators) de-briefing held after each session, video evidence of each session, and follow up observation by participants' probation officers.

The rehearsal of personal situations was considered to be an important, and successful, part of the course. Feed-back from some of the participants' partners was also encouraging, including reports that levels of aggression had significantly reduced in the home since the individual had joined the group. This was directly linked (by the participants) to the exploration and rehearsal of non-aggressive strategies through role play and Forum techniques. There were a number of reported incidents which demonstrated that offenders were trying out rehearsed strategies in real life with rewarding success. For example Pete, a group member in Bury, told the group how someone had tried to 'wind him up' to start a fight, Pete had used a strategy practised in the group a couple of weeks before, and had simply ignored the person by walking away. The participants became highly engaged in looking at problems using role play, not only in the demonstration of certain key skills, but in suggesting strategies from their own experience. This gave the sessions a very pragmatic appeal, allowing group members to explore their personal situations in a positive and safe environment.

However, the Probation team did feel that there was more need for victim perspective work. In both groups it was noted that there were different degrees of victim denial and justifications of violent actions. For example in Salford, some participants expressed a belief that 'women needed to be beaten to keep them in their place'. These types of patriarchal beliefs, encountered frequently during the course, highlighted the need to develop the course towards a much greater emphasis on the partner's experience. It became increasingly clear that promoting belief change in abusive men required that the process within the men's group be directed and informed by the effects of men's beliefs and actions on their partners. This links to the pro-feminist arguments that behavioural and/or skill training interventions were based on inappropriate conceptualisations of the problem. Equally clear was the indication from the participants that 'thinking of other people' scored low on their course feedback. The problem was that the Pump course was designed for all types of violent offenders, and had to address these problems equitably. In the longer term, Greater Manchester Probation Service has developed a specific domestic violence course that can focus on comprehensive and sustained change in men's interactions with and attitudes toward their partners. Therefore, the Pump course has become more orientated to other categories of violent offender, street violence, G.B.H., A.B.H., etc. However, as I will discuss later, the pro-feminist perspective is still relevant and applicable.

Exercises that looked at individual patterns of behaviour (most notably in The Jack section) were sometimes compromised due to a shortage of course time. The idea of The Jack is that it enables participants to identify past patterns of behaviour that lead to violence. Because there are only two sessions of The Jack, it means that there is only enough time to look at one, or maybe two people's individual patterns. These sessions also tend to go into a great deal of detail, focusing on one individual, which means that other members in the group find some of the material irrelevant or of little interest. Some offenders also tended to offer stories that were either very minimal anger situations ('I tripped over the carpet'), or irrelevant to their offending behaviour. There was a need for the team to be more direct about the types of stories that were relevant to the group, and to push for these to be included and explored. However, some offenders, most notably in Bury, seemed more motivated to talk openly and in more depth without very much prompting.

In general the evaluation showed that in both locations (though in Salford to a lesser degree) objectives for each of the sessions were met satisfactorily. There was also strong evidence to support good levels of programme integrity. Through observing the participants during the session (plus video evidence) it was suggested by the independent Probation observer that a majority of the participants found the concepts and language (Pumps, Knocks, and Wind ups) easy to understand and apply to their own lives. For example, in discussing problems group members were able to analyse situations using the Pump terms accurately. The staff feedback identified that the drama-based techniques facilitated a more positive and effective learning environment. Staff believed that participants' who were expected to contribute little to the groups, were perceived to have become engaged in the process. Compared with previous challenging violence groups run by staff, the Pump programme introduced 'interesting, participatory exercises which enabled the group to explore their problems to much greater effect'. [12]

Evaluation of behaviour outcomes: questionnaires.

In the psychometric model of man it is assumed that any given behaviour is a linear function of ability traits, temperamental traits, motivational traits, moods and the situation in which an individual finds themselves. [13] The definition of personality implicit in the model is that it is the sum total of the characteristics (traits) of an individual which contribute to one's behaviour, to being oneself,

---

[12] ibid., p.17

[13] Kline, P. (1980) 'The Psychometric Model of Man', in A. Chapman and D. Jones (eds) *Models of Man*, Leicester, BPS.

different from others. Two types of probation service psychometric questionnaires were used for the TIPP Centre course, one was Crime-PICS II (see appendix 7), the other was State-Trait Anger Expression Scale (STAXI) (see appendix 7). The latter scale is particularly important in measuring the impact of emotion and stressful events on behaviour.

The distinction between states and traits.
The difference between states and traits is considered to be an important psychological point and one that cannot be minimised. [14] This distinction may be exemplified by anger.

State anger is caused by some particular event: someone jumps a queue, a car deliberately 'cuts you up' on a motorway, someone insults you. Trait anger is the general anger level of an individual when nothing traumatic or provoking has happened or is about to happen. At any given moment the actual anger level of an individual is composed of state and trait anger. Measuring these components separately, state anger could be expected to fluctuate over time, while trait anger would probably not vary quite so much. There is an interaction between state and trait anger; the stolid, low-anger individual reacts little to events that make the highly trait-anger subject highly 'explosive'. Therefore, in general, traits are relatively stable over time; states show considerable fluctuation.

In the evaluation for the Pump programme, the pattern of scores available imposed two restrictions. First, given the small numbers it made no sense to analyse the data for the two locations (Salford and Bury) separately; they were therefore pooled for analysis (though even then the combined number was small). Second, since data is only really usable for participants available at both pre- and post- test, the pooled sample size became seven for STAXI, and five for Crime-PICS.

---

[14] ibid

The best that can be said about the questionnaires is that there are encouraging trends and with a larger sample or a slightly stronger effect may prove to be statistically significant.

Findings.

The questionnaires are, at present, one of a few accepted Home Office psychometric tools designed to test changes in attitude of participants. However there is no direct evidence to suggest that degrees of attitude change manifestly influence behaviour, although results from attitude questionnaires may provide an indication that there is the possibility of a change in behaviour. I will come back to this issue of the limitation of questionnaires later.

Results from the STAXI questionnaire should highlight four areas of concern:

- current state of angry feelings (State-Anger),
- personality traits of anger (Trait-Anger),
- sense of control over angry emotions (Anger Control) and
- how anger is expressed (Anger Expression).

Crime-PICS deals more specifically with attitudes to offending behaviour, and categorises five main areas:

- general attitude towards offending;
- anticipation of re-offending;
- acknowledgement of victims of crime;
- evaluation of crime as a worthwhile lifestyle;
- rationalisation of offending behaviour as a justifiable solution to personal problems.

A detailed breakdown of the results is available in appendix 7b, however what follows here is a summary of the findings. Dr James McGuire, a psychologist at the University of Liverpool, analysed the data and came up with the following notes: [15]

> The data on most subscales of the measures show trends in the favoured direction. None of the pre-to-post test differences is statistically significant, but some approach it. The following positive findings are worth noting:
>
> 1. The decline in mean trait anger scores (general level of anger when nothing traumatic or provoking has happened or is about to happen) from 23.67 to 19.00.
>
> 2. The increase in mean anger control scores from 15.78 to 23.00
>
> 3. The decline in mean anger expression scores from 35.22 to 26.14
>
> 4. The decline in mean general attitude to crime scores from 40.50 to 35.00
>
> 5. The decline in mean problem scores (rationalisation of offending behaviour as a justifiable solution to personal problems) from 33.25 to 27.00

Analysis.

The five significant findings that McGuire highlights, point to areas of the course which have had the most impact on offenders. Although it is hard to pin-point with any degree of accuracy which aspects of the course relate to the data in the findings, it may be worth attempting to make feasible links between the two.

The Trait Anger scores show a reduction in overall inclination towards anger as a positive response to stressful situations. I would like, tentatively, to suggest that this might be a result of the consistent use of Forum Theatre to look at the impact of different ways of responding to high risk situations. The group members on both courses used the methods of Forum to explore how best to deal with their anger. I think the 3 Pump workshops, which sought to distinguish between situations that were Knocks, Wind ups and Pumps also may have contributed to offenders *perceiving* many situations in less aggressive terms and thus reducing the Trait Anger level. However, without other evidence to provide justification for this view, it remains conjecture at this point.

---

[15] GMPS (1995) op,cit.

The increase of participants' sense of control over anger suggests that the aspects of the course which looked at strategies of self control were effective. This relates to exercises such as aggravating language, thought stopping (reversing pumping thoughts), and finding pragmatic ways of winding down and relaxing.

The decrease in anger expression highlights two things. Firstly, simply the creation of a group to discuss difficult situations seemed to be helpful in reducing the level of anxiety and stress. Several offenders noted that they felt much less tense as a direct result of putting aside two hours a week to talk and focus on their problems. Secondly, that some partners of participants also noted a reduction in their normal anger levels. This raises a question of whether the course participants continued to feel less anxious after completing the group, or whether levels increased again after they were no longer able to off-load stress through the group meetings. The evidence from other evaluation suggests that the levels of stress and anxiety gradually rise up again over a period of time and that the strength of the course 'inoculation' tends to wear off. [16] The decline in mean Problem scores might further suggest that offenders' view of their personal difficulties lessened during the course because they felt that they were dealing with situations as and when they arose.

Using drama as evaluation.

The TIPP Centre also experimented with the use of dramatic forms of measurement, which, as far as I am aware, are original to the project. For example in the first session group members brain-stormed what specific situations triggered their anger or violence. From this material the group were asked to short-list 5 'trigger' situations which might lead to violence, to make a tableau of each situation and to then stand on a continuum line to identify how much of a personal provocation they thought it was. The tableaux were photographed and

---

[16] Wilkinson, J. (1994) 'Does offence-focussed work reduce re-offending in the long term?', What Works? Conference 1994, Salford University.

the position on the continuum lines was recorded. These trigger situations were then re-introduced in the last session, and the group members were asked to stand on the continuum line where they now thought they were in relation to the risk of violence. The most common of these trigger situations found in the two groups were family violence and violence in public places (pubs, streets, football matches). [17]

It is an important process for the programme and for the men in the group to identify at an early stage where they perceive their anger or violence problems to lie. The continuum also allows the group to evaluate their own progress during the course; where they feel they have changed, where they feel justified in using violence. The continuum lines are used to structure discussion both at the start and at the end of the course. When used at the beginning of the programme participants are not unsurprisingly reluctant to admit to personal problems, this can be for a number of reasons: they are anxious about revealing themselves to the group; they have no trust in the programme yet; it is part of their denial and minimisation of their behaviour; they are unconscious of specific 'at risk' situations; they do not want to disclose information about themselves, etc. As the course progresses it is possible to refer back to the results of this exercise, and at the end of the course the exercise is re-done to see if offenders' self awareness or motivation to admit to certain actions has changed. For the facilitator the exercise is a way of gathering initial information about the group members, and getting a feeling for the context in which the offenders' violence occurs.

In the pilot programmes participants were not challenged to discuss their personal stories. What was found was that unless there was one person particularly motivated to offer detailed information about himself, the group members would suggest ridiculously 'low risk' material about their situations. For example, when asked to fill-in anger diaries, the information would relate to instances like 'when

---

[17] *For reasons of confidentiality these photos are not included in the appendix.*

I tripped over a wire in the pub'. The selection of this type of 'low risk' material allowed for the minimum investment in the process. Sometimes this low investment was dispersed as the course progressed and a more trusting environment was established, at other times this type of selection was maintained throughout. In order to address this situation, the facilitator needs to help set the 'level' of group investment, by setting out more specifically what type of material is required. For example, in the first session, the offences participants have committed are recorded, so that from the very beginning, the discussion of anger and violence is connected to real events.

The data revealed through this process should not be viewed as a precise appraisal of the participants' attitude, but it can be a strong indicator of the issues which are important for group members. As an evaluation process the material gained from the continuum exercise needs to be put in context and properly interpreted. For example participants can quite easily deny they have a problem with any of the trigger situations and stand at the lower 'no risk' end of the continuum. However depending on the participant, and what the team knows about that individual, his denial of anger can be identified through this process because he constantly (and quite improbably) stands at the 'low risk' end of the line. Because the groups identified slightly different situations, the results have been broken down into locations.

There is a detailed breakdown of results available (in appendix 8), however here is a summary of findings. The impact of the programme on the two locations seems markedly different; with the Bury group showing consistent trends in the favoured direction, but Salford showing little or no change in results. In Salford there was a slight increase towards a perception that arguments with partners could lead to violence. In this case a single client went against the general trend of the group, and as before if this result was excluded a significant difference would have been achieved. It is interesting to note that this is the same individual identified in the questionnaires as showing an opposite trend to the group. This produces a correlation between different evaluation exercises. The following positive findings are worth noting:

1. The decline in 'wind ups' (as a perceived provocation) score from 6.0 to 1.6
2. The decline in 'feeling rejected' (as a perceived provocation) score from 4.6 to 1.3
3. The decline in mean 'feeling threatened' (as a perceived provocation) score from 6.0 to 3.3
4. The decline in 'family row' (as a perceived provocation) score from 4.0 to 2.0
5. The decline in 'drink' (as a perceived factor) score from 2.5 to 1.2

Summary of evaluation results.

In order to summarise the findings of The Pump pilot evaluation I have analysed the comparative data and attempted to draw some tentative conclusions. The evaluation does suggest that a number of conclusions can be validly made:

1. *The course attained a good level of programme integrity, meeting learning aims and objectives for each session successfully.* Comparing the three different sections of the course, The Jack section demonstrated slightly weaker learning outcomes than the other two. There was a perceived increase in participants' confidence in controlling their anger, and a general reduction in anger as a trait in dealing with situations.

2. *Further understanding of the background to participants' violent behaviour.* Two common factors emerged from running the groups, first that seven out of the nine participants committed acts of violence only when under the influence of alcohol (the other two were related to drug abuse, and mental health). The conclusion of the team was that alcohol was a strong factor in violence. Second, that domestic violence figured strongly in the backgrounds of the men, even if they had been convicted of other violent crimes. Though the course was targeted at any form of violent behaviour, the personal stories

that emerged were in the majority of cases related to incidents in the home and primarily with female partners or children.

3. *Where specific personal problems were focused on, by using certain theatre techniques, the Pump course seems to have had a significant affect on participants' ability to deal with those problems in reality.* The evaluation data indicated a significant statistical improvement in participants' ability to cope with problems (decline in mean Problem Score). Where stories were not relevant to group members there seemed to be a weakening in impact of the programme, particularly when key social skills were modelled or demonstrated. It was also observed that participants needed to be encouraged to focus on their specific personal problems. If this was not done participants tended to offer very 'safe' stories which did not address their problems in any meaningful way. These types of stories demonstrate a reluctance by the participant to engage or focus on situations in which violence was a real possibility.

4. *Impact on the two pilot groups different.* One of the clearest pieces of evidence to emerge from the evaluation findings was that the course had a varying degree of impact in the two different locations. The questionnaire, continuum, participant and staff feed-back all suggest that the programme consistently achieved higher degrees of impact in Bury than in Salford. It is possible that the programme can have quite different outcomes when replicated in different contexts.

5. *Although the sample size was small the evaluation suggests that the TIPP Pump course achieved a small, but significant reduction in the likelihood of further violent offences by some of the participants.* It was interesting to note that the text-in-situation was subject to a complex set of contextual factors. By assessing the contextual factors it is sometimes possible to identify in what way the course is being delivered and received differently. For example early evidence from more recent Pump courses run solely by Probation teams, but

trained by the TIPP Centre, suggests a significant decrease in overall programme impact. This implies two things, first, that perhaps the skills transference in the training received by Probation staff was not adequate, and second, that there was a value in the combination of skills that TIPP and Probation staff brought to the course that is weakened when one, or other, is absent.

From the positivistic perspective this issue of replication is crucial for pilot demonstration projects such as The Pump. A demonstration project can only usefully inform policy and practice if its results are repeatable. However, no drama based educational course can ever be absolutely replicated, just as no two theatrical performances can ever be exactly the same. Even if it were possible to reproduce the course absolutely, the context in which it is received will always be different. So, although a scientific rationalist might wish for absolute reproduction, it is in fact an impossibility. The point here is that it should be accepted that education programmes may produce tolerable levels of variance in levels of achievements and results. Replication studies, therefore, should study why and how differences come about, so that there is an increase in understanding of what works in what situations and with whom.

I believe that the research methods did take into account these issues. A number of different techniques were used to evaluate different elements of the study and some of the outcomes. However, in selecting attitude questionnaires as the only method of analysing behavioural outcomes this limited the evaluation in this area to a positivistic approach. It would have been my intention, if there had been more resources available, to follow up participants' progress through interviews and perhaps role-play evaluation sessions. This was not done because of financial limitations and the inevitable restriction of information after a participant has served his probation condition.

Criticisms and alternatives to a positivistic social sciences approach.

The use of questionnaires, continuum feedback, and other psychometric (i.e. self-statement measures) forms of evaluation needs to be carefully considered. These and other measures are often used in the evaluation literature because they 'look' valid, have been used in the past, and have produced some (seemingly) meaningful results, even though sufficient attention has not been paid to questions of validity. [18] Take for example the psychometric tests used in The Pump programme (see appendix), what are these measures actually assessing? Are they really giving an accurate, veridical measure of participants' internal dialogue, or attitudes to crime and anger?

Meichenbaum and Cameron have speculated on the meaning of self-reports of cognitive activity. [19] They conclude that the report of no activity may not necessarily indicate the absence of thoughts, but rather the inability to describe verbally one's cognitive experience, lack of motivation, or the operation of implicit ('unconscious') rules. On the other hand, the report of specific cognitive activity does not imply it is really experienced. Meichenbaum and Cameron suggest that in some reports individuals have inferred from behaviour what s/he 'must have been thinking'. For example, one of the participants in Salford had problems dealing with his ex-wife without getting angry. When he was asked to role-play a telephone call to his wife to discuss picking up the children, he picked up the phone, but then slammed it down after two rings. Even though he may not have experienced a particular thought, the participant endorsed having the thought, 'I can't do this', on a self-statement inventory. Perhaps he has inferred from his behaviour that, since he quit in the middle of the task, this is a likely thought for him to have had at the time.

---

[18] Glass, C.R. & Merluzzi, T.V. (1981) 'Cognitive assessment of social-evaluative anxiety', in T. Merluzzi, C.R. Glass, & and M. Genest (Eds.) *Cognitive Assessment*, New York, Guildford.
[19] Meichenbaum, D. & Butler, L. (1981) 'Issues in cognitive assessment: an overview', in T. Merluzzi, C.R. Glass, & and M. Genest (Eds.) *Cognitive Assessment*, New York, Guildford.

I think it is highly unlikely that participants who report having certain thoughts 'very frequently' on a self-statement inventory really have these exact thoughts. For one thing, our thought processes (a) are probably highly idiosyncratic, automatic, and non-conscious (b) do not occur in the form of complete sentences, (c) may sometimes rely heavily on image and not language, and (d) have probably not been tallied or counted by the individual.[20] So what are participants really saying when they circle a '5' on such an inventory, indicating on the five-point scale that they had this thought quite often?

There appear to be at least four possibilities. Firstly, the report of having had a thought 'very frequently' may reflect not the frequency but the impact or importance of the thought. The participant may read the statement on the questionnaire, feel that it really hits home, and thus infer that s/he must have had that thought frequently. There is certainly a difference between feeling as if you have had a thought quite often and actually thinking it.[21] Secondly, the endorsement may reflect a translation from the idiosyncratic or fragmented thoughts to the grammatical complete sentence on the inventory. With the possibility of enhanced self-esteem through 'recognition' of its 'clarity'. Thirdly, the self-report may represent the decision that the thought 'matches up' with one's self-concept, presentation of self to others, and/or personal construct system. This raises the interesting question of whether the self-concept of being a failure predisposes an individual to actually think negative self-statements or just report them. Fourthly, it may be that participants are 'translating' affective experiences into a language-based self-statement format. [22] Although an individual may experience physiological signs of anger, such as increased heart rate or sweaty

---

[20] Vygotsky, L.S. (1962) *Thought and Language*, E. Hanfmann and G. Vakar,(eds. and trans.), Cambridge, Massachusetts, MIT Press.

[21] Goldfried, M.R. (1980) 'Assessment strategies for cognitive-behavioural interventions', symposium presented at the meeting of the Association for Advancement of Behaviour Therapy, New York.

[22] Glass, C.R. and Arnkoff, D.B. (1982) Issues in Cognitive Assessment and Therapy, in P.C. Kendall (ed.) *Advances in Cognitive-Behavioural Research and Therapy vol. 1*, New York, Academic Press.

palms, he may not be aware at the time of any cognitive activity or specific anger-related thoughts. Yet on a self-statement inventory, the participant may give a high endorsement to the thought, 'I am very angry'. The intensity of the emotional experience becomes expressed in thought-related terms, even though such thoughts were not necessarily formulated at the time.

These four hypotheses may also be relevant to other forms of assessment, like attitude questionnaires such as Crime-Pics II and STAXI. In much the same way as self-statement inventories, attitude questionnaires seek to approximate language-based thoughts and raise similar concerns regarding whether the individual has really had these thoughts. And, as discussed previously, if we take into consideration the motivation to 'play the system', it is not unreasonable to be concerned about the validity of these methods.

These criticisms about qualitative methodology echo the anti-positivist perspective that 'scientific' procedures in the social sciences are mechanistic and reductionist and, by definition, exclude notions of choice, freedom, individuality and moral responsibility. William Blake, noted:

> ....they (the 'scientists') reduce 'life' to conceivable measurement, but such a conception of life does not embrace the most evident element of all: that life can only be known by a living being, by 'inner' experience. No matter how exact measurement may be, it can never give us an experience of life, for life cannot be weighed and measured on a physical scale. [23]

I think the use of quantifiable measures in the arts is particularly problematic. The positivistic approach concentrates exclusively on notional aspects of the person; responding to the world in a repetitive and predictable way; on the external rather than the internal world. But it is not that qualitative assessments in themselves are

---

[23] Nesfield-Cookson, B. (1987) *William Blake: Prophet of Universal Brotherhood*, Crucible, p.23

wholly objectionable, it is more that their elevated status in social research as the only means of establishing a valid relationship to reality is in question:

....the sciences, in their relentless pursuit of objectivity, raise alienation to its apotheosis as our *only* means of achieving a valid relationship to reality. Objective consciousness *is* alienated life promoted to its most honorific status as the scientific method. Under its auspices we subordinate nature to our command only by estranging ourselves from more and more of what we experience, until the reality about which objectivity tells us so much finally becomes a universe of congealed alienation. [24]

To avoid this idea of 'congealed alienation' I think it is important to go back to the notions of what the drama or educational programme is attempting to do. In chapter two I discussed Husserl's notions of 'epoche' or 'bracketing' of reality, and how this related to what a drama practitioner may be aiming to achieve in a workshop. The 'bracketing' of an experience may be an equally valid approach to evaluation, as it is an assessment which attempts to increase awareness and degrees of consciousness about the nature of a phenomenon (a project). Certainly alternatives to positivism, like phenomenology (Husserl, 1952; Schultz, 1962), ethnomethodology (Garfinkel, 1968) and symbolic interactionism (Mead, 1934), move away from the demands that nothing may be regarded as real unless proven by empirical science.[25] Instead of quantitative outcomes, these theoretical perspectives argue that individual behaviour can only be understood by attempting to share frames of reference. This calls for an emphasis on subjectivity rather than objectivity:

---

[24] Roszak, T. (1970) The Making of a Counter Culture, in Cohen, L. and Manion, L. (1994) *Research Methods in Education*, London and New York, Routledge, p.24

[25] Husserl, E (1952) *Ideas: General Introduction to Pure Phenomenology*, translated by W.R. Boyce, London, George Allen and Unwin; Schultz, A. (1962) *Collected Papers*, Nijhoff, The Hague; Garfinkel, H. (1968) *Studies in Ethnomethodology*, Englewood Cliffs, New Jersey, Prentice-Hall; Mead, G.H. (1934) *Mind, Self, and Society*, (ed.) Charles Morris, Chicago, University of Chicago Press.

(T)he purpose of social science is to understand social reality as different people see it and to demonstrate how their views shape the action which they take within that reality. Since the social sciences cannot penetrate to what lies behind social reality, they must work directly with man's definitions of reality and with the rules he devises for coping with it. While the social sciences do not reveal ultimate truth, they do help us to make sense of our world. What the social sciences offer is explanation, clarification and demystification of the social forms which man has created around himself. [26]

I think subjective approaches to evaluation, as suggested by the anti-positivists, are closely aligned with programmes which have an interest in the intentional and 'creative' (opening up new ways of perceiving) aspects of individuals. The cognitive theories of Novaco and the pro-feminists come from a humanist psychological perspective, and this should be reflected in the research methodology of programmes developed from these theoretical standpoints. As one critic has argued: 'For scientific purposes, treat people as if they were human beings.' [27]

In terms of evaluation practice, phenomenology is concerned with the study of direct experience and the way we classify and organise our everyday world. These classifications are learned through our biographical situation and influenced by our social context, leading to the conclusion that 'knowledge of everyday life is socially ordered'. [28] This everyday knowledge by which we are able to come to terms with reality varies from situation to situation. And so it is the way in which people classify reality in which a phenomenology researcher is interested. Accounts, case studies, personal testimonies are the key techniques used to research this area.

---

[26] Beck, R.N. (1979) *Handbook in Social Philosophy*, New York, Macmillan, p.9
[27] Harre, R. and Secord, P. (1972) The Explanation of Social Behaviour in Cohen, L. and Manion, L. (1994) *Research Methods in Education*, London and New York, Routledge, p.27
[28] Burrell, G. and Morgan. G. (1979) *Sociological Paradigms and Organizational Analysis*, London, Heinemann Educational Books.

Ethnomethodology, however, challenges this notion of sociologically ordered reality, stressing the presence of multiple realities co-existing simultaneously.[29] The emphasis in ethnomethodology is on seeking to understand in which way people negotiate the social contexts in which they find themselves; how people make sense of and 'construct' order from their environment. Ethnomethodology researchers may use similar techniques to a Phenomenologist, but will reflect the differing emphasis found in these different theories. [30]

Of importance to both phenomenology and ethnomethodology, is the human faculty of reflexivity. The ability to turn back on oneself; to look and respond in reaction to a different imputation of meaning. This element of reflexivity is one of the main underlying factors involved with cognitive intervention programmes; that human beings react according to the meaning given to the situation, but that the attribution of meaning is a continuous process and subject to change. This is as relevant to the participants as it is to facilitators leading a programme. I found that the different reactions from the participants to the Pump programme demanded an eclectic and reflexive response from the facilitating team. For example, some of the more introspective participants resisted taking action based on their self-discoveries; other participants were 'doers' but disliked examining their actions; for some talking through problems with a minimum of action seemed to be useful, for others action seemed to be the only way in which to clarify how to deal with a situation. The assessment of each participant is usually an informal, instinctive and reflexive one which continues throughout the life of the programme.

In rejecting the positivistic image of a passive, determined, predictable human organism and focusing on an interactional model, social researchers may find a more complex world, governed by intangibility, multiple meanings, and shifting

---

[29] Garfinkel, H. (1968) *Studies in Ethnomethodology*, Englewood Cliffs, New Jersey, Prentice-Hall.
[30] ibid.

perspectives. However, this is a particularly relevant approach when attempting to assess the nature of programmes such as The Pump. The use of an interaction model implies human beings acting in relation to each other, taking each other into account, acting, perceiving, interpreting, acting again - precisely the focus of a cognitive educational programme. In evaluatory terms, phenomenology and ethnomethodology share a common characteristic with the kind of concentrated social action found in group work rooms, an action characterised by participants and facilitators '.....continually adjusting, reckoning, evaluating, bargaining, acting and changing'. [31]

Therefore, one alternative to a positivistic approach to evaluation is to focus on individuals and their interpretations, rather than quantitative collections of group data (characterised by statistical outcomes). In particular the emphasis is on theory which emerges from particular situations, rather than theory which is hypothesised and then tested. Theory, the anti-positivists argue, 'should not precede research but follow it'. [32] From this perspective the hope of a universal theory, which characterises the positivist outlook, gives way to multifaceted images of human behaviour as varied as the situations and contexts supporting them.

It is important to reiterate that whilst quantitative measures in social research are limited in their view of the complexity of human behaviour (and of situations in which human beings interact), this does not negate their contribution to multi-method approaches to evaluation. My criticism has been directed against the emphasis on quantitative techniques (typified by the attitude tests), by Probation and Home Office researchers, as being the only valid indicator of outcomes. I think that exclusive reliance on one method may bias or distort the researcher's picture of the particular slice of reality s/he is investigating. A researcher needs to be confident that the data generated are not simply artefacts of one specific

---

[31] Woods, P. (1979) *The Divided School*, London, Routledge and Kegan Paul, p. 46
[32] Cohen, L. and Manion, L. (1994) op.cit., p. 37

method of collection. [33] Further the more the methods contrast with each other, the greater the researcher's confidence may be.

Conclusion.

To conclude the chapter I want to discuss how the evaluation findings affected the aims and agendas of the project team, both from a probation and a theatre perspective. The evaluation data suggested that it was feasible to pre-plan structured and objective-led sessions, that probation and theatre practitioners could work together to ensure programme integrity. The Pump programme has developed an approach to using a range of delivery styles, not just drama-based techniques. For the TIPP Centre facilitator this has meant responding to a general need from this type of group to allow space for participants to talk about their problems. Understandably, some men attending the group have found it hard to openly discuss their violence in front of others, and for many it is the first time they have articulated how and why they are violent. The programme facilitators have had to respond to this situation, by being sensitive to the style in which these 'discussions' take place. For a theatre practitioner there is a strong instinctive need to get the group 'up on their feet' and getting used to working with tableau or role-play. For the probation officer the level of 'honest' discussion and commitment to addressing offending behaviour is important. However it is one of the strengths of the programme that clear learning aims and objectives have been set, and that through a combination of theatre and discussion these targets can to some extent be met.

To an extent the programme agenda limits the scope of each session to what has been pre-planned. This suggests little flexibility to the needs of each group. However, what happens when this structure loses shape is that the energy and sense of purpose in the group dissipates; rather than learning together as a group, participants become isolated, bored and frustrated by the sense that the session is

---

[33] Lin, N. (1976) *Foundations of Social Research*, New York, McGraw-Hill.

meandering. Whilst the structure sets the learning agenda, it has also had to be adapted to the responses to the material and content generated by the participants on the course. For example, as discussed in the last chapter, although the situations described and role-played by the men varied greatly, they had in common a perceived threat to the man's sense of personal integrity, his pride, and his mastery of the social environment. Take the story about the participant who assaulted a Housing Officer. This could be an angry provoking situation for anyone being treated in a patronising way. For the participant, however, the situation was transformed into one of power. The issue, for the participant, became one of social hierarchy. 'It felt good to smack him. He had it coming. No-one should treat me like that, why shouldn't I get respect?' It was clear from discussing the situation with the participant that even before he hit the officer he knew it would jeopardise the case, and that he would be arrested for it. It was the insult of being made to wait to process the case by 'a social inferior' who was 'being patronising'. It is an inherent slight to his dignity.

Beyond the two pilot courses the Pump programme has had to develop responses to this type of material. The facilitators have had to become reflexive to the issues which have been presented by men attending the group. This, I think, has led to sessions becoming more responsive to participants' stories, and led to developments which have moved away from the original aims and agenda of the programme. It has been one of the strengths of the partnership between the TIPP Centre and Greater Manchester Probation Service that this on-going development has been supported, and that the re-assessment of some of the theories which informed the initial project has been adapted in response to the practical experiences of the facilitating team. However the negotiation of this agenda has been based on qualitative evaluation work that has highlighted areas in which the programme could be effectively developed. For example in the interim evaluation of the two pilot projects it was already clear that through the practice a better understanding of the background to participants' violent behaviour was emerging;

the extent to which alcohol featured in violent incidents; the high rate of domestic abuse in participants who had not been convicted of violence against their partners. After two years of running the programme, it is also becoming clearer that anger as a theoretical explanation for criminal violence is less valid then originally proposed by the TIPP and Probation team who developed the Pump. It certainly is a factor in male violence, but as the pro-feminists argue, anger is only a means to the end - to establish or regain power and control in a situation. It is this re-emphasis that the programme has had to develop as a direct response to the practical experience.

The function of evaluation for a programme of this nature is to attune itself to the responses of participants, facilitators and outside observers. Not in an effort to create a fixed structure which can be repeated and replicated with uniform results, but as an antenna which responds and is reflexive to the problems and experiences of the group; which can feed into a process of continued development and refinement.

Conclusions

At the beginning of this monograph I set out to investigate the potential efficacy of drama based educational programme for violent offenders, and to highlight potential areas of conflict within the TIPP field. The crucial question for the TIPP field is whether, given the contradictions of creative work in a system orientated as much to punishment as to rehabilitation, it is possible for theatre organisations to be aware of the paradoxical and complex interactive context, and through practice, attempt to make the attendant tensions transparent. In this conclusion, I hope to draw together ideas and arguments relating to this question. I will be considering efficacy in relation to the micro level of the facilitator-participant context and the arts-probation partnership, and also to the macro level, of the relationship between theatre and the criminal justice system in general.

Drama with offenders.

One of the important issues discussed in this monograph was the theoretical and practical significance of the self as an agent of change. The theory of autonomy and responsibility are the foundation of the empiricist definition of the criminal offender. But in order to avoid the theoretical myopia of selecting 'atomistic caricatures of human nature and simplistic notions of social order' it has been important to emphasise a pluralistic and reflexive approach to a complex range of social theories. [1] In other words the notion of autonomy needs to be set against

---

[1] Young, J. (1994) 'Incessant chatter: recent paradigms in criminology', in McGuire, M., Morgan, R.and Reimer, R. (1994) *Oxford Handbook of Criminology*, New York, Clarendon Press, p. 70

other theoretical explanations for criminal behaviour, and these need to be considered in practical policies and drama-based educational intervention work.

However, while acknowledging the influence of socio-cultural, biological and/or economic influences on criminal behaviour, the approach in this thesis has asserted the value and validity of work with individuals as part of an overall strategy to deal with anti-social behaviour. As I discussed in Chapter Two, there is research to suggest that some drama-based methods, like re-enactment of crimes, role-reversal and social skills training, are efficacious in helping offenders change attitudes linked to criminal actions.[2]

The Pump programme aimed to extend these drama methods to challenge, and help violent offenders deal with their aggression. The main theoretical perspectives which informed the Pump programme argued that when people (men in particular) perceive some barrier, personal or interpersonal, to their freedom to choose a course of action, they will act to restore their sense of freedom. Novaco argued that this loss of freedom triggers men to try and restore their freedom, either directly or indirectly through expressions of hostility towards the person or thing that is implicated in their loss of freedom. [3] The pro-feminists argued that whilst the loss of freedom can result in anger and violence, the feelings of being out of control are directly related to patriarchal expectations of what those

---

[2] Chandler, M.J. (1973) 'Egocentrism and anti-social behaviour: the assessment and training of social perspective-taking skills', *Developmental Psychology*, **46**, pp. 326-332; Sarason, I.G. (1968) 'Verbal learning, modelling and juvenile delinquency', *American Psychologist*, **23**, pp.245-266; Sarason, I.G. (1978) 'A cognitive social learning approach to juvenile delinquency', in R.D. Hare and D. Schalling (eds.) *Psychopathic Behavior: Approaches to Research*, New York, Wiley; Sarason, I.G. and Ganzer, V.J. (1973) 'Modelling and group discussion in the rehabilitation of juvenile delinquents', *Journal of Counselling Psychology*, **20**, pp.442-449; Scopetta, M.A. (1972) A comparison of modelling approaches to the rehabilitation of institionalised male adolescent offenders implemented by paraprofessionals, unpublished doctoral dissertation, University of Miami; Ollendick T.H. and Hersen, M. (1979) 'Social skills training for juvenile delinquents', *Behaviour Research and Therapy*, **17**, pp. 547-554; Spence,S., and Marzillier, J.S. (1979) 'Social skills training with adolescent male offenders: 1. Short term effects', *Behaviour Research and Therapy*, **17**, pp. 7-16
[3] Novaco, R W. (1975) *Anger Control*, Massachusetts, Lexington Books.

freedoms *should* involve.[4] The crucial theoretical implication for the Pump programme was to explore these dual issues of control/loss of control and the attendant issues of power derived from patriarchal and masculine expectations, beliefs and social rules.

The Pump programme team wanted to promote a need for reflexivity to the environment. It was not simply a question of 'learning new tricks', but there was a constant need to adjust and re-adjust one's perceptions of life in response to interactions. The crucial role of creativity in the process is to promote the idea that the 'art of life' lies in a constant readjustment to our surroundings.[5] The phenomenological perspective, in particular, suggests that meaning and interpretation of reality is infinite and multiple. These philosophical principles are supported by cognitive-behaviourists and pro-feminists who argue that intransigence and fixity in thinking and social rules are often characteristic of men who are violent.

One of the factors in assessing the efficacy of the Pump programme, therefore, is the extent to which these principles may be communicated to the participants. It may be argued that the programme's strength, in suggesting pragmatic solutions to potentially violent situations, eclipsed the more philosophically complex notions of multiple meanings in reality. There was a tendency for solutions to be found to what were very often confusing and frustrating personal problems, rather than promoting an exploration of the complexity of social interactions. I think these limitations were due partly to having to focus in on 'personal problems' and the 'actual' rather than expanding the aesthetic to include the fictional and the 'possible'. While the re-creation of real-life experience can facilitate self-critical awareness, it does far less to *extend* the capacity of the individual into more imaginative realms of response/interpretation.

[4] Dobash, R.E. and Dobash, R.P. (1990/91) *The CHANGE Project Annual report 1990 and 1991*, University of Stirling.
[5] Okakura, Kakuzo (1991) *The Book of Tea*, Tokyo, Kodansha International.

The critical point is that perception of the self as an effective agent was important and therefore had implications for the way in which the programme dealt with participants. The efficacy of the rehabilitative goal needs to be measured against the extent to which the programme could promote the security of the group members in their sense of agency *and* to introduce acceptable forms of disruptive challenges to the way in which they operated that power and control - namely violent or aggressive behaviour. The Vermont case study highlighted the need to create a way to motivate offenders to address and challenge their anti-social behaviour, whilst at the same time respecting their dignity and rights.   In considering whether the Pump programme was efficacious in these terms, it is relevant to understand the specific function of theatre that the TIPP Centre sought to promote:

> ...at its best [theatre] is dialogic - transitive. It takes as much from the audience as it gives. It develops dialogue and the practitioner should always learn as much as the participant. It is based on pedagogic practice that does not preach or fill up its audience with information - it should develop critical abilities and make the participants, audience members subjects of the process. [6]

Drawing on the feed-back and evaluation, and from my own subjective observations, I believe that the Pump programme was able to create a relatively dialogical and egalitarian learning environment. The re-enactment and analyses of violent incidents, the rehearsal of social skills, and the use of role reversal were all elements which group members said they found helpful. Also the non-judgemental role of the theatre practitioner meant that oppositional debates about the validity of values and morals were displaced by a rational approach governed by participants: deducing principals from practice; comparing different courses of action in the same situation; and observing and testing results.

---

[6] Thompson, J. (1997) *Theatre and Offender Rehabilitation; Observations from the US,* unpublished.

The motivation and/or resistance of the learner-participants is a critical factor in the efficacy of compulsory arts-education programmes. If, as Freire argues, it is the participant who is the agent of change, then the general efficacy of a programme is, at least partially, reliant on individual motivation and/or a programme's ability to encourage motivation.[7] The limitation of a programme like the Pump is that it is has a very short period of time in which to present oppositional or alternative modalities of thinking and behaviour. The brevity of time means that for some individuals the ideas of dialogism and phenomenology, which underpin the process, may lead to a condition which Witkin refers to as 'disjunction':

> Action in the world becomes increasingly difficult as the individual succumbs to a motivational crisis in which he finds himself either with behaviour for which he has no impulse, or impulse for which he has no behaviour. [8]

There is not sufficient evidence to suggest 'disjunction' occurred in the Pump programme, but Witkin's term does highlight the need for caution in discussing efficacy with reference to the extremes of success *or* failure. [9] What is crucial is to be sensitive to the multifarious impact that a programme, like the Pump, may or may not have on its participants, and moreover, to expect and be reflexive to the unexpected outcomes.

The implication for TIPP practice is that although autonomy and change provide a valid premise from which to approach the work, in practice, the participants on the Pump programme expressed personal problems which reflected the complexity of theoretical perspectives e.g. that individual autonomy is one of many explanations

---

[7] Freire, P. (1974) *Education For Critical Consciousness*, London, Sheed & Ward.

[8] Witkin, R.W. (1974) *The Intelligence of Feeling*, London, Heinmann Educational Books, p.28

[9] The Pump programme consisted of 8 x 2 hr session. This can be contrasted with a similar (though non-drama based) course in the US which runs over two years, two times a week, in both prison and when the men are released on a community supervision order. Info: Bush, J. (1995) Teaching Self Risk Management to Violent Offenders, in McGuire, J. (Ed.) *What Works: Reducing Reoffending*, Chichester, John Wiley and Sons.

222

and/or solutions to violent behaviour. Erikson described this approach as 'triple-book keeping'.[10] An approach which takes into consideration the relationship between biological, social and developmental aspects of personal identity. From the biographical information of the Pump participants (see appendix 4) it is possible to suggest a wide range of factors connected with violent behaviour, for example, the effects of alcohol and/or drugs, problems in early childhood, mental health issues, learnt behaviour, the need for power and control in intimate relationships - in effect all these influences may be drawn together in one individual. Identity is complex and the approach to working with violent men needs to reflect that complexity. As discussed earlier, autonomy is limited as a single rationale. This re-emphasises the need for an egalitarian and reflexive approach which creates a challenging, dialogical learning environment in which each individual is respected as a human being first, and offender second.

Working with criminal justice agencies; creating effective partnerships.

The question of efficacy, in relation to theatre and education programmes in probation, may be thought of as a problem of dialogical balance - so much aesthetic freedom against so much educational (probation) duty. A perpetual dialogue exists in relations between these two potentially opposite qualities. However, as Raymond Williams notes, in paradoxical mode, 'in an important sense the first duty of the artist is to be free and [that] the first duty of social provision in the arts is to ensure freedom'. [11] These arguments are certainly not new or unique to TIPP practice. Brecht faced similar arguments in relation to his teaching plays in the 1930's:

---

[10] See Erikson, E.H. (1968) *Identity: Youth and Crisis*, London, Faber; Erikson, E.H. (1975) *Life History and the Historical Moment*, New York, Norton; Erikson, E.H. (1950) *Childhood and Society*, New York, Norton.
[11] Williams, R. (1989) 'Art: Freedom as Duty', in *Resources of Hope*, London, Verso, p.88.

Generally there is felt to be a very sharp distinction between learning and amusing oneself. The first may be useful, but only the second is pleasant...Well, all that can be said is that the contrast between learning and amusing oneself is not laid down by divine rule; it is not one that has always been and must continue to be...Theatre remains theatre, even when it is instructive theatre, and in so far as it is good theatre it will amuse. [12]

In defining theatre in probation terms, there is a possibility that the aesthetic language and methodology becomes '...manipulated and twisted, with the result that [community] artists are increasingly told what to do, how to do it, by people whose motivations often [directly] contradict the alleged aims of the community arts movement'. [13] For example, during the development of the Pump programme the TIPP Centre created ideas which were thought to be too 'aesthetic' or 'not probationary enough' by probation representatives.[14] There are limits to what an agency may endorse, even if an arts practitioner believes this may be the best way to approach the subject with offenders.

The inherent risk is that drama and role-play become determined by the context, and are used to 'emotionally buckle' or hold offenders 'accountable' by proscribing behaviour and/or blaming and shaming them.[15] This is evidenced by the example of the sex offender injunction case in the US as described in Chapter Two. The risk in forgetting the aesthetic argument for theatre in prisons and probation is that the arts become swallowed up by the wider punitive, political, psychological, rehabilitative, therapeutic goals of the agencies. This, in my view, is something to be resisted. Theatre practitioners in prisons/probation, whilst acknowledging the common ground with colleagues in those domains, need also to be quick to identify theoretical and methodological conflicts - and make these

---

[12] *In* Willett, J. (1974) 'Theatre for pleasure or theatre for instruction', (about 1936), reprinted in *Brecht on Theatre*, London, Methuen, pp 72-3.

[13] Kelly, Owen (1984) *Community, Art and the State: Storming the Citadels*, London, Comedia, p.3

[14] This is a reference to the archetypes of the Puppeteer, the Buddha, the Jack in the Box, the Punchbag.

apparent in their partnerships and practice. This requires that TIPP practice has a sense of identity within the system, that it becomes more assured in its sense of what theatre/art can and cannot do. My general point is that theatre practitioners who have established partnerships with criminal justice agencies need to be more confident in developing, influencing, informing, resisting and, if needs be, transcending probation or prison agendas which may over emphasise the educational and compromise or understate the aesthetic.

One of the ways in which drama may be compromised is in the on-going pressure to prove programme efficacy in terms acceptable to the Home Office. Probation researchers tend to use traditional methods of evaluation and assessment - quantitative methodologies characterised by statistics. This may be a necessary evil. However, in the long term, as I argued in Chapter Four, the limitations of these evaluation methodologies affect the potential qualitative and aesthetic aims of a programme by reducing its elements to measurable and quantifiable effects. This, in my view, needs to be resisted or transcended, by creating programmes that may have an element of measurability, but have the potential to develop the aesthetic nature of the work beyond the pragmatism of social skills training. Although these elements will problematise the quantifiable nature of evaluation, therein, I believe, lies the greater potential of theatre and the arts in prisons and probation. Drama is 'as multifaceted in its images, as ambivalent in its meanings as the world of mirrors...that is one of its main strengths, its characteristic as a mode of expression'.[16] The point is that drama and the arts may be as effective when being ambivalent and indirect, as when they are directive and loaded with an educational agenda:

I believe that involvement in the creative arts process often mirrors exactly what is being attempted in cognitive behavioural programmes. The Drumming

---

[15] Thompson, J. (1997) op.cit., p.7
[16] Esslin, M. (1976) *An Anatomy of Drama*, London, Abacus, p.118

workshop.....required every person to control and co-ordinate themselves physically, it required a complex interaction and communication with other members of the group, it required listening, it required team work, it required an exhausting expression of energy. The Cuban-American drummer running the group was the perfect cognitive behavioural therapist.[17]

While there is a risk that theatre and probation partnerships may lead to a compromising of an aesthetic agenda, the relationship may also promote a process in which aims, skills and experience develop reflexively with one another. A positive, creative and dialogical partnership should not depend on either party accepting the terms of any particular alignment as given.

A partnership, based on dialogical principles, between probation and theatre practitioners, offers a number of useful functions. At the most obvious level, drama-based techniques aim to make probation group work practice more accessible, to engage participants who might not otherwise feel involved in an educational process traditionally delivered by instruction, discussion, or paper and pen exercises. In applying theatrical conventions to probation group-work spaces, theatre practitioners crucially alter established relationship patterns between 'the worker' and 'the participant'. The 'them and us' culture so established in probation and prison contexts can become temporarily suspended (although it is always present), so that the relationships in a group are more direct and flexible, less mediated by formality and procedures that can govern the probation/offender interaction. The use of games, of team building drama exercises, of devising performances and creating role-plays, can all promote this egalitarian aim and develop dialogical relationships.

A second function of the dialogical model is that it suggests a relativity to the context in which one operates. This relativity is relevant if both partners seek to develop and adjust the programme in response to what is learnt from the practical environment. For example the Pump programme underestimated the influence of

---

[17] Thompson, J. (1997) op.cit., p.12

the socio-cultural environment and its support and endorsement of violence. But the Pump programme, and the theatre and probation team, developed in response to these observations by extending pro-feminist theories to non-domestic violent incidents. In relation to the theatre/probation partnership even a positive process of dialogue and negotiation implies a shared ability to compromise. The negotiation involves constraints and limitations on the freedoms of both the parties involved.

TIPP practitioners also need to recognise the strengths and weaknesses of drama-based methods. Drama may not be able to translate all probation objectives into drama-based methods. For example the TIPP Centre's most recent project is part of a multi-method, multi-agency approach in which there is a mixture of facilitators and learning techniques used. The development of TIPP practice with agencies, therefore, lies in TIPP practitioners establishing long term relationships in which genuine dialogue informs both theatre and probation practice.

Working within the criminal justice system.

In Chapter One I explored the wider concerns of the criminal justice system and society. I looked at theories of rehabilitation and socialisation in relation to educative work in prisons. I want to conclude these arguments by suggesting that theatre practitioners delivering a programme like The Pump need to be careful to negotiate and strengthen their position within the theoretical and philosophical framework of criminology. Specifically, the application of an egalitarian, dialogical and phenomenological model to practical drama work needs to be considered in terms of its influence on the wider concerns of the criminal justice system. I believe it is important to consider the relationship between the inmate and the prison, and the probationer and the community - and in what ways theatre may discover connections and seek to influence these external institutional and socio-cultural environments.

The significance of the socio-cultural environment on the individual and his behaviour has been evidenced by both the theories and practice of the Pump programme. The patriarchal justification and rationalisation for violence was one of the key areas which the programme attempted to address. In orientating itself to an anti-violence perspective, it promoted violence as a behaviour that could be, and should be, avoided. This type of statement was sometimes greeted with derision and scepticism from Pump programme participants: 'you know nothing about our world outside of this room. You talk about no violence - and maybe that works for you in your world - but in our world violence means survival'. [18]

In a prison setting particularly this is extremely difficult to circumvent, because the system may implicitly endorse violence as a means to solve problems and conflicts between inmates:

> I was...always on the verge of exploding. The place had been structured to encourage boredom....the only thing left to do was clash with each other, which didn't bother the screws. [19]

The probationer may also be influenced by the strength of a sub-culture which legitimises violence. The crucial point is that the efficacy of educational programmes is dependent not only on what happens in the group-work space, but also the environment to which participants return. Therefore there is a need to consider initiatives which build dialogue between individual change and community change, and *vice versa*.

It is relevant to refer back to Kohlberg's innovative trials in setting up penal 'just communities' in which the inmates and guards agreed to work together to democratically arrive at decisions about how to govern their community, and how

---

[18] *Participant on a Pump course, personal notes*
[19] Boyle, J. (1977) *A Sense of Freedom*, London, Pan Books, p.185

to enforce the rules they made. [20] Kohlberg's model provides a useful example of how dialogical and egalitarian principles can be applied to the system and not just the individual. The Barlinnie Special Unit was set up from a similar impulse; to link self efficacy with an environment in which rights and responsibilities were part of a rational critical process:

> ....[There] were things I had to learn as I had come from a world where decision making was taken out of my hands. If I wanted a cup of water, the toilet, soap, etc...etc then I had to ask for it. Now I was having to cope with not only these decisions but to think in terms of other people and it was pretty frightening...This is what made the Special Unit such a tough place to live in - the fact that every single one of us had to look at himself, warts and all, probably for the first time in his life. [21]

If the development of the self in dialogue is a significant rehabilitative factor, then it is important to implement and extend dialogical principles from the micro level - a two hour workshop in one room - to the macro level - the social community in which an individual exists. The implication for TIPP practice is that it is not enough to be simply aware of the theoretical territory of the criminal justice system. If one is to be efficacious it is important to attempt to change the landscape. Otherwise theatre and creative rehabilitative initiatives may continue to be regarded as a localised effort and tokenistic to the overall concerns of the institution and/or system.

Though the ideal of egalitarian spaces governed by rationality and dialogue between criminal justice staff and inmates has been attempted by the Prison Service, the examples are few - HMP Barlinnie, HMP Grendon. The system is locked into a complex theoretical and practical debate, governed by the three main stays of punishment, retribution and rehabilitation. Theatre and arts make a small

---

[20] Kohlberg, L., Scharf, P. and Hickey, J. (1975) 'The Just Community Approach to Corrections: the Niantic Experiment', in L. Kohlberg (Ed) *Moral Development and Behaviour*, New York, Holt, Rinehart and Winston.

contribution to a minute element of the system. However its principles of egalitarianism - of treating people with equity; of dialogism - promoting debate and critical consciousness; and phenomenology - suggesting 'a living contract with the unfinished, still-evolving contemporary reality (the open-ended present)' may well be crucial factors from which to develop more radical and efficacious work in the criminal justice system: [22]

> The key to the whole thing lies in the relationships of the people within the group, and the understanding that no one person is bigger than the Community, that the commitment is to the Community and not the individual....[23]

If a model based on egalitarian, dialogical and phenomenological concepts may be extended from the rehearsal in the theatrical group-work space to the actual in the social environment, the validity of both may genuinely reap rehabilitative efficacy. This generates new forms of dialogue, which change the nature of the space. In Bakhtin's words 'the work and the world...enter the real world and enrich it, and the real world enters the work and its world as part of its creation...in a continual renewing of work through the creative perception' of participants and those committed to the egalitarian space. [24]

Implications for TIPP practice.

Although the concept of correctional and community rehabilitation continues to face economic, theoretical and practical challenges, [25] recent data suggests that many interventional programmes have resulted in significant improvements in the

---

[21] Boyle, J. (1977) op.cit., p.247
[22] Bakhtin, M. (1981) *The Dialogic Imagination*, ed. Michael Holquist, trans. Caryl Emerson and Michael Holquist, Austin, University of Texas Press, p.7
[23] Boyle, J. (1977) op.cit., p.252
[24] Bakhtin, M. (1981) *The Dialogic Imagination*, ed. Michael Holquist, trans. Caryl Emerson and Michael Holquist, Austin, University of Texas Press, p.254
[25] Lab, S. and Whitehead, J. (1988) 'An analysis of Juvenile Correctional Treatment', *Crime and Delinquency*, **34**, pp. 60-83

behaviour and adjustment of both youthful and adult participants. [26] This is supported by the evidence discussed in Chapter Two, and from some of the evaluation of the Pump programme. [27]

It is therefore possible to suggest that drama-based educational programmes can be a potentially useful and efficacious educational and rehabilitative approach to working with offenders. However the Pump programme does also demonstrate that learner motivation and the nature of the learning environment (the agency and the institution) are critical factors in facilitating change. The nature of individuals, social interaction in a learning environment, and the macro-social context, need to be viewed as being in complex interaction and dialogue. The character of each is changed by its interaction with the other and yet each has its decisive impact:

> People are determined, but they also determine the institutions that they create...We operate within constraints, which we are free to change, but we are not free to abolish the principle of living within constraints. [28]

TIPP practitioners need to have an awareness of the theoretical and practical contradictions of prison/probation and move towards clarifying the nature of theatre's efficacy and what the role of the arts practitioner might be in criminal justice work. TIPP practitioners, I believe, also need to develop an approach to the work which not only accounts for interactions at the micro level, but at the macro-institutional level. TIPP practice needs to build on its understanding of the system by developing links not only with criminal justice agencies but with others in the wider community. The crucial Freirian notion of efficacy is based on the concept

---

[26] *See generally*, Wilson, J.Q. (1982) 'What Works? Revisited: New Findings on Criminal Rehabilitation, in *Legal Process and Corrections*, N. Johnston and L. Savitz, eds., New York, John Wiley and Sons; *and* McGuire, J., and Priestly, P. (ed.)(1995) *What Works: Reducing Re-offending*, Chichester, Wiley.
[27] See footnote no.2
[28] Kelly, Owen (1984) op.cit., p.4

that there is no dichotomy between personal and social change, that dialogue between these two elements needs to be strengthened and developed.

TIPP practice is similar to the other fragmented groups which form part of a 'mercurial' alternative theatre movement in the 1990's. In terms of the general efficacy of oppositional efforts of the movement the perceived need is for 'an imaginative synthesis' of the fragmented, incoherent elements that make up the eclectic network. [29] In order to continually reinvent itself, to transcend the constant pressure and influence of the criminal justice system, TIPP practice needs to find ways of linking its practice with other practices, 'generalising' its 'successes' while 'maintaining within each project the control and self-determination which is essential to competence'. [30] This does not diminish the value of partnerships with Probation or projects like The Pump, it merely suggests a way forward that builds on the strengths of these initiatives, and seeks to minimise the limitations of its weaknesses. It may also offer a way forward that generates new methodologies to enhance the general efficacy of theatre in prisons and probation, while exploring the notion of 'theatre that brings us into contact with what exists or with what it is possible to do, theatrically, with what exists'. [31]

[29] Kershaw, Baz (1992) *The Politics of Performance*, London, Routledge, p. 256
[30] Kelly, Owen (1984) op.cit., p.132
[31] States, Bert O. (1985) *Great Reckonings in Little Rooms*, California, University of California Press, p.37

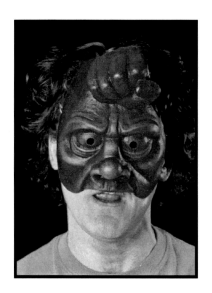 

Geese Theatre Company Fragment Masks
Photo 1. Mr. Fist 2. Bullshit Artist 3. Good Guy
(reproduced with kind permission from Geese Theatre Company)

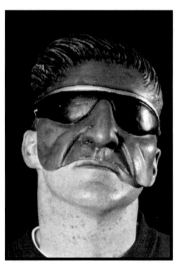

Geese Theatre Company Fragment Masks
Photo 4. Victim Mask 5. Stone Wall 6. Mr. Cool
(reproduced with kind permission from Geese Theatre Company)

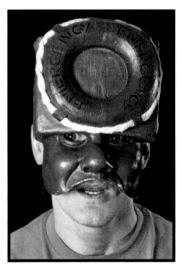

Geese Theatre Company Fragment Masks
Photo 7. Angel Mask 8. The Joker 9. Rescuer Mask
(reproduced with kind permission from Geese Theatre Company)

**THE TIPP CENTRE'S CHALLENGING VIOLENCE
PROGRAMME.**
**A FIST LIKE HEAD PUMPED UP BY ANGER AND READY TO
EXPLODE.**

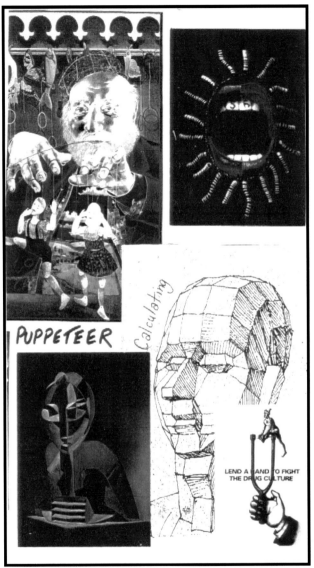

THE TIPP CENTRE'S CHALLENGING VIOLENCE PROGRAMME.
THE CONCEPT OF THE PUPPETEER WHO USED ANGER AS A WAY TO CONTROL AND GAIN POWER IN HIS RELATIONSHIPS.

The Jack Box.

THE TIPP CENTRE'S CHALLENGING VIOLENCE PROGRAMME.
THE JACK IN THE BOX PROP USED IN SOME OF THE SESSIONS.

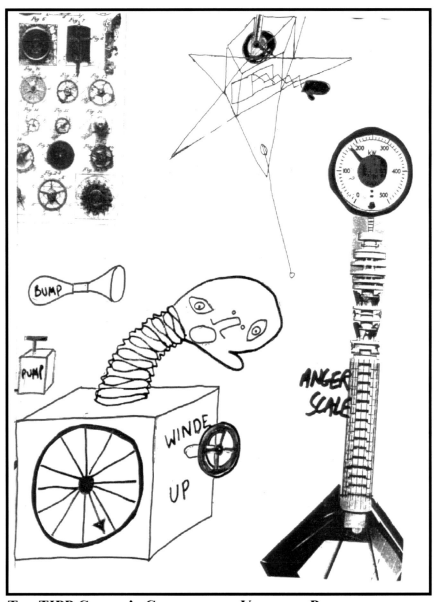

THE TIPP CENTRE'S CHALLENGING VIOLENCE PROGRAMME.
INITIAL DESIGNS FOR THE JACK BOX AND ANGER 'THERMOMETER'.

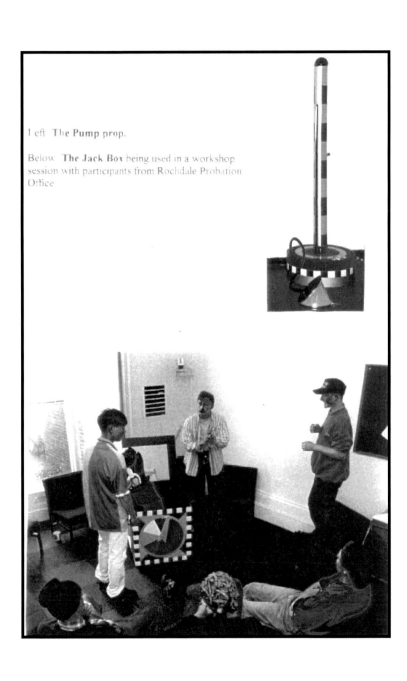

Left **The Pump** prop.

Below **The Jack Box** being used in a workshop
session with participants from Rochdale Probation
Office

APPENDIX

CONTENTS

Appendix 1. Background

The Theatre in Prisons and Probation (TIPP) Centre, based at the University of Manchester, began in 1992. The Centre was started as an initiative from Paul Heritage and James Thompson after a successful conference, Acting For a Change, which for the first time in UK brought together criminal justice workers and arts practitioners to discuss prison/probation issues. The TIPP Centre has developed several 'themed' programmes: - Blagg! (general offending behaviour); The Pump challenging violence programme; Bully; CLEVER (employment and training); Dealing with Drugs; Living Together (for bail hostel residents) and Drama in Group Work (training for probation/prison staff).

These five projects that have been developed work on a unique two year model. The first year is spent in researching and consultation with relevant agencies and community groups (including offenders); from this stage work on the actual programme is started, and as the structure of the workshop evolves, the techniques are piloted with different groups (offenders, probation/prison staff). After about a year a draft manual is written of the programme, and in the second year the sequence and structure of the workshop is tested and evaluated by as many different groups as possible. By the end of the second year, TIPP Centre staff will be able to confidently train criminal justice staff in the programme. This dissemination of the work, in consultation with the Centre, is an important part of the TIPP Centre ethos. The Centre trains between 300-400 members of staff in a range of programmes, from basic drama in group work skills, to running the drama-based anger management course. The Centre views its programmes as the source of creative ideas for people working in prisons and probation, and has deliberately focused on extending the skills of criminal justice staff.

My involvement in the Centre began in 1994, when I was employed to help research and develop the anger management programme described in this monograph.

The **Practice Development Unit** is a research section of Greater Manchester Probation Service. The P.D.U. has been closely associated with the TIPP Centre since 1992. The Unit has not only commissioned the development of four of the Centre's programmes, but takes a 'hands on' approach to the support and evaluation of programmes. The P.D.U. is responsible for the development, evaluation and dissemination of a range of probation practice initiatives, not just drama-based projects. For the last 6 years the unit has co-ordinated a series of influential international conferences in the development of probation practice: the What Works? conference, held every two years at Salford University, aims to promote and present research findings on what approaches to working with offenders help reduce offending behaviour.

Appendix 2. The TIPP field

There are currently at least five arts organisations working full time in prisons and probation (including TIPP Centre). There are many crossovers between the organisations, and indeed, some joint collaboration on projects, but there are also different philosophical approaches to the work. The key difference is in how the drama practitioner perceives his/her role within the system. The Unit for Arts and Offenders defines two different approaches to TIPP practice; companies that specialise in rehabilitative theatre work with offenders (TIPP Centre, Geese Theatre Company, Plan B Arts); and companies that provide opportunities for ex-offenders to perform and train in the use of theatre and allied arts (Clean Break Theatre Company, Insight Arts Trust, Escape Artists). All the organisations are part of a joint committee, S.C.A.P. (Standing committee on arts and prisons), which meets to develop policy initiatives, and all have been involved in co-organising events such as the 2nd European Conference on Theatre in Prisons, held at University of Manchester, in April 1996.

Insight Arts Trust offers creative arts opportunities to ex-prisoners, those on probation and parole. They run regular workshops in drama and creative writing as well as directing performances with workshop attendees and offering advice to those wishing to take further training in the arts. Insight believes the arts can play a major role in the process of rehabilitation; the ex-offender finding an outlet for their imagination, their emotions and their need for support from a group. The experience of drama in particular develops mutual trust and understanding, reduces a sense of being different and generates enthusiasm.

Geese Theatre Company (UK) is a touring group working in prisons, young offenders institutions and probation centres. Since beginning work in August 1987, the company has toured extensively throughout England, Wales, Scotland

and Ireland. Their work includes live performances, workshops on a wide variety of themes, long term programme work, staff training and week long residencies for forming and training inmate and ex-offender drama groups. The team of professional actors and actresses are dedicated to the idea that theatre in prison and probation can be a valuable teaching, learning and rehabilitative tool. Recent programme work with the probation service has concentrated on specialist work with violent offenders and sex offenders.

Clean Break Theatre Company was founded in 1979 by two women during their prison sentences at HMP Askham Grange. The company aims to produce original theatre performances which provide a voice for women prisoners, ex-prisoners and ex-offenders. It also seeks to expand employment opportunities and personal choices. Clean Break Theatre Company believes that theatre is a means by which individuals can develop their skills, creativity and self-esteem. The development of a positive self-image, is in the company's view, one of the keys to breaking the cycle of crime. Clean Break encourages access to the theatre by people who would not normally attend established arts venues or training organisations.

Escape Artists were set up in 1996 as a theatre company employing mainly ex-offenders. It provides vocational training for ex-prisoners in all areas of theatre practice, and aims to produce 'professional' touring performances featuring ex-offenders. The company is 'committed to championing theatre as a means of reaching and challenging people', and as an educational force which will hopefully dispel many of the preconceptions, prejudices and myths which exist about prisons and prisoners' (Escape Artists newsletter, Issue 1, October 1996)

Unit for Arts and Offenders was established in 1992 in response to numerous enquiries received by the Centre for Research in Social Policy following its publication of reports on the arts in prisons and in special hospitals. These reports demonstrate that creative arts programmes using participatory work in drama, dance, music, film and the visual arts and crafts offer significant benefits of a personal/therapeutic, educational, social, recreational and commercial nature both to the offenders and to the establishments in which they are held.

Plan B Arts was founded in 1995. It was set up to provide arts opportunities, training and support for prisoners, ex-offenders, arts and criminal justice agencies within Yorkshire. The company's work has included drama programmes that explore offending behaviour issues, the making of video films, murals and the creation of books that raise awareness of various social issues, including HIV/AIDS and homelessness. Plan B Arts' main aim is to 'enable prisoners and ex-offenders to reintegrate into society by encouraging personal development through shared experience and participation in arts opportunities of the highest quality' (Info: Unit for Arts and Offenders (1996) *Arts in Prisons 'A good doss' or purposeful activity?* Loughborough, Centre for Research in Social Policy).

Appendix 3. The Pump Programme – course outline

1. **Pump session (1).** Introduction of Pump prop and terms.
2. **Pump session (2).** Strategies for dealing with external and internal provokers.
3. **Pump session (3).** Practice on own stories.
4. **Jack introduction.** What is Jack? Evaluation work. Thinking Reports. Triggers.
5. **Jack session (2).** New jack stories - thinking reports - triggers. Jack's Out - victim perspective and consequences.
6. **The behaviour box session (1).** Introduction of the four behaviours – Jack/violent behaviour, Indirect aggression, 'Bottling' behaviour and Assertiveness. Power and control issues.
7. **The behaviour box session (2).** The consequences of different types of behaviour.
8. **Review and evaluation.**

The Sessions

Pump Session 1.

Session aim: to introduce the group to Knocks, Wind-ups and Pumps and examine situations in which they occur.

Session objectives: at the end of the session participants will have:

- Been introduced to the course aims and objectives
- Had the ground rules explained
- Been introduced to the participatory style of the group
- Been introduced to the idea of an 'anger thermometer' and had the terms Knock, Wind-up and Pump practically explained.

1. **Introduction to course**.

   The whole course aims and objectives are briefly explained. Any questions on these and the practical arrangements for the course are to be answered.

2. **Rules of the group.**

3. **Introduce session aims and objectives** (reference to the Pump prop).

4. **Warm up**

   Explain to the group that the course takes an active, participatory approach to work. The course will ask people to participate in role plays and 'on their feet' exercises. The warm ups are to develop the group's focus, relax them and introduce them to each other. There are two types of 'ice breakers' – mental/low-profile and physical/high-profile. It's generally best (but not always) to start a first session with a low profile exercise to demonstrate and re-assure participants that they are not going to be made to do 'stupid' things like 'pretend to be a tree'.

   Example: Mental/low-profile. Name game

Everyone says their name and is asked to remember as many of the groups names as possible. One person is 'it' and has to try and say another persons name three times, before that person says it once. So if I am 'it' and am trying to get out Tom, I would call out Tom, Tom, Tom – and Tom simply has to try and say his name once in the time it takes me to say his name three times. If I achieve this Tom is it and has to try and get someone else out. It's a difficult game to explain, so its best to do a couple of dry runs while people get the hang of it.

Example: Physical/high profile. Fruit bowl

A classic. Very rarely fails. The group needs to be sitting in a circle. Facilitator stands and removes his/her chair. Go round the circle giving each person a fruit name – apple, orange and pear (in a group of 8 have about 3 types of fruit). Facilitator stands in centre and calls out a type of fruit, if it's yours you have to get up and find a new seat. The person in the middle also tries to find a seat. This leaves a different person in the middle. They then repeat this process. The person in middle can also call out fruit bowl which means that everyone needs to change chairs. Facilitator can also slowly remove chairs, so that there are more and more people in centre and fewer and fewer people sitting.

5. **What's the Story?**

Ask for two volunteers. Ask one volunteer to stand facing the rest of the group, and the other to stand to one side, slightly behind, the first. Ask the group the open question 'What do you see?' Accept the responses, and develop the question. 'What's the story?' Accept all the replies, and collect as many stories as possible. Ask the group for their favourite interpretation. Go over to the volunteers and ask the group to come up with one line of dialogue for each 'character'. Make sure volunteers know their lines.

Tell the group they are about to see the best performance of their lives, and that after the lines have been said they must burst into 'spontaneous, rapturous applause'. Count to 3, and let the performance begin. Afterwards, thank the performers and explain that the acting on the course is rarely going to be harder than that.

6. **Introduce group to Pump prop**.
   Example: 'This session looks at 3 prompts which can fuel an angry or violent reaction. They are 'Knocks', 'Wind-ups' and 'Pumps'. Don't worry about the terms; we will learn about them as we go along. Over here is a door knocker - this signifies a 'Knock'.

7. **'Knocks'**.
   a. Explanation: 'Knocks' are given facts that can't be changed. If I go out and it starts to pour with rain and I get annoyed then this is a 'Knock'. If the T.V. set blows up or breaks down - another 'Knock'. It is a fact. *You can't blame anyone for a 'Knock'*.
   b. Demonstration: Tableau with Postman delivering a Council tax bill to someone (this can be pre-arranged using a co-worker and a volunteer). What's going on? Where is the 'Knock' in this scene?
   c. Try Out: In pairs ask group members to discuss a situation that involves a 'Knock'. Create a tableau or scene of the situation.
   d. Analysis of 'Knocks': Making it clear what is and is not a 'Knock'.

8. **Wind ups**.
   a. Explain: 'A 'Wind up' is a deliberate act. It can be an attitude someone has, or an action that provokes (the fingers up) or it can be a straight forward taunt. 'Wind ups' can occur at the same time as a 'Knock'.

b. Tableau of postman delivering a bill and laughing at the person opening it.

c. Working in the same pairs ask group members to add a 'Wind up' to their 'Knock' scenes.

d. Group analysis where and how wind up occurs in the scene.

9. **'Pump' Thoughts**.

a. Explain: A 'Pump' is an internal thought. It is not an ordinary thought, such as 'what a nice day it is today' or 'I must have a brew'. A 'Pump' is a thought that internally winds you up; thoughts that lead to an increase in anger and sometimes a moment of violence.

b. Return to the tableau of the postman laughing at the person receiving the bill saying 'this scene will end in violence; the person hits the postman'. Ask group members to create 4 tableaux of moments leading up to the punch - record the specific 'Pumping' thoughts that occurred.

c. Ask group members to repeat the above exercise on their own scenes.

d. Discuss the results.

10. **Spot the 'Knock'/ 'Wind up'**.

a. Group divides into two teams. Each team must present a potentially aggravating scene that demonstrates 2 'Knocks' and 2 'Wind ups'. The two teams must analyse where and when the 'Knocks' or 'Wind ups' occurred. The group must also record possible 'Pumping' thoughts.

b. Ask teams to repeat the scenes. This time the observing group can freeze the action and add in additional 'Knocks'/Wind ups' which the performance group must deal with. Record how character's anger rate is affected. If there is time repeat scenes again, this time giving the observer group the objective of bringing the scene to a positive and realistic conclusion.

11. **Discussion and close.**

Session 2.

Deflating the Pump!

Session aim: to introduce the group to the strategies for dealing with Knocks, Wind-ups and Pumps.

Session objectives: at the end of the session participants will have:

- Discussed the physiological signs of anger
- Suggested and practised strategies for dealing with Knocks and Wind-ups.
- Examined and practised thought stopping and self-calming statements

1. **Recap last session.**
2. **Introduce the aims and objectives of the session.**
3. **Warm-up.**
4. **Physiological factors**.

    Chart what physical symptoms of anger the group have experienced. Chart physical strategies that can be used to counter the physical effects of anger (deep breathing, relaxation).

5. **Strategies.**

    Ask group members to identify general strategies for coping with 'Pumps', 'Knocks' and 'Wind ups'. Reinforce suggestions by saying for example: 'Knocks' have to be accepted, 'Wind ups' ignored, and 'Pumps' controlled. Accepting or ignoring a situation does not mean that you become passive to everything, but that you deal with the situation positively.

    a. Controlling a 'Pump'.

    'You have shown in your scenes how 'Pumping' thoughts can lead to extreme violence and anger. What strategies will counter the strong effect of these thoughts?' Record suggestions.

    b. Demonstrate Thought Stopping.

'In the postman scene we recorded four thoughts leading to the character becoming violent. Given that we want this character to avoid violence what thoughts might stop him?' Write up the group members' suggestions - use them in a scene.

c. Self calming statement.

A Giro or domestic scene. 4 tableaux leading to a moment of intense anger with corresponding thinking reports. What statements can be found to calm and prevent the anger level rising? Record. Activate the scene with one person acting as an internal counsellor/adviser feeding in calming statements.

d. You game. In pairs.

A mundane domestic disagreement, for example: the washing up has been left for 3 days and there are no more plates. Both people in scene blame each other. Start scene. Once the argument begins to develop stop the scene. Say to the pair that they should continue the scene only this time they are not allowed to use the word 'you'. The exercise should demonstrate how language can be a 'Wind up' in an argument. And that certain key words are more antagonising than others.

6. **Consequences; action breeds reaction.**

Follow up scene used in 3c. Ask if the character were to return home without having dealt with the situation in what way might the residual anger and frustration affect his actions and behaviour. Ask group members what type of behaviour might the character show? 'Bottle it up'? Silence? Try and keep the lid on anger? Be irritated - slam doors, kick a table? Activate 2-3 suggestions. Record what the consequences might be for the partner and for the character. Discuss best option and why certain actions have certain consequences.

7. **Discussion and close**

Session 3.

Deflating the 'Pump' (2)

Session aim: to strengthen the understanding of the strategies for dealing with Knocks, Wind-ups and Pumps. To examine the consequences of not dealing with them.

Session objectives: at the end of the session, participants will have:

- Examined incidents in their lives
- Explored their Pumps and possible self-calming statements
- Practised calming the scenarios of other group members
- Examined the consequences of not dealing with Knocks, Wind ups and Pumps.

1. **Recap on last week.**
2. **Introduce the aims and objectives of this session.**
3. **Warm-up.**
4. **High Risk Situations.**

   Explain that High Risk situations are physical spaces in which anger can often occur - in the car, at home, outside the pub, etc. Ask group members to identify in which environments they are most likely to become angry.

5. **Group Stories.**

   Ask group members to fill in an 'anger diary' listing an angry/violent incident. The information should include where the incident occurred, how many 'Knocks' and 'Wind ups' there were and what the 'Pumping' thoughts were. Divide group into pairs and ask them to make a tableau of one of these situations from which the rest of the group have to identify the 'Knocks'/'Wind ups' and guess the 'Pumping' thought.

6. **Strategy practice.**

Use one of the stories to explore a high risk situation in more detail. Do 4 tableaux of the situation, record 'Pump' thoughts and anger rate. Analyse with group where 'Knocks'/ 'Wind ups' occur. Ask group members to suggest 4-5 possible strategies or alternatives to deal with the situation more positively; thought stopping, deep breathing, time out, etc. Role-play some of the strategies and practise them in a scene. Discuss with offenders what strategy worked best and why. Repeat exercise using another story.

7. **Discussion and close.**

Let the group know that the focus of the next session will change and concentrate more directly on their own violence.

Session 4.

Introduction to Jack

Session aim: to concentrate on and examine in detail violent incidents in the lives of participants.

Session objectives: at the end of the session participants will have:

- Discovered which violent situations are relevant for the whole group
- Examined real situations in detail
- Examined the triggers to those situations

1. **Recap on last session**

2. **Introduce the aims and objectives of the session**

Explain to the group that the next sessions will be dealing in more detail with violent scenarios. Go through aims and objectives. Briefly introduce Jack box prop, and say that you will be explaining this later.

3. **Continuums**

Ask group to imagine a line on the floor that stretches from one side of the room to the other. Explain that you will make a statement and the group have to stand on the line according to how much they agree or disagree with the statement. Designate one end of the line 'strongly disagree' and the other 'strongly agree'. Start with a basic statement:

'I find it difficult getting up in the morning' or 'White bread is nicer than brown'.

Ask participants why they have put themselves in a particular place. Concentrate at first on those who are furthest apart and according to the exercise are therefore in most disagreement. Develop the discussion with a few contributions before moving on to the next question.

The questions can get more serious and/or you can ask the group to pose questions about themselves.

4. Violence tableaux and continuum.

Ask the group to come up small still images of moments that would lead them to violence in their lives. This can either be done in pairs, or as a whole group. Look at each image. Examine these by identifying what the story is, who the characters are, where it takes place, what the conflict is, and thoughts and feelings of all characters. You can also bring back into play Knocks, wind-ups, pump thoughts etc. The main intention is to clarify the nature of the incident. Give a short title to the image, or a specific pump thought that seems to be a trigger, e.g.: 'I hate it when my wife laughs at me'. It's sometimes useful to take a Polaroid to record it for later reference.

Once all group members have created an image of a violent moment – re-introduce the continuum. Using the scene titles re-create the continuum and ask the group to stand on the line, according to how likely it would be for them to respond to the situation with violence. It is useful to record this process on paper, putting a dot and initials for where individual group members stand.

Ask each person to say why they choose to stand on a particular place on the line. If two people are at different ends of the continuum, ask the group/them why there might be such a difference of attitude.

The exercise should give a clear idea of the **key trigger situations** for this group.

5. What is Jack?

Feedback on the prop (if using). Explain to group that all violence has some form of trigger. That different situations cause different reactions and behaviours in different people. Identifying personal triggers help to create awareness about when and where an individual is most at risk of 'exploding' (demo of jack-in-the-box jumping out).

6. **Select a story.**

If a participant offers a personal incident ask him to take the 'story' seat. The group members must then ask the volunteer questions about the incident to establish what happened. The objective for the group is to get a full picture of the incident; was there a lead up to the moment; were drugs or alcohol involved; was the individual already angry about something before the moment of violence? etc.

Once the story has been told, ask the individual to work with other members of the group to come up with an image of the moment of violence. Record the thoughts and feelings of all involved.

If using the prop explain: the red section of the dial represents the moment of violence. The facilitator can take the arrow back to other sections and ask what was happening before the violent incident that led to this moment. Ask the group members to make a tableau for each of the stages (about 3-5 is about usual). These stages might represent seconds, minutes, hours, or days before the build up to the incident. Check on what the person was thinking and feeling throughout this process, and also comment on the Knocks and Wind-ups that occurred. Check too on what other people involved in the scene were thinking and feeling.

Once this process has been thoroughly explored, ask the group to go back to the earliest image before the moment of violence. You want to see all the 4-5 images shown in rapid succession to see how the moment of violence was created. As you clap your hands the group should change to the next image. With each change group members can shout out what triggers the next image e.g. pump thought, alcohol, high anger, wind up.

Ask group to discuss exercise, ask what triggers them in similar situations, what are triggers?

9. **Close**

Explain that in session 5 they will be repeating many of the exercises from session 4, but on a new person's incident. Ask them to consider if they would like to concentrate particularly on their material.

Week 5.

Jack Session 2.

Session aim: to examine in detail a violent incident and also concentrate on the victim's perspective.

Session objectives: at the end of the session participants will have:

- Examined another real life situation
- Examined the triggers to that situation
- Examined the effects of violence on a victim
- Explored the long-term consequences of violence for a victim.

1. **Recap on last week.**
2. **Introduce the aims and objectives of the session**
3. **Warm up**
4. **Personal stories**
   - ➢ Select a story, and turn into a series of tableaux
   - ➢ Thinking and feeling report on each tableau.
   - ➢ Triggers that move stages on (a statement or attitude).

5. **Jack's Out.**

   Ask the group to create a tableau of a moment of violence. Try and use a personal story that has already been discussed. Tell the group that the focus of this section is the victim not the perpetrator. The incident has happened.

a. Create tableaux of the effect on the victim of the violence, and generate thinking and feeling reports from victim's point of view.

b. If it is domestic violence, activate scenes that show how the violence has effected the relationship. Constantly check for minimisation and denial. Would she really trust the man again so easily? How does she feel when she is with the man?

c. Interview 'victim' using individual involved and/or other group members. Emphasise that there are always two (or more) sides to a story.

6. **Discussion and Close.**

Check with group that they have understood the material covered in the session. Explain that the next session will move onto a different area – the Behaviour Box.

Week 6.

The behaviour box (1).

Session aim: to examine in detail the links between violent and other behaviours.

Session objectives: by the end of the session participants will have:

- Explored the four elements of the behaviour box
- Examined the differences between violent behaviour, indirect aggression, 'bottling' behaviour and assertiveness.
- Examined how each of the behaviours respond to dilemma situations.
- Explored the characteristics of people who use each type of behaviour.

Session preparation:

Masking tape. Use the masking tape to set out a cross on the floor ' +'. Have a flip chart or wipe board available to draw up a cross to record the information that the group give for each section.

1. **Recap on last session.**

2. **Introduce aim and objectives.**

3. **Warm up.**

4. **Introduction to the box**

Explain to the group that the room is split into four quarters to indicate four different but related types of behaviour. Physically stand in the space as you do this. The first area is violence or directly aggressive behaviour. The second area is 'indirect aggression', the third is 'bottling' behaviour and the fourth is 'assertiveness'. These behaviours are not fixed - it is quite easy to move from one box to the next in the space of a few seconds. Re-assure the group not to worry about the terms for the moment as they will be explained as the session develops.

In order to explain the behaviour box, the group need to be taken through each box following the following pattern:

Part A: Explanation

Part B: Tableaux

Part C: Dilemma

Part D: Characteristics

5. **Jack! Or Violent Behaviour**

   A. Explanation

   Explain that this area of the box is not about people, but about specific forms of behaviour – violent and directly aggressive behaviour.

   B. Tableaux

   Set up a tableau of violent behaviour with one or two volunteers.

   What is the story? Record thoughts and feelings of character that shows violent behaviour.

   C. Dilemma

   Set up a dilemma situation e.g. two characters in a lift on the 5th floor, one character wants to go to the 7th floor, the other wants to go to the 3rd. One of the characters is going to show violent/aggressive behaviour to get what he wants. What action will he take? Record. Review character information so far.

   D. Characteristics.

   Ask group members how they would describe the character to someone who has never met him before. Record on wipe board.

6. **Indirect Aggression**

   A. Explanation

   Move to the next box. Explain to the group that violence is not only physical. Intimidation, threatening behaviour, coercion are also forms of violence - mental violence, if you like. This behaviour is a bit like a puppeteer who pulls the strings of a puppet and makes it do what s/he wants. But in this corner the puppeteer is pulling strings to manipulate real people to do things s/he wants them to do. Indirect aggression is a way of getting what you want no matter whom you hurt.

B. Tableaux

Tableau of an argument. A. is a character standing over B. with a menacing stance, B. sits in a defensive position. What is going on in scene? What is being said? Record thinking report.

C. Dilemma.

Using same tableau as above. Explain to the group that the male character in the scene wants to go out drinking with his friends but his partner wants him to stay home to help look after the kids. The character will show indirect aggression - what action will he take to get his own way? Record.

D. Characteristics.

Ask group members for a list of characteristics of character. Record on wipe board.

7. **'Bottling' behaviour.**

A. Explanation

Move to next box. Explain to the group that someone in this box manages to keep the lid on Jack/violent behaviour. But instead of dealing with a difficult situation the anger is kept inside and allowed to fester away inside the person. In this corner someone might take anger out on himself or inanimate objects. But for most of the time the person in this corner is shy, passive and withdrawn.

B. Tableaux

'Bottling' tableau: A is slumped in a chair in a 'withdrawn' position. B is sitting opposite trying to talk to A. Record thoughts and feelings of A. and B.

C. Dilemma

Replay the lift/elevator scene, but this time with someone using 'bottling' behaviour. Record thinking and feeling, and explore how this behaviour differs from the others.

D. Characteristics.

Ask group members for a list of characteristics of character. Record on wipe board.

8. **Assertiveness**

A. Explanation

Explain that this area of the box represents assertiveness. Assertiveness is a tricky term which is often misunderstood for aggression. The first point to make is that assertiveness is a way of dealing with conflict honestly and positively - and doesn't therefore belong to the other boxes. An assertive person respects others and understands they are responsible for their own life.

B. Tableaux.

Re-create the tableau from the direct aggression box. Record thoughts and feelings of the assertive person as the conflict develops. Enable a discussion about the context of the situation, the behaviour demonstrated, the tone of the voice, the manner of the behaviour.

C. Dilemma.

Replay lift/elevator dilemma discussing what actions someone being assertiveness might take. Replay the scene a number of times with different participants, finding different assertive strategies.

D. Characteristics.

Ask group members for a list of characteristics of character. Record on wipe board.

9. **Discussion and close.**

Remind group that these behaviour types are not fixed. It is easy to move from one box to another. Having established the four behaviour types explain to the group that each of the behaviours has consequences and outcomes. The outcome of violent behaviour has had implications because they are here in the group. The outcome of indirect aggression will also have an effect on participants and the people that they love. They may not get arrested for this type of behaviour, but it will have very definite consequences. The same applies to people who deal with their anger by 'Bottling ' behaviour, by not dealing with problems they turn in on themselves, they tighten up inside and may become more and more isolated. Equally, Assertive behaviour has a direct impact on the way conflicts in life can be managed. Say to group that the next session will look at the consequences of different types of behaviour.

Week 7

The behaviour box (2)

Session aim: to examine the behaviour boxes in more detail and practise using assertive behaviour

Session objectives: at the end of the session participants will have:

- Explored whom the four types of behaviour affect
- Examined the consequences of violent behaviour, indirect aggression, 'bottling' behaviour and assertiveness.
- Discussed strategies for mitigating the worst effects of these behaviours
- Practised dealing assertively with difficult situations

Session preparation:

As session 6

1. **Recap on last session.**

2. **Introduce aim and objectives.**

3. **Warm up.**

4. **Re-introduction to behaviour box**

As with the previous session, session 7 runs to a fixed sequence repeated in each of the four box areas. This sequence is as follows:

a. Tableau of characteristics

b. Who is affected?

c. Thoughts and feelings

d. Consequences

e. Strategies

5. **Jack! Or Violent behaviour**

a. Tableau of characteristics.

Working from violent characteristic board (used in the last session) ask volunteers to pick out a characteristic and create a tableau - the rest of the group members have to guess which characteristic is being portrayed.

b. Who is affected?

Take one of the tableaux and place the person at the centre of the Jack box. Ask group - who is affected by this type of behaviour. Record and get group to create tableau of these people and place them in the Box with the character showing violent behaviour.

c. Thoughts and feelings.

Record thoughts and feelings of people affected. The scene can be activated by finding a sentence or comment to demonstrate what each person is thinking/feeling.

d. Consequences.

Ask group what the consequences of Jack/violent behaviour is on the people affected. Record.

e. Strategies.

Ask group members what strategies could the character use to stop being violent. Record.

6. **Indirect aggression.**

Repeat the five parts above in the indirect aggression area.

a. Tableau of characteristics.

b. Who is affected?

c. Thoughts and feelings.

d. Consequences.

e. Strategies.

7. & 8. **Repeat exactly the same stages for 'Bottle it up' behaviour and Assertiveness.**

9. Walking through stories

Have a brief discussion about the box and consequences. Ask the group for stories that relate to the Jack/violence Box. Walk through the story and ask the group how the character can get from the Jack/violence Box to the Assertive Box. Discuss the various alternatives and then activate the scene and see which options resolve the situation the most positively. Discuss and underline what skills were used and how effective they were. Repeat exercise for indirect aggression and 'Bottling' behaviour boxes.

10. Discussion and close

Check with the group that they have understood the material covered in this session.

Week 8

Review and Evaluation

Session aim: to get feedback on the course and make plans for the future

Session objectives: at the end of the session participants will have:

- Offered feedback on exercises and the relevance of the course to their lives
- Examined any changes they anticipate in their dealing with dangerous situations in the future
- Chosen a personal strategy for the future
- Created personal action plans

1. Recap on last session.

2. Introduce aim and objectives.

3. Warm up.

4. Continuums

Re-do continuum exercise from the first Jack session week, asking how likely is it that the situations would lead to a violent incident. Ask them to revisit where they would place themselves on the line. Note this down and record. Has anybody moved? If so, in what direction? Show any moves to the group and use them to develop a discussion.

5. Feedback on course.

i) The props

ii) The exercises

iii) How much of what they have learnt can they apply to their own lives?

6. Questionnaires

If pre and post course questionnaires are used – ask group to fill in.

7. Close

Close with a final group exercise, to end the course positively.

Appendix 4. Profile of the two pilot groups.

Planning for an 'ideal' group is a difficult if not impossible task. But there are some important points to bear in mind when enrolling individuals on an anger management course. The types of questions that can be asked are: should different ages be mixed, what is the ideal number of group members, should offenders with different types of violent offences be kept separate or are mixed crime groups better? Very often in Probation there is very little scope for dictating such matters. 'We have to work with what we get' is a common phrase used by officers.

The group members for the two pilot courses were selected on the basis of two criteria; circumstance and suitability. The men had been convicted for a violent incident but most of them had a history of (recorded and unrecorded) violence. Issues of domestic violence featured strongly in both courses. In addition misuse of alcohol and in some cases drugs featured highly:

Total number; Bury/Salford = 9
Drink related violence (6/9) = 67%
Drug related violence (1/9) = 11%
Mental Health Issues (1/9) = 11%
None of the above   (1/9) = 11%

Participant's background.

The group in Bury comprised three men; Pete (early 20's); Johnnie (mid 30's) and Stan (mid 30's). All were on the course as a condition of their sentences. The names and details of these offenders have been changed to protect their identities.

Pete

Pete was a slim, sallow 'Lancashire lad' with short dark hair normally combed forward. He dressed in trainers, jerseys and chinos. He often wore the hooded-eyed, expressionless mask which passes for cool on the streets. If not then he was pumped up with anger and frustration. He was once described by his probation officer as the proverbial angry young man. He was offending from the age of 16, usually petty theft or street brawls as a gang member. He had several convictions and many of his gang were now either in young offender institutions or on Probation. Pete's 17 year old girlfriend had recently become pregnant so they were applying to the local housing department for a place to share together.

Pete was referred to the course after a serious assault on his room-mate, a sex offender, whilst staying at a Bail Hostel awaiting trial for another offence. My first impression of him was of a bull venting his rage in a china shop. He entered the group workroom in an aggravated state, and he seemed irritated at having to come to the session. He kicked the door behind him, banged down his cup, and hit a table top. He seemed nervous as well as anxious. The background to his irritation was his perception that what he had done to the sex offender was 'right', so therefore what use was a course aimed at managing his anger?

This entry tantrum seemed designed to make a point, because as soon as the session commenced Pete got involved with the exercises with the minimum of resistance. In the first session he was more obviously shy then the other men, perhaps owing to some discomfort about being in a group discussing 'feelings'. The other two group members were also older and were more able to be open about their feelings and experiences. At first the age gap seemed to intimidate Pete, but as the course progressed the older men talked about their own experiences of being young which he could relate to well and they often offered him 'fatherly' advice and support.

By the third week Pete was much more comfortable in the group. His girlfriend had told him that she wished the group meetings were every day as he came home much less argumentative. He told the group that he and his partner had been having frequent rows and that he often caused arguments if he wanted to go out for the night, because he knew that after a couple of hours' shouting his girlfriend would tell him to get lost. When asked what he did when his girlfriend wanted to go out, he replied:

'Sometimes I let her go, other times I stand in front of the door and stop her'.

Pete became uncomfortable after saying this, and wanted to change the subject.

Johnnie

Johnnie's offence was a serious assault (a 'head-butt') on his partner during an argument.

Johnnie was in his middle 30's, tall and built like a heavy weight boxer. He had a deep, gruff Northern voice that reminded one of Les Dawson. He was in full time employment with a local paving contractor, and also looked after his daughter from a previous relationship. Johnnie had a great deal of warmth and charm, was intelligent and perceptive, but often seemed confused about his feelings - particularly about his current relationship. He showed great motivation in examining his own problems, however, and was also able to support and challenge other group members in a positive way.

Throughout the course he had continuing difficulties with his partner. The couple had been to RELATE but their turbulent on-off relationship had continued unabated. He showed some signs of manipulative and controlling tendencies. For example he admitted to the group that he was beginning to feel more in control of himself 'during arguments with my partner', and realised he could 'wind her up' by saying to her - 'look I am in control, why can't you be?'

Johnnie seemed to have false expectations of his partner. He once said: 'I'm putting in lots to the relationship. I know what I want to get back but she does not give me what I want'.

There was no doubt that the relationship was a very negative one for both of them.

Stan.

Stan was referred to the programme after a serious assault on his step son.

Stan was thin to the point of being undernourished. Dark skinned, with short black hair which was always a little greasy. His posture made him look smaller then he actually was. He was not hunched, but he looked vulnerable.

After a disastrous home life which included a great deal of physical and mental violence from his father, he escaped to join the Army at a young age. He had been in the Army for 17 years, serving in Northern Ireland and in the Gulf, and he was now employed on night shift at a local factory.

We learnt from his Probation officer that Social Services had placed a court order on him not to live with his family for a trial period. He was also told that when visiting his family he should not intervene in any domestic rows. The Probation Officer told us that Social Services suspected Stan of violence towards his partner, but his partner did not see this as a problem and wanted more than anything else to keep the family together. Stan and his partner looked after three boys, the youngest of whom was Stan's son, the older boys being his partner's from a previous relationship. It was the oldest of the boys that he had assaulted.

Stan was a good participant but tended to offer work-related examples of his anger rather than talk about domestic difficulties. As the course progressed he opened up a little about some of his family problems and was able to rehearse new strategies and recognise how to deal with his anger more positively. Stan's harsh and disciplinarian father had taught him not to talk about his problems and to deal with situations 'like a man'. His army training had only served to reinforce his belief that to share one's problems was a weakness. He often played a jocular 'I'm all right' character in group, and though a lively and helpful contributor, he remained guarded about his problems.

The Salford group:

Mick

Mick was referred to programme after an assault occasioning Actual Bodily Harm against his ex-wife. He was still living with her and their three children. Mick was a reticent figure in his mid thirties, well built, quiet, with slow, rather tense movements. He rarely smiled, and when he talked it was in a faltering, disconnected voice which often tailed off in the middle of a sentence. From his probation report it was clear that he and his partner had a long history of alcohol abuse, and that violence played a regular part in the relationship. When charting up his offence in group he described the A.B.H. incident as 'a slap', yet when asked what injuries his partner had incurred told us that she had two black eyes, broken ribs, a broken nose and a cut to the head. He was a reluctant participant and would often take a back seat in the group. He found it hard to learn many of the anger management skills, and he did not seem to have much motivation to change. In some ways Mick was not ready for this type of programme as he still used a lot of denial and minimisation when talking about his violence. It was quite obvious that he was still drinking heavily, and there was some cause to believe that he was continuing to be violent during the course. On one occasion he told the group how his ex-wife had come home drunk in the afternoon and fallen asleep on the sofa. Mick felt that she was winding him up and said he had slapped her because 'she never knew anything about it when she woke up'. Mick had already breached the original court order and had been charged again after causing property damage to his ex-wife's house.

Eddie

Eddie was a volunteer on the programme. He had recently come out of a de-tox centre and had attended the Alcohol Abuse group. Eddie was in his early thirties, stocky but athletically built. He had an open friendly face with long sandy brown hair normally kept in a ponytail. His enquiring blue eyes reflected his warm and intelligent personality. I was very aware of his self determination and strength of character - a trait that was admirable and an obvious saving grace. He had spent the last fifteen years drinking very heavily, and would have continued if his body had not started failing, and his best friend had not died from an alcohol-related disease. He did not admit to committing any serious violent acts but did suffer from aggressive tantrums and had a healthy disregard for authority. He also hinted that his relationships were not entirely violence free. Despite all this Eddie responded extremely well to the course and was an intelligent and lively contributor. He was also supportive of the others in the group and encouraged them to be honest and to open up about their problems.

Luke

Luke was a volunteer on the programme and was in his early 20's. He had already completed one anger management course. Luke was tall, good-looking and stylish, usually dressed in a snappy jacket and baseball cap, with wide flared jeans and smart trainers to signify his cool street credentials. He was a natural extrovert, noisy, disruptive, but relentlessly cheerful with an infectious, garrulous charm. Luke also had a violent temper and the strength to act on it. Most of his stories were connected with heavy drinking, and often 'casual violence' - in which he seemed to look for violent situations intentionally. His original conviction was for assaulting someone who was chatting up a mate's girlfriend. He later encountered the same lad and beat him up once again. He also offered the group stories of how he had gone to football matches and intentionally wound up the other team's supporters so that a fight would ensue. His personal motto was 'always have the last word', or in his case the last punch. On several occasions when talking about his violence he would say that he had hit out 'just like my father used to'. On the surface he seemed to have little regard for people, but in fact his cocky front hid a much more sensitive and caring side. He was fiercely loyal to his friends and one or two of the Probation staff who had helped him in the past. Unfortunately his attention seeking and sulking ploys won him few friends in the group, and he became more and more disruptive as the course progressed. After a particularly difficult session he was politely asked to make more of an effort to participate or to sign off from the programme. He opted to sign off.

Jimmy

Jimmy was another 'graduate' volunteer from the last anger management course. He had originally been convicted of an assault occasioning Grievous Bodily Harm on a (former) friend several years ago. Jimmy was in his mid 30's, overweight, scruffy and a keen attendant of the Probation Office - coming in first thing everyday and leaving after the afternoon events. Jimmy suffered from loneliness and depression and was socially isolated from everyone except his mother and some caring female members of staff. Jimmy had a history of Mental Health problems and it was sometimes hard to know what was truth and what was fiction in his many stories. The richness of his fantasies extended to his belief that he was the manager of the local Salford Football Club, and in order to back this claim up he came to sessions complete with kit and footballs. Most people at the Probation Centre knew this story was not true. The other offenders tolerated him and only occasionally did he become the subject of their mockery. He was not an ideal participant on the programme, and he soon found the going rather 'heavy' and dropped out mid way.

Bobby

Bobby was a small, wiry lad of 19, quiet, shy, hunched and often found wrapped up in his anorak with a woollen hat to give himself anonymity. Bobby's story was that he was falsely charged for a Section 18 (a stabbing) and remanded to a Bail Hostel at the age of 17. Whilst he was at Hostel he attempted to rob a shop. When challenged by the owner a fight ensued, ending with Bobby throwing the owner through the shop window and then smashing up the shop. At the time he was on

180 mls of Tamarzipan. Bobby's childhood was extremely troubled. He was born addicted to heroin, put into care at 3, adopted at the age of 4, put back into a home at 11, was in prison at 17 and was currently on probation living at a local Bail hostel. Despite this unfortunate background he had a sensitive, polite and disarmingly pleasant manner. Bobby was highly influenced by what was going on in the immediate vicinity, impulsive and rather prone to using and abusing drugs. Bobby told us that his childhood experiences of a drugged and alcoholic mother, of the austere and indifferent attitudes encountered in Care Homes and Bail Hostels had left him without the capacity to trust anyone. His current girlfriend brought out the worst of these insecurities and he told the group how even if she went out for a bottle of milk he suspected her of doing something behind his back. However Bobby showed a good application to the course work and found that after rehearsing difficult situations he was able to apply lessons to real life. He always seemed grateful for the support and advice of the group and he said that the course had taught him that there were positive alternatives to violence.

David.

David, was in his early 40's, over 6 foot, with large, powerful arms, and the general look of the archetypal farmer (which he was). He seemed an outsider to the generally youthful Probation culture. He wore dirty a dirty Barbour and tough work boots and liked to hang about the cattle market on a Thursday. He was on the programme as a condition of his court order for arson and attempted arson on his ex-girlfriend's car. The incident followed the break-up of his relationship, and the fact that his former girlfriend owed him a sum of money which she told him she would not repay. After drinking 12 pints David had gone up to his ex-girlfriend's house 'torched' her car and attempted to 'torch' her new boyfriend's car. He said that he had not drunk since, though he had previously drunk a lot after the break up with his wife. David had on-going problems with his wife, and was very confused emotionally. By the end of the course it was apparent that he needed long term counselling work as well as an anger management course. David often talked about his 20 year relationship with his partner, and how difficult it was to stop wanting to know where she was and who she was with. Even after her walking out with the children he continued to 'spy on her' and monitor who was visiting the women's hostel where she stayed. He confessed that he sometimes felt that the only way to get rid of these feelings was to kill her. He said that being on the anger management course had calmed him down, but the day after the group session he would get depressed and suspicious again about his partner. From his own admissions the relationship with his wife had been dominated by his insecurity, violent temper, and the need for absolute power and control over his wife's actions. Stories from his marriage demonstrated that he sought to control the relationship and family absolutely, and that when his authority failed he stopped at nothing to threaten and intimidate his wife. It became clear as the course went on that although David participated well and was able to use the programme language to analyse situations he was growing more and more depressed and confused and needed professional counselling help.

Appendix 5. Participant evaluation

Due to the relatively small number of participants results from the two locations were analysed together. The letters a - d represent the scoring of participants on the Salford course, whilst e - g represent the responses of the Bury group. The questions asked:

1. How effective did you find *the props* used in these sessions?
2. How effective did you find *the exercises* used in these sessions?
3. How much do you feel you have learnt about practical intervention strategies (for avoiding angry or violent situations) from this section of the course?

Participant feed-back

The Jack section

Question	Salford a-d a.	b.	c.	d.	Bury e-g e.	f.	g.	Total	%
1.Props	1	2	5	4	5	4	5	26/35	74%
2.Exer.	1	3	4	5	4	4	5	26/35	74%
3.Learn	3	4	5	3	5	5	4	29/35	82%
Total	5	9	14	12	14	13	14	81/105	77%

The Pump section

Question	Salford a-d a.	b.	c.	d.	Bury e-g e.	f.	g.	Total	%
1.Props	1	1	4	5	5	5	5	26/35	74%
2.Exer.	2	4	4	5	5	5	5	30/35	85%
3.Learn	4	4	3	4	5	5	5	30/35	85%
Total:	7	9	11	14	15	15	15	86/105	82%

The Box section

Question	Salford a-d a.	b.	c.	d.	Bury e-g e.	f.	g.	Total	%
1.Props	4	3	2	5	5	5	5	29/35	82%
2. Exer.	4	5	4	4	5	5	5	32/35	91%
3.Learn	3	3	4	4	5	5	5	29/35	82%
Total:	11	11	10	13	15	15	15	90/105	85%

Appendix 6. Feed-back comments from the two anger management groups.
Thinking a problem through.

'It made me think a lot more - back to things that I've done in the past - and I try and work out why they happened'.

'The exercises helped break things down and by seeing that it made you understand better'.

274

Thinking before acting, speaking, or offending

'The Jack session taught me to think first before acting. I think a lot now before I do anything'.

'I think you can apply what we learned every day - every situation you come across you can stop and think'.

'The prop explains things very well. When I am in a situation now I see the prop in my head and ask myself - am I being wound up, is it a Knock, am I pumping myself up?'

'Acting out the situations made me see how quickly I could move from one box to another. In the scene that we did I had every intention of staying calm, but I ended up in the indirect aggression box. It made me realise how easy it is to move. But you can make yourself stay in the assertive box - if you think about what you say and how you say it'.

Applying strategies to real life

'I've tried to apply new strategies every day. First thing I do when I get in the house is sit down and have a brew and think about how I am going to play the situation. Then I go and do it. Not like before when I'd go straight in and shout at the kids to get up. I don't lose my temper half as much'.

'If someone tries to wind me up now, I just ignore them'.

'It helps you to see that there are different ways of seeing things. You don't have to be frightened about saying things - you can say it but in a certain way that calms the situation down instead of making it boil up. Or you realise when not to say something - that it's sometimes better to leave it be'.

Thinking of others

'It made you think that there is always another side to someone's story'.

Appendix 7. Results from pre and post questionnaires.

Crime-pics and STAXI evaluation.
Offender numbers completing measures:

		STAXI	Crime-PICS
Bury:	Pre-test	3	3
	Post-test	3	3
Salford:	Pre-test	6	5
	Post-test	3	3
Total:	Pre-test	9	8
	Post-test	6	6

STAXI Pre and post-test data for all offenders

	STAXI Mean	Pre-test Min.	Max.
State-Anger	12.56	10.0	24.0
Trait-Anger	23.67	11.0	30.0
Anger Control	15.78	8.0	22.0
Anger Expression	35.22	28.0	43.0

	STAXI Mean	Post-test Min.	Max.
State-Anger	12.00	10.0	20.0
Trait-Anger	19.00	15.0	29.0
Anger Control	23.00	17.0	31.0
Anger Expression	26.14	14.0	37.0

Crime-PICS Pre and post-test data for all offenders

	Crime-PICS Mean	Pre-test Min.	Max.
General attitude towards offending	40.50	27.0	55.0
Anticipation of re-offending	12.75	7.0	18.0
Victim hurt denial	6.62	3.0	11.0
Eval. crime as a worthwhile lifestyle	10.25	6.0	18.0
Problem inventory	33.25	25.0	51.0

	Crime-PICS Mean	Post-test Min.	Max.
General attitude towards offending	35.00	19.0	47.0
Anticipation of re-offending	11.67	6.0	19.0
Victim hurt denial	5.67	3.0	10.0
Eval. crime as a worthwhile lifestyle	8.50	4.0	13.0
Problem inventory	27.00	19.0	31.0

Figure 1. Pre and post-test means on STAXI subscales (n=7 clients)

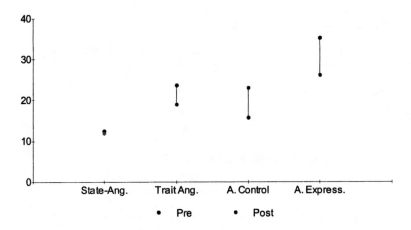

Figure 2. Pre and post-test means on Crime-Pics subscales (n=5 clients)

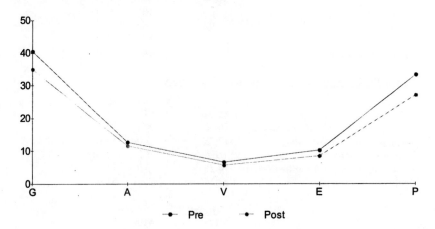

Appendix 8. Continuum results

Participants on the Pump course were asked for a list of situations which might cause them to become angry, aggressive or violent. Images of these 'trigger' situations were created and recorded. The participants then stood on a continuum line to demonstrate how likely the situation would negatively affect them. The positions were marked by a co-worker, and the results gained by using a scale of 1-8.1 being least likely, 8 being more likely. The post test was simply a repeat of the images and questions in week 8.

Pre and Post test continuum data in Bury (n = 3 clients)

How likely is it that the following situations might lead to violence:

	Pre-test			Post-test		
	Mean	Min.	Max.	Mean	Min.	Max.
When I feel threatened (street/pub)	6.0	5.0	8.0	3.3	2.0	4.0
When I feel rejected (by partner)	4.6	1.0	7.0	1.3	1.0	2.0
Someone questions my authority	2.3	1.0	5.0	2.3	2.0	4.0
A family row	4.0	1.0	8.0	2.0	1.0	3.0
When someone winds me up	6.0	5.0	7.0	1.6	1.0	2.0

Pre and Post test continuum data in Salford (n = 4 clients)

How likely is it that the following situations might lead to violence:

	Pre-test			Post-test		
	Mean	Min.	Max.	Mean	Min.	Max.
When someone winds me up	2.5	1.0	6.0	2.5	1.0	4.0
When I have been drinking	2.5	0.0	5.0	1.25	0.0	5.0
When I am frustrated	3.25	1.0	5.0	3.25	1.0	5.0
A row involving money	4.0	1.0	6.0	4.0	1.0	5.0
An argument with partner	3.75	2.0	6.0	4.0	1.0	6.0

Pre and Post test means on continuum subscales in Bury (n=3 clients)

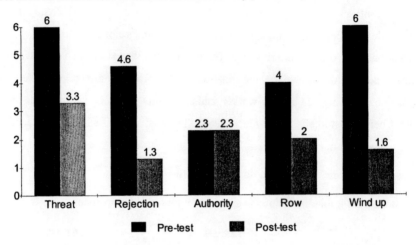

Pre and Post test means on continuum subscales in Salford (n=4 clients)

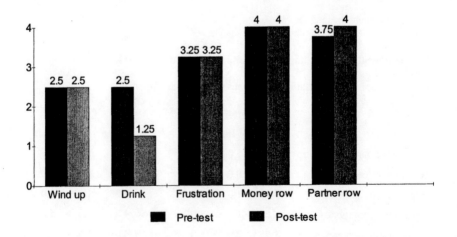

BIBLIOGRAPHY

Aichorn, A. (1965) *Wayward Youth*, New York, Viking Press.

Akers, R (1968) 'Problems in Sociology of Deviance: Social Definitions and Behaviour', *Social Forces*, **46**, Spring.

Andrews, D. (1990). 'The Role of Antisocial Attitudes in the Psychology of Crime', Paper presented to the *Canadian Psychological Association*, Ottawa.

Andrews, D.A., Zinger, I., Hoge, R.D., Bonta, J., Gendreau, P. and Cullin, F.T. (1990) 'Does correctional treatment work? A clinically relevant and psychologically informed meta-analysis', *Criminology*, **28**.

Argyle, M. (1969) *Social Interaction*, London, Tavistock.

Arnkoff, D.B. (1981) Flexibility in practicing cognitive therapy, in G. Emery, S. Hollin, and R. Bedrosian (eds.) *New Directions in Cognitive Therapy*, New York, Guilford.

Ashworth, A., McDonald, C., McCarthy, J., Mosson, L. (1994) 'Working with Violence -Lakes Conference March 1994', Letter to *The Probation Journal* April 1994.

Bakhtin, M.M. (1981) *The Dialogic Imagination: Four Essays*, edited by Michael Holquist, translated by Caryl Emerson and Michael Holquist, University of Texas Press.

Bakhtin, M.M. (1984) *Rabelais and his World*, translated by Helene Iswolsky, Indiana University Press.

Baim, C. (1993) Interview with author.

Bandura, A. (1973). *Aggression: A Social Learning Analysis*, Englewood Cliffs, N.J., Prentice Hall.

Bandura, A (1977) *Social Learning Theory*, Englewood Cliffs, N.J., Prentice-Hall.

Bandura, A., Ross, D. and Ross, S.A. (1961) Transmission of aggression through imitation of aggressive models, *Journal of Abnormal and Social Psychology*, **63**, 575-82.

Barnes, D. (1969) *Language, the Learner and the School*, London, Penguin.

Bates, B. (1986) *The Way of the Actor*, London, Century Hutchinson.

Beccaria, C. (1963 [1764]) *Of Crimes and Punishments*, Indiana, Bobbs-Merill. First published in Italian as *Dei Delitti e Delle Pene*.

Beck, A.T. (1976). *Cognitive Therapy and the Emotional Disorders*, New York: International Universities Press.

Beck, A.T., Rush, A.J., Shaw, B.F., & Emery, G. (1979) *Cognitive Therapy of Depression*, New York: Guilford Press.

Beck, A.T.(1987). *Recidivism of Young Parolees*, Washington D.C., Bureau of Justice Statistics Special Report

Beck, R.N. (1979) *Handbook in Social Philosophy*, New York, Macmillan.

Bergman, J. (1989) unpublished article, transcript available from the TIPP Centre.

Bergman, J. (1996) *Drama Therapy and the Sex Offender*, unpublished article.

Bergman, J. and Hewish, S. (1996) 'The Violent Illusion, Dramatherapy and the Dangerous Voyage to the Heart of Change', in *Arts Approaches to Conflict*, ed. Marian Liebmann, London, Jessica Kingsley Publishers.

Bernard, J.L., & Bernard, M.L. (1984) 'The Abusive Male Seeking Treatment; Jekyll and Hyde', *Family Relations*, **33**, pp. 543-54

Bernard, T.J. (1990) 'Angry aggression among the truly disadvantaged,' *Criminology*, **28**.

Blatt, M. and Kohlberg, L. (1971) 'The Effects of Classroom Moral Discussion Upon Children's Level of Moral Judgement', research report in *Collected Papers on Moral Development and Moral Education*.

Blatner, A. and Blatner, A. (1988) *The Foundations of Psychodrama. History, Theory and Practice*, New York, Springer Publishing

Boal, A. (1979) *Theatre of the Oppressed*, London, Pluto Press

Boal, A. (1992) *Games for Actors and Non-Actors*, London, Routledge.

Boal, A. (1995) *Rainbow of Desire*, London, Routledge.

Bolton, G. (1979) *Towards A Theory Of Drama In Education*, London, Longman.

Bottomley A.K. (1979) *Criminology in Focus*, Oxford, Martin Robertson.

Boyle, J. (1977) *A Sense of Freedom*, London, Pan Books.

Brown, R and Herrnstein, R.J., (1975) *Psychology*, London, Methuen.

Burrell, G. and Morgan. G. (1979) *Sociological Paradigms and Organizational Analysis*, London, Heinemann Educational Books.

Bush, J. (1995) Teaching Self Risk Management to Violent Offenders, in McGuire, J. (Ed.) *What Works: Reducing Reoffending*, Chichester, John Wiley and Sons.

Campbell, A. (1993) *Out of Control: Men, Women and Aggression*, New York, Pandora.

Campbell, D.T. (1975) 'On the Conflicts Between Biological and Social Evolution and Between Psychology and Moral Tradition', *American Psychologist*, **30**.

Carlson, M. (1992) 'Theater and Dialogism', in Janelle G. Reinelt and Joseph R. Roach (eds.) *Critical Theory and Performance*, Michigan, University of Michigan Press.

Chandler, M.J. (1973) 'Egocentrism and anti-social behaviour: the assessment and training of social perspective-taking skills', *Developmental Psychology*, **46**, pp. 326-332

Chapman, J.R. & Gates, M. (Eds.) (1978) *The Victimization of Women*, Beverly Hills, California, Sage.

Clean Break Theatre Company *Annual Report 1993*.

Clear, T. and O'Leary, V. (1983) *Controlling the Offender in the Community*, Lexington, Mass., Lexington Books.

Cohen, L. and Manion, L. (1994) *Research Methods in Education* (4th Ed.), London and New York, Routledge.

Colby, A., Gibbs J, and Kohlberg, L. (1978*) The Assessment of Moral Judgement: Standard Form Moral Judgement Scoring*, Cambridge, Mass., Moral Education Research Foundation.

Collins, C. (1944) *The Vision of the Fool*, London, Penguin.

Community Sentences Committee (1994) *Probation and the Arts, A Briefing Paper*, Association of Chief Officers of Probation, Wakefield.

Cook, P.(1982) Evaluating Drama in *2D Dance/Drama*, Vol.2, No.1, Autumn.

Cooley (1902) *Human Nature and the Social Order*, New York, Schoken Books.

Cox, M. (ed.) (1992) *Shakespeare Comes To Broadmoor*, London, Kingsley.

Culbertson, F.M. (1957) 'Modification of an emotionally held attitude through role playing', *Journal of Abnormal and Social Psychology*, **54**, pp 230-233.

Curtis, B. (1978) *Phenomenology and Education*, ed. Bernard Curtis and Wolfe Mays, London, Methuen.

Damon, W. (Ed) (1978) *New Directions for Child Development: Moral Development*, **2**, San Francisco, Jossey-Bass Publishers.

D'Andrade, R.G. and Romney, A.K. (1964) Summary of Participants' Discussion, *American Anthropologist*, **66**.

Davidoff, L. and Greenhorn, M. (1991) 'Violent Crime in England and Wales', paper presented at the British Criminology Conference, York.

De Certeau (1984) *The Practice of Everyday Life*, Berkeley, Los Angeles, London, University of California Press.

De Marinis, M (1993) *The Semiotics of Performance*, Bloomington and Indianapolis, Indiana University Press

Derrida, J (1978) 'Structure, Sign and Play', in *Writing and Difference*, Chicago, University of Chicago Press.

Derrida, J. (1981) *Positions*, trans. Alan Bass, Chicago, University of Chicago Press.

Devon Probation Service (1994) Paper delivered by Probation team at What Works Conference 1994.

Dobash, R.E. and Dobash, R.P. (1979) *Violence Against Wives*, New York, The Free Press

Dobash, R.E. and Dobash, R.P. (1981) 'Community response to violence against wives: charivari, abstract justice and patriarchy', *Social Problems*, **28**, 5, pp 563-581.

Dobash, R.E. and Dobash, R.P. (1990/91) *The CHANGE Project Annual report 1990 and 1991*, University of Stirling.

Dobash, R.E. (1994) *'What Works?'* Conference Presentation 1994, Salford University.

Dodge, K.A. (1986) 'A Social-information processing model of social competence in children', in M. Permutter (Ed.) *Minnesota Symposium on Child Psychology*, Hillsdale, N.J., Erlbaum, p.18

Dodge, K.A., and Newman, J.P. (1981) 'Biased decision-making processes in aggressive boys', *Journal of Abnormal Psychology.*, **90**, pp. 375-9.

Dreyfus, H. L., Rainbow, P. (1982) *Michel Foucault: Beyond Structuralism and Hermeneutics*, New York, Harvester Wheatsheaf

Dufrenne, M. (1973) *The Phenomenology of Aesthetic Experience*, translated by Edward S. Casey, Albert Anderson, Willis Domingo, Leon Jacobson, Evanston, Northwestern University Press.

Dunne, N. (1993*) An Evaluation of the Staffordshire HIV and AIDS Theatre in Health Education Programme*, Birmingham, T.H.E. Trust

Durkheim, E. (1961) *Moral Education: A study in the Theory and Application of the Sociology of Education*, New York, Free Press.

Durkheim, E. (1974) *Sociology and Philosophy*, New York, Free Press.

D'Zurilla, T. and Goldfried, M. (1971) 'Problem solving and behaviour modification,' *Journal of Abnormal Psychology*, **78**, pp.107-126.

Edwards, S.S.M. (1985) 'A socio-legal evaluation of gender ideologies in domestic violence, assault and spousal homicides'. *Victimology*, **10**, pp 186-205.

Ellis, A. (1973) *Humanistic Psychology: The Rational-Emotive Approach*, New York, Julian Press.

Erikson, E.H. (1968) *Identity: Youth and Crisis*, London, Faber.

Erikson, E.H. (1975) *Life History and the Historical Moment*, New York, Norton.

Erikson, E.H. (1950) *Childhood and Society*, New York, Norton.

Esslin, M. (1976) *An Anatomy of Drama*, London, Abacus.

Eysenck, H.J. (1970) *Crime and Personality*, St. Albans, Paladin

Eysenck, H.J. (1985) *The Decline and Fall of the Freudian Empire*, Harmondsworth, Viking.

Falloon, I.R.H., Lindley, P., McDonald, R., and Marks, I.M. (1977) 'Social skills training of out-patient groups: a controlled study of rehearsal and home-work', *British Journal of Psychiatry*, **131**, pp. 599-60

Faure, S. (1914) *La Ruche: son but, son organization, sa portee sociale*, Rambouillet, La Ruche.

Felson, R. (1978) 'Aggression as Impression Management,' *Social Psychology Quarterly*, 41.

Ferrer, F. (1913) *The Origins and Ideals of the Modern School*, London, Watts.

Fischer-Lichte, E. (1992) *The Semiotics of Theatre*, trans. Gains, J. and Jones D.C, Bloomington/Indianapolis, Indiana University Press.

Fransella, Fay & Dalton, Peggy (1990) *Personal Construct Counselling in Action*, London, Sage Publications

Freedman, L.W., Rosenthal, L., Donahoe, C.P., Schlundt, D.J., and McFall, R.M. (1978) 'A social-behavioural analysis of skill deficits in delinquent and non-delinquent children', *Journal of Consulting and Clinical Psychology*, **46**, pp. 1448-1462.

Freeman, M.D.A (1980) 'Violence against women: does the legal system provide solutions or itself constitute the problem?' *British Journal of Law and Society*, **7**, 2, 215-241.

Freire, P.(1972) *Pedagogy of the Oppressed*, London, Penguin.

Freire, P. (1974) *Education For Critical Consciousness*, London, Sheed & Ward.

Fromm, E. (1968) *The Heart of Man: Its Genius for Good and Evil*, New York, Harper and Row.

Frost, A., Yarrow, R. (1990) *Improvisation in Drama*, London, MacMillan

Foucault, M. (1972) *Archaeology of Knowledge*, trans. AM Sheriden Smith, London, Tavistock.

Foucault, M. (1973) *The Birth of the Clinic*, London, Tavistock.

Foucault, M. (1979) *Discipline and Punish*, London, Penguin.

Fox, R. (1977) 'The Inherent Rules of Violence', in *Social Rules and Social Behaviour*, ed. P. Collett, Oxford, Basil Blackwell

Fyvel, T.R. (1963) *The Insecure Offenders*, London, Penguin

Gahagan, J. (1984) *Social Interaction and its Management*, London, Methuen

Gahagan, J. (1994) 'The management of social relationships', in J. Anderson and M. Ricci (eds.) *Society and Social Science*, Milton Keynes, Open University Press.

Garfinkel, H. (1984) *Studies in Ethnomethodology*, Cambridge and Oxford, Polity and Blackwell

Garvey, D.M. (1971) 'A catalogue of judgements, findings and hunches', in *Educational Aspects of Evaluation*, P.J. Tansey (ed.), London, McGraw Hill p.218

Gayford, J.J. (1975) 'Wife battering: a preliminary survey of 100 cases', *British Medical Journal*, (January), pp. 194-197

Geese Theatre Company Programme 1993

Geese Theatre Company Programme notes for Hooked On Empty.

Geese Theatre Company From Insult to Injury - course manual.

Gendreau, P and Andrews, D.A. (1990) 'Tertiary prevention: what the meta-analysis of the offender treatment tells us about "What Works"?, *Canadian Journal of Criminology*, **32**.

Gerson, R.P., and Damon, W. (1978) Moral Understanding and Children's Conduct, in Damon, W. (Ed) *New Directions for Child Development: Moral Development*, **2**, 19-39, San Francisco, Jossey-Bass Publishers.

Gibbons, D.C., (1965) *Changing the Law Breaker*, Englewood Cliffs, N.J., Prentice Hall

Gibbons, D. C. (1977) *Society, Crime and Criminal Careers - an introduction to Criminology* (3rd ed) New Jersey: Prentice Hall Inc.

Glass, C.R. & Merluzzi, T.V. (1981) 'Cognitive assessment of social-evaluative anxiety', in T. Merluzzi, C.R. Glass, & and M. Genest (Eds.) *Cognitive Assessment*, New York, Guildford.

Glass, C.R. and Arnkoff, D.B. (1982) Issues in Cognitive Assessment and Therapy, in P.C. Kendall (ed.) *Advances in Cognitive-Behavioural Research and Therapy vol. 1*, New York, Academic Press

Greater Manchester Probation Service (1989) *Anger Management Manual*.

Greater Manchester Probation Service (1995) *The Pump Programme: Interim report*.

Godwin, W. (1946) *Enquiry Concerning Political Justice*, Toronto, University of Toronto Press.

Godwin, W. (1966) *Four Early Pamphlets*, Gainsville, Florida, Scholer's Facsimilies and Reprints.

Goffman, E. (1959) *The Presentation of Self in Everyday Life*, Middlesex, Pelican.

Goldfried, M.R. (1980) 'Assessment strategies for cognitive-behavioural interventions', symposium presented at the meeting of the Association for Advancement of Behaviour Therapy, New York.

Goldstein, A. (1988) *The Prepare Curriculum*, Champaign, Research Press.

Gondolf, E (1984) 'How Some Men Stop Battering: An Evaluation of a Group Counselling Program.' Paper presented at the second *National Conference for Family Violence Researchers*, Durham, NH.

Gondolf, E and Russell, D. (1986) 'The Case Against Anger Control Treatment Programs for Batterers', *Response*, **9**, No 3

Gordon, C. (ed) (1980) *Power/Knowledge, Selected Interviews and Other Writings 1972-1977 Michel Foucault*, Brighton, Harvester Press

The Guardian, 12.7.97., p.5

Haag, E. van den (1975) *Punishing Criminals*, New York, Basic Books.

Hagan, J. (1987) *Modern Criminology: Crime, Criminal Behaviour and its Control*, NY, McGraw-Hill.

Halleck, S. (1967) *Psychiatry and the Dilemmas of Crime*, New York, Harper and Row.

Hamilton, D. (1976) *Curriculum Evaluation*, London: Open Books.

Hamilton, V.L. (1976) 'Role play and deception: a re-examination of the controversy', *Journal for the Theory of Social Behaviour*, **6**, 233-50.

Harre, R. and Secord, P. (1972) *The Explanation of Social Behaviour*, Oxford, Basil Blackwell.

Harris, R.N. and Bologh, R.W. (1985) 'The dark side of love: blue and white collar wife abuse'. *Victimology*. **10**, pp 242-252.

Hawks, T. (1977) *Structulism and Semiotics*, London, Metheun.

Hecker, E.A. (1910) *A Short History of Women's Rights: From the Days of Augustus to the Present Time*, London, Putnam's Sons.

288

Henderson, M. (1986) 'An empirical typology of violent incidents reported by prison inmates with convictions for violence', *Aggressive Behaviour*, **12**.

Herson, M. (1979) 'Modification of skill deficits in psychiatric patients', in A.S. Bellack and M. Herson (eds.) *Research and Practice in Social Skills Training*, New York, Plenum Press

Hewitt, H. (1984) *Self and Society: A Symbolic Interactionist Social Psychology* (3rd edn.) London, Allyn and Bacon.

Hildebran, D. and Pithers, W.D. (1989) 'Enhancing offender empathy for mental abuse victims', in D.R. Laws (ed.) *Relapse Prevention with Sex Offenders*, New York, Guilford, pp.236-243

Hitchcock, G and Hughes, D. (1989) *Research and the Teacher*, London and New York, Routledge.

Hogan, R. (1975) 'Moral Development and Personality', in D.J. DePalma and J.M. Foley (eds*.) Moral Development: Current Theory and Research*, Hillside, N.J., Erlbaum Associates.

Hollin, C. R. (1992) *Criminal Behaviour: A Psychological Approach to Explanation and Prevention*, London and Washington D.C., Falmer Press.

Holmes, Mark and Lundy, Colleen. (1990) 'Group Work For Abusive Men: A Profeminist Response', *Canada's Mental Health*, Vol. **38**, December 1990.

Home Office (1947*) Report of the Commissioners of Prisons and Directors of Convict Prisons for the Year 1946*, Cmd. 7271, London, HMSO

Home Office (1992) *Prison Statistics England and Wales 1990*, Cmnd. 1800, London, HMSO.

Homer, M. *et al* (1985) 'The burden of dependency', in N. Johnson (Ed.) *Marital Violence*, Sociological Review Monograph, London, Routledge and Kegan Paul.

Horney, K. (1950) *Neurosis and Human Growth*, New York, Norton.

Howells, K. (1989) 'Anger-Management Methods in Relation to the Prevention of Violent Behaviour', in J. Archer and K. Browne (eds.) *Human Aggression*, London, Routledge.

Humphrey, C and Carter, P and Pease, K (1992) A Reconviction Predictor for Probationers, in *British Journal of Social Work*, **22**, p.33-46.

Husserl, E (1952) *Ideas: General Introduction to Pure Phenomenology*, translated by W.R. Boyce, London, George Allen and Unwin

Husserl, E. (1960) *Cartesian Meditations: An Introduction to Phenomenology*, trans. Dorion Cairns, The Hague, Martinus Nijhoff.

Itzin, C. (1980) *Stages In The Revolution*, London, Methuen.

Jackson, T. (ed.) (1980) *Learning Through Theatre*, Manchester, Manchester University Press

Jackson, T. (ed.) (1993) *Learning Through Theatre* (2nd edition) London and New York, Routledge.

Jeffries, J. (1991) 'What We Are Doing Here Is Defusing Time Bombs' in Holmes and Karp (ed.) *Psychodrama - Inspiration and Technique*, London and New York, Routledge.

Jennings, S. (1990) *Dramatherapy with Families, Groups and Individuals. Waiting in the Wings.* London. Jessica Kingsley.

Kalmuss, D.S., & Strauss, M.A. (1981) 'A wife's marital dependency and wife abuse', *Journal of Marriage and the Family*, (May), pp. 277-286.

Katz, J. (1988) *Seductions of Crime: Moral and Sensual Attractions of Doing Evil*, New York, Basic Books.

Kear-Colwell, J. and Pollock, P. (1997) 'Motivation or confrontation: Which approach to the child sex offender?' *Criminal Justice and Behaviour*, **24**, No.1, pp.20-33

Kelly, G.A. (1955) *The Psychology of Personal Constructs*, New York: Norton.

Kelly, G.A. (1986) *A Brief Introduction to Personal Construct Theory*, London, Centre for Personal Construct Psychology.

Kelly, O. (1984) *Community, Art and the State: Storming the Citadels*, London, Comedia Publishing Group

Kendall, P., & Hollon, S. (1979) *Cognitive Behavioural Interventions*, New York, Academic Press.

Kerlinger, F.N. (1970) *Foundations of Behavioural Research*, New York, Holt, Rinehart and Winston.

Kershaw, B. (1992) *The Politics of Performance*, London, Routledge

Klein, D (1982) 'Battered wives and the domination of women'. In Rafter, N. H. and Stanko, E. (Eds,). (1982). *Judge, Lawyer, Victim, Thief: Women, Gender Roles and Criminal Justice*. Boston, Mass: Northeastern University Press.

Kline, P. (1980) 'The Psychometric Model of Man', in A. Chapman and D. Jones (eds) *Models of Man*, Leicester, BPS.

Kline, P. (1984) *Personality, Measurement and Theory*, Hutchinson University Library, London.

Knight, M. (1994) Interview with author.

Kohlberg, L., Scharf, P. and Hickey, J. (1975) The Just Community Approach to Corrections: the Niantic Experiment, in L. Kohlberg (Ed) *Moral Development and Behaviour*, New York, Holt, Rinehart and Winston.

Konecni, V.J. (1975) 'The mediation of aggressive behaviour: Arousal level vs. anger and cogntive labelling', *Journal of Personality and Social Psychology*, **32**, pp 706-712.

Lab, S. and Whitehead, J. (1988) 'An analysis of Juvenile Correctional Treatment', *Crime and Delinquency*, **34**.

Landy, R.J. (1986) *Drama Therapy: Concepts and Practices*, Springfield, Illinois, Charles C. Thomas.

Lange, J. (1921) *Verbrechen Als Soshicksal*, Leipzig, Verlag.

Levi, M. (1994) 'Violent Crime', in McGuire, M., Morgan, R. and Reimer, R., *Oxford Handbook of Criminology*, New York, Clarendon Press.

Levi-Strauss, C (1969) *The Elementary Structures of Kinship*, Boston, Beacon Press.

Lin, N. (1976) *Foundations of Social Research*, New York, McGraw-Hill.

Lipsey, M.W. (in press) (1991) 'Juvenile delinquency treatment: A meta-analytical inquiry into the variability of effects', in K.W. Watcher and M.L. Straf (eds.) *Meta-Analysis for Explanation: A Casebook*, New York, Russell Sage Foundation.

Lipton, D., Martinson, R. and Wilks, D. (1975) *The Effectiveness of Correctional Treatment*, New York, Praeger.

Llosa, M.V. (1996) *Making Waves*, John King (ed) London & Boston, Faber and Faber

Lovejoy, A.O. (1961) *Reflections on Human Nature*, Baltimore, John Hopkins University Press.

Mahoney, M.J., & Arnkoff, D.B. (1978) Cognitive and self-control therapies, in S.L. Garfield and A.E. Bergin (eds.) *Handbook of Psychotherapy and Behaviour Change* (2nd ed.) New York, Wiley.

Mair, G. (1994) *'Questioning Reconviction Rates'*, unpublished paper presented at *What Works? Conference*, Salford University, 1994.

Mannheim, K. (1943) 'Diagnosis of Our Time', in P. Freire (1974) *Education For Critical Consciousness*, London, Sheed and Ward.

Martinson, R. (1974) 'What works? - Questions and answers about prison reform', *Public Interest*, **35**, pp 22-54.

Masson, J. (1989) *Against Therapy*, London, Harper Collins.

Mayhew, P., Maung, N.A. & Mirrlees-Black, C. (1993) *The 1992 British Crime Survey*, Home Office Research Study No. 132, London, HMSO.

McDougall, C. and Barnett, R.M and Ashurst, B. and Willis, B. (1987) 'Cognitive Control Of Anger', in B. McGurk, D. Thornton & M. Williams (Eds.) (1987) *Applying Psychology To Imprisonment Theory and Practice*, London, HMSO, p 303 - 313

McGregor, L., Tate, M., Robinson, K. (1977) *Learning Through Drama*, London, Heineman Educational Books.

McGuire, J. and Priestly, P. (1985) *Offending Behaviour*, London, B.T. Batsford.

McGuire, J., and Priestly, P. (ed.)(1995) *What Works: Reducing Re-offending*, Chichester, Wiley

McGuire, M., Morgan, R., and Reimer, R. (1994) *Oxford Handbook of Criminology*, New York, Clarendon Press

McIvor, G. (1995) *What Works: Reducing Re-offending*, edited by McGuire, J., and Priestly, P., Chichester, Wiley

McLeod, W.T. (ed.) (1982) *The New Collins Dictionary of the English Language*, London, Collins.

McVicar, J. (1993) 'A Response to Geese', *Plays and Players Theatre Yearbook*.

Mead, G.H. (1934) *Mind, Self and Society*, Chicago, University of Chicago Press.

Meichenbaum, D. (1975) 'Self-instructional methods', in F.H. Kanfer and A.P. Goldstein (eds.) *Helping People Change*, New York, Pergamon Press.

Meichenbaum, D. (1977) *Cognitive Behaviour Modification*, New York, Plenum Press.

Meichenbaum, D. & Novaco, R.W.(1978) 'Stress Innoculation: A Preventative Approach'., in C. Spielberger and I. Sarason (eds) *Stress and Anxiety*, vol **5**, New York, Halstead Press.

Meichenbaum, D. & Butler, L. (1981) 'Issues in cognitive assessment: an overview', in T. Merluzzi, C.R. Glass, & and M. Genest (Eds.) *Cognitive Assessment*, New York, Guildford.

Merleau-Ponty, M. (1962) *Phenomenology of Perception,* trans. C. Smith, New York, Humanities Press

Merton, R.K. and Kendal, P.L. (1946) 'The focused interview', *American Journal of Sociology*, **51**, pp. 541-57.

Metcalf, I. (1996) *The Pump anger management evaluation report*, Practice Development Unit, Greater Manchester Probation Service.

Mid Glamorgan Probation Service (1992) *Straight Thinking on Probation - One year on*. Evaluation study available from Mid Glamorgan Probation Service.

Moore, P. (1997) *Acting Out: Therapy for Groups*, Aldershot, Arena

Morash, M. (1986) 'Wife Battering', *Criminal Justice Abstracts*, June 1986, 252-271

Moreno J.L. (1963) 'Reflections on my methods of group psychotherapy, *Ciba Symposium II*: 148-57.

Mouly, G.J. (1978) *Educational Research: the Art and Science of Investigation*, Boston, Allyn and Bacon.

Much, N.C., and Scheder, R.A. (1978) Speaking of Rules: The Analysis of Culture in Breach, in Damon, W. (Ed) *New Directions for Child Development: Moral Development*, **2**, 19-39, San Francisco, Jossey-Bass Publishers.

Mummendey, A. (1994) *Aggressive Behaviour, in Introduction to Social Psychology*, Hewstone, Miles, Stroebe, W., Codol, J.P. and Stephenson G.M. (eds) Oxford, U.K. & Cambridge, USA, Blackwell.

Nesfield-Cookson, B. (1987) *William Blake: Prophet of Universal Brotherhood*, Crucible.

Novaco, R W. (1975) *Anger Control*, Massachusetts, Lexington Books.

Novaco, R W. (1976) Treatment of Chronic Anger Through Cognitive and Relaxation Controls, *Journal of Consulting and Clinical Psychology*, **44**, p 681.

Novaco, R W. (1979) 'The Cognitive Regulation of Anger and Stress', in P. Kendall and S. Hollon (Eds.) *Cognitive-behavioural Interventions: Theory, research and Procedures*, New York, Academic Press.

Novaco, R W. (1983) *Stress inoculation Therapy for Anger Control: A Manual for Therapists*, Irvine, University of California Press.

Okakura, Kakuzo (1991) *The Book of Tea*, Tokyo, Kodansha International.

Ollendick T.H. and Hersen, M. (1979) 'Social skills training for juvenile delinquents', *Behaviour Research and Therapy*, **17**, pp. 547-554.

Pahl, J. (1985) *Private Violence and Public Policy*, London, Routledge

Palmer T., (1992) *The Re-Emergence of Correctional Intervention*, Newbury Park, Sage

Parker, T. (1995) *The Violence Of Our Lives*, London, Harper Collins

Pavis, P. (1982) *Essays in Semiology of Theatre*, New York, Performing Arts Journal Publications

Peay, J. (1994) 'Mentally Disordered Offenders' in in McGuire, M., Morgan, R. and Reimer, R. (1994) *Oxford Handbook of Criminology*, New York, Clarendon Press, pp.1119-1160.

Pelfrey, W. (1980) *The Evolution of Criminology*, Cincinnati, Ohio, Anderson Publishing Co.

Pence, E. & Paymar, M. (1986) *Power and Control: Tactics of Men Who Batter*, Minnesota Program Development, Inc., Duluth.

Pervin, L. A. (1984) *Personality: theory and research* (4th ed.). New York. John Wiley and Sons, Inc.

Piaget, Jean (1965) *The Moral Judgement of the Child*, New York, The Free Press.

Pithers, W.D. (1997) 'Maintaining Treatment Integrity with Sexual Abusers', *Criminal Justice and Behaviour*, Vol. **24**, No.1

Pitzele, P. (1991) 'Adolescents Inside Out', in Holmes and Karp (ed.) *Psychodrama: Inspiration and Technique*, London, Routledge.

Pojman, L.P. (1978) Kierkegaard's theory of subjectivity and education, in *Phenomenology and Education,* (ed.) Bernard Curtis and Wolfe Mays, London, Methuen.

Powell, J. (1969) *Why Am I Afraid to Tell You Who I Am?* Illinois, Argus Communications.

Priestly, P., McGuire, J., Flegg, D., Hemsley, V., Welham, D., and Barnitt (1984) *Social Skills in Prisons and in the Community*, London, Routledge and Kegan Paul.

Prins, H. (1990) 'Mental abnormality and criminality: an uncertain relationship', *Medicine, Science and Law*, 30/3, pp. 247-58.

Quinn, A. (1994) 'In Defence of Geese', *The Probation Journal*, June.

Rabinow, P (ed) (1984) *Foucault Reader*, London, Penguin.

Radzinowicz, L. (1966) *Ideology and Crime*, London, Stevens.

Radzinowicz, L. (1986) *A History of the English Criminal Law and its Administration, from 1750*, 5 vols., London, Stevens.

Rathus, S. (1988) *Psychology*, New York, Holt, Rinehart and Winston.

Read, H. (1982) *Meaning of Art*, London, Faber and Faber.

Redington, C. (1983) *Can Theatre Teach?* London, Pergamon Press.

Reinelt, J.G. and Roach, J.R. (1992) *Critical Theory and Performance*, Michigan, University of Michigan Press

Rest, J. (1976) 'The Research Base of the Cognitive Developmental Approach to Moral Education', in T.C. Hennessy (ed.) *Values and Moral Development*, New York, Paulist Press.

Robinson, K. (1993) Evaluating TIE, in T. Jackson (ed) *Learning Through Theatre, New Perspectives on Theatre in Education* (Second edition), London and New York, Routledge.

Rogers, C. (1990) *The Carl Rogers Reader*, Kirschenbaum, H., Henderson, V.L. (ed.) London, Constable.

Roszak, T. (1970) *The Making of a Counter Culture*, London, Faber and Faber.

Rowe, D.C. (1990) 'Inherited dispositions toward learning delinquent and criminal behaviour: New evidence', in L. Ellis and H. Hoffman (Eds) *Crime in Biological, Social and Moral Contexts*, NY, Praeger.

Rowe, D.C. and Osgood, D.W. (1984) 'Heredity and sociological theories of delinquency: A reconsideration', *American Sociological Review*, **49**.

Roy, M (1977) *Battered Women*. New York: Van Nostrand Reinhold.

Sacks, S. (Ed.) (1979) *On Metaphor*, Chicago and London, University of Chicago Press

Sarason, I.G. (1968) 'Verbal learning, modelling and juvenile delinquency', *American Psychologist*, **23**, pp.245-266.

Sarason, I.G. (1978) 'A cognitive social learning approach to juvenile delinquency', in R.D. Hare and D. Schalling (eds.) *Psychopathic Behavior: Approaches to Research*, New York, Wiley.

Sarason, I.G. and Ganzer, V.J. (1973) 'Modelling and group discussion in the rehabilitation of juvenile delinquents', *Journal of Counselling Psychology*, **20**, pp.442-449.

Sartre, J.P. (1966) *The Psychology of Imagination*, trans. B. Frechtman, New York, Washington Square Press.

Schattner, G. and Courtney, R. (eds.) (1981) *Drama in Therapy*, New York, Drama Book Specialists.

Scheter, S. (1982) *Women and Male Violence,* London, Pluto Press.

Schmidt, S. J. (1973) Texttheorie/Pragmalinguistik, in Hans Peter Althaus, Helmut Henne, and Herbert Ernst Wiegand, eds., *Lexikon der germanistischen Linguistik*, Tubingen: Niemeyer p 233-44.

Schultz, A. (1962) *Collected Papers*, Nijhoff, The Hague.

Scopetta, M.A. (1972) *A comparison of modelling approaches to the rehabilitation of institutionalised male adolescent offenders implemented by paraprofessionals*, unpublished doctoral dissertation, University of Miami.

Scott, M. (1993) *A Cognitive-Behavioural Approach to Clients' Problems*, London and New York, Tavistock/Routledge.

Scott, P. (1970) 'Henry Maudsley', in Hermann Mannheim (ed.) *Pioneers in Criminology*, Montclair, N.J., Patterson Smith.

Siann, G. (1985) *Accounting for Aggression: perspectives on aggression and violence*, London, Allen and Unwin.

Siegal, L.J. (1986) *Criminology* (2nd ed.) St. Paul, MN, West Publishing.

Siegal, L.J. and Senna, J.J. (1990) *Introduction to Criminal Justice* (5th ed.) St. Paul, MN, West Publishing.

Slaby, R.G. and Guerra, N.G. (1988) 'Cognitive mediators of aggression in adolescent offenders: 1. Assessment', *Developmental Psychology*, pp. 580-8.

Smith, L.J.F. (1990) *Domestic Violence: an overview of the literature*, London, HMSO.

Smith, M. (1983) *The Libertarians and Education*, London, Unwin.

Smith, P. (1968) *Cesare Lombroso, Crime Its Causes and Remedies*, Montclair, N.J.

Spence,S. and Marzillier, J.S. (1979) 'Social skills training with adolescent male offenders: 1. Short term effects', *Behaviour Research and Therapy*, **17**, pp. 7-16

Spence, S. (1979) 'Social skills training with adolescent offenders: a review', *Behavioural Psychotherapy*, **7**, pp 49-56.

Spitzer, S. (1980) "Left Wing" Criminology - An Infantile Disorder?' in J. Inciardi (ed), *Radical Criminology*, Beverly Hills, Sage.

States, B. O. (1985) *Great Reckonings in Little Rooms*, California, University of California Press.

Stevens, R. (1985) 'Personal Worlds', Block 4 of D307, *Social Psychology: Development, Experience and Behaviour in a Social World*, Milton Keynes, The Open University Press.

Stevens, R (1991) 'Personal Identity', Block 5, D103, *Identities and Interaction*, Milton Keynes, The Open University Press.

Strauss, M.A. (1977) 'A sociological perspective on the prevention and treatment of wife-beating', in M. Roy (Ed.) *Battered Women*, New York, Van Nostrand Reinhold, pp 194-239.

Suinn, R. and Richardson, F.(1971) 'Anxiety management training: A non-specific behavior therapy program for anxiety control', *Behavioral Therapy*, **2**, pp. 498-510.

Tarling, R. (1993) *Analysing Offending: Data, Models and Interpretations*, London, HMSO

Taylor, I., Walton, P., and Young, J. (1973) *The New Criminology*, London, Routledge and Kegan Paul

Thibaut, J and Kelly, H.H. (1959) *The Social Psychology of Groups*. New York: Wiley.

Thomson, J.B. (1867) 'The Effects of the Present System of Prison Discipline on the Body and Mind', *Journal of Mental Science*, **12**.

Thompson, J. (1997) *Theatre and Offender Rehabilitation; Observations from the US*, unpublished.

The Times Educational Supplement. 27.4.90

Toch, H. (1969) *Violent Men*, Chicago, Aldine Publishing Co.

Tolstoy, L. (1967) *Tolstoy on Education*, trans. Leo Wiener, Chicago, University of Chicago Press.

Tomalin, D. (1995) General report on drama work in Probation in *The 1995 NACRO Annual Report*, NACRO

Tomalin, D. (1996) Interview with the author.

Tyler, R. W. (1949) Basic Principles of Curriculum and Instruction, Chicago, University of Chicago Press, reprinted in D. Hamilton, D. Jenkins, C. King, B. MacDonald and M. Parlett (eds) *Beyond the Numbers Game*, London: Macmillan Education.

Vygotsky, L.S. (1962) *Thought and Language*, E. Hanfmann and G. Vakar,(eds. and trans.), Cambridge, Massachusetts, MIT Press.

Wehman, P., and Schleien, S. (1980) 'Social skills development through leisure skills programming', in G. Cartledge and J.F. Milburn (eds.) *Teaching Social Skills to Children: Innovative Approaches*, New York, Pergamon.

West Midlands Probation Service (1986) *Anger Management Manual*

Wethered, A.G. (1973) *Drama and Movement in Therapy*, London, Macdonald and Evans.

Willet, J. (1977) *The Theatre of Bertolt Brecht*, London, Methuen.

Willet, J. (ed. & trans.) (1986) *Brecht on Theatre*, London, Methuen.

Wilson, E (1983) *What Is To Be Done About Violence Against Women*. Harmondsworth: Penguin.

Wilson, J.Q. (1982) 'What Works? Revisited: New Findings on Criminal Rehabilitation, in *Legal Process and Corrections*, N. Johnston and L. Savitz, eds., New York, John Wiley and Sons.

Williams, R. (1989) 'Art: Freedom as Duty', in *Resources of Hope*, London, Verso

Witkin, R.W. (1974) *Intelligence of Feeling*, London, Heinemann Educational Books.

Whitehead, A.N. (1962) *The Aims of Education and Other Essays,* London, Ernest Benn.

Wolfgang, M. and Ferracuti, F. (1967) *The Subculture of Violence*, New York, Barnes and Noble;

Woods, P. (1979) *The Divided School*, London, Routledge and Kegan Paul.

Young, J. (1994) 'Incessant chatter: recent paradigm's in criminology', in McGuire, M., Morgan, R.and Reimer, R. (1994) *Oxford Handbook of Criminology*, New York, Clarendon Press.

Young, J. (1981) 'Thinking seriously about crime' in *Crime and Society: Readings in History and Theory*, London, Routledge.

Young, J. (1975) 'Working Class Criminology', in I. Taylor, P. Walton, and J. Young (eds.) *Criminal Criminology*, London, Routledge Kegan Paul.

Young, J. (1979) 'Left Idealism, Reformism and Beyond', in B. Fine *et al*, (eds.), *Capitalism and the Rule of the Law*, London, Hutchinson.

INDEX

STUDIES IN THEATRE ARTS

1. J.R. Dashwood and J.E. Everson (eds.), **Writers and Performers in Italian Drama From the Time of Dante to Pirandello: Essays in Honour of G.H. McWilliam**

2. David P. Edgecombe, **Theatrical Training During the Age of Shakespeare**

3. Bryant Hamor Lee, **European Post-Baroque Neoclassical Theatre Architecture**

4. Diane Hunter (ed.), **The Makings of Dr. Charcot's Hysteria Shows: Research Through Performance**

5a. Jan Clarke, **The Guénégaud Theatre in Paris (1673-1680): Volume One: Founding, Design and Production**

5b. Jan Clarke, **The Guénégaud Theatre in Paris (1673-1680): Volume Two: The Accounts Season by Season**

6. James Strider, Jr., **Techniques and Training for Staged Fighting**

7. Steve Earnest, **The State Acting Academy of East Berlin–A History of Actor Training From Max Reinhardt's** *Schauspielschule* **to the** *Hochschule für Schauspielkunst "Ernst Busch"*

8. Calvin A. McClinton, **The Work of Vinnette Carroll, An African American Theatre Artist**

9. Linda Mackenney, **The Activities of Popular Dramatists and Drama Groups in Scotland, 1900-1952**

10. Kazimierz Braun, **Theater Directing–Art, Ethics, Creativity**

11. Jerry Rojo, **An Acting Method Using the Psychophysical Experience of Workshop Games-Exercises**

12. Tony Williams, **The Representation of London in Regency and Victorian Drama (1821-1881)**

13. Lloyd Anton Frerer, **Bronson Howard–Dean of American Dramatists**

14. Roy Connolly, **The Evolution of the Lyric Players Theatre, Belfast: Fighting the Waves**

15. Bonnie Milne Gardner, **The Emergence of the Playwright-Director in American Theatre, 1960-1983**